RENUNCIATION AND REALIZATION

Volume 4

SUBHAS CHANDRA BOSE

Renunciation and Realization

Correspondence 1926–1932

Netaji Collected Works
Volume 4

edited by
SISIR KUMAR BOSE
SUGATA BOSE

Netaji Research Bureau
in association with
permanent black

Published by

PERMANENT BLACK

'Himalayana', Mall Road, Ranikhet Cantt,
Ranikhet 263645

perblack@gmail.com

and

NETAJI RESEARCH BUREAU

38/2 Lala Lajpat Rai Road
Kolkata 700020

Distributed by

ORIENT BLACKSWAN PRIVATE LTD

Bangalore Bhopal Bhubaneshwar Chandigarh Chennai
Ernakulam Guwahati Hyderabad Jaipur Kolkata
Lucknow Mumbai New Delhi Patna
www.orientblackswan.com

First published in hardback 1982
First paperback printing 2016

ISBN 978-81-7824-491-2

Acknowledgement

Sarat Chandra–Bivabati Bose Collection
Emilie Schenkl-Bose, Anita B. Pfaff, Basanti Devi,
Dilip Kumar Roy, Santosh Kumar Basu, Gopal Lal Sanyal,
Haricharan Bagchi, Amrita Lal Chattopadhyaya, Aroti Dutt

Printed and bound by Sapra Brothers, New Delhi 110092

FOREWORD

The fourth volume of Netaji's Collected Works being released on the 112th birth anniversary of Deshbandhu Chittaranjan Das is a continuation of the fascinating collection of Netaji's correspondence of the period 1923 to 1932, the first part of which has been published in the third volume. Taken together these two volumes provide a most valuable and varied collection of material relating to the first phase of Subhas Chandra Bose's public life of which two and half years were spent in prison in far away Burma.

The collection is of diverse character. The letters are written mostly by Netaji and his brother and life-long comrade Sarat Chandra and the rest by his other relations, including his parents and sister-in-law Bivabati, by his fellow workers in social welfare organisations in South Calcutta and in the Calcutta Corporation and by his political comrades. There are also some provocative ones written by Netaji to jail authorities and the Government.

The subjects dealt with in the correspondence cover a wide field, viz., currents and cross-currents in Bengal politics of the twenties and early thirties ; the North Calcutta election to the Bengal Legislative Council in which Subhas Chandra himself was the Congress candidate *in absentia*, Hindu-Muslim unity and separate electorates, problems of social work under voluntary auspices, role of the Anglo-Indian press in public affairs, municipal questions, the *Statesman* case in which Bose himself was a litigant, management of the Swarajist daily *Forward*, personal and family problems, the woes of a political prisoner under British rule, etc., etc.

Some indication is available from this correspondence of the great variety and nature of the books that Bose was reading at the time, particularly during the time that he was in prison. Moreover, they show how a person with a deeply philosophical mental constitution was simultaneously deeply involved in family matters, viz., studies and training of his many nephews and nieces, their marriage and future career and so on. They also show how doggedly he was fighting the unjust prison conditions. Some of his letters to his elder Sarat are so deeply emotional, idealistic and philosophical. Once again there is an opportunity to study the relationship of the two brothers whom, as we saw later, nothing but death could part. The crisis in Subhas Chandra's life that resulted from his refusal to accept conditional release in 1927 even at the risk of death comes out as the most moving episode of this period of his life.

A number of interesting letters, some of them very personal to Basanti Devi and others, written from Shillong where he was convalescing after his release, are a valuable addition to this volume.

There is not much available in the way of correspondence between 1928 and 1931 because in the case of Subhas Chandra Bose letters proliferated only when he was in prison or ill. This was the time when he emerged on the Indian national scene as the Leader of Youth and together with Jawaharlal Nehru as the protagonist of a new left wave in Indian politics. His writings and speeches of this period, of great historical importance, will follow in the fifth volume now in preparation.

His arrest and imprisonment in the beginning of 1932 brought forth a fresh bunch of letters again of varied nature ending with the one to his sister-in-law Bivabati of October 1932 from Madras Penitentiary. He was subsequently and finally transferred to Jabalpur Central Jail where he spent some time with his brother Sarat before leaving for Europe in the beginning of 1933.

When this volume was in press, twenty letters written between 1925 and 1927 were passed by the Research Division to the Publishing Department of the Bureau. As the letters belong very much to the period and subjects covered in the third and fourth volumes and are very relevant and pertinent to them, we decided to include them as Addenda in this volume. This meant disturbing the chronology which the reader may please overlook.

Readers will find the material given in the Appendices

of uncommon interest. It begins with a secret despatch from the Viceroy to the Secretary of State in Britain proposing the arrest of Subhas Chandra Bose and others in 1924, followed by confidential exchanges among officials of the Home Department in Burma on Bose, correspondence carried on by Sarat Chandra Bose with the Government on the question of his brother's release and finally documents relating to the Dakshin Kalikata Sevasram, a social welfare organisation sponsored by Bose and his associates which is still in existence.

As in the preceding volume we have appended some Notes on Bengali expressions and persons mentioned in the text for the benefit of the non-Bengali reader.

The Research Division and the Publishing Department of the Bureau are being reorganised and further strengthened for heavier tasks ahead in terms of analysis, translation and organisation of material for the fifth and sixth volumes to be published in 1983 in rapid succession. In all this we seek the support and goodwishes of Netaji's countrymen and our readers all over the world. Our printers deserve our sincere thanks for their patience and diligence in the midst of the continuing and oppressive power crisis.

We acknowledge once again with sincere appreciation the financial assistance of the Government of India, Ministry of Education, which has enabled us to maintain the high quality of production.

As we advance another step forward in our ambitious project we seek the blessings of our countrymen and friends of India everywhere and pledge to do our best.

Jai Hind
SISIR K. BOSE

Netaji Bhawan
38/2 Lala Lajpat Rai Road
Calcutta 700 020 India
The 6th September 1982

CONTENTS

Subhas Chandra Bose as Mayor of Calcutta, 1931

Subhas Chandra Bose in Lahore, October 1929

Introduction to the Paperback Edition

SUGATA BOSE

SUBHAS CHANDRA BOSE came to regard *tyaga* and *amrita* (renunciation and realization) as "two faces of the same medal" during his long stay in Mandalay Jail. "To attain hundred per cent and to sacrifice hundred per cent," he proclaimed, had become a passion with him.[1] This volume opens with Bose's prison letters written during the last year he spent in Burmese prisons in 1926–7 (plus twenty additional letters of 1925 that could not be included in volume 3, published here as addenda). Between 1928 and 1931 Subhas was in and out of prison even as he emerged as the leader of students, youth, and labour across India. The volume closes with another set of his prison letters written from many different jails during the second phase of the civil disobedience movement in 1932.

The correspondence between the Bose brothers, Sarat and Subhas, continues to provide fascinating insights into the mental make-up of the younger brother. New elections to the Bengal legislative council were due late in 1926. Deprived of any legal remedy to free Subhas, who had been held without trial since October 1924, Sarat resorted to the Sinn Fein tactic of nominating political prisoners for election based on the principle "Vote him in, to get him out". At first Subhas rejected the suggestion to stand for election as he was getting disgusted with members of the councils who were not doing any good work for the country. He thought that the time had come

[1] Subhas Chandra Bose to Jatindra Nath Chakrabarty, April 2, 1927.

for the pendulum to swing back in the old Gandhian anti-council direction. Sarat got him to realize, however, that there was "good reason" behind his advice. Subhas agreed to be put up in the north Calcutta constituency against Jatindra Nath Basu, a stalwart of the Liberal Party who had beaten the Swarajist candidate in 1923. "God willing, we shall give him a damned hollow defeat," wrote Sarat, who was confident of his younger brother's prospects. Subhas could not even release his manifesto on account of political prisoners not being permitted to issue appeals to the public.[2] Sarat managed Subhas' election campaign as well as his own with consummate skill from the University constituency throughout the autumn of 1926. Both were rewarded in the winter with thumping victories. The supporters of the Bose brothers celebrated with fireworks, and "Victory to Subhas Chandra" in glittering Bengali letters illuminated the Calcutta sky.[3] The colonial authorities in India, however, proved more obdurate than their counterparts in Ireland. Winning the vote was not sufficient to get Subhas out of jail.

Subhas chose to be philosophical about his continued imprisonment. "The purpose for which Providence sent me here still remains unfulfilled," he wrote to Basanti Devi, "and my apprenticeship in prison is yet incomplete." Since he did not accept *sannyasa*, the asceticism of a world renouncer, memories of the outside world did cause him sorrow. But he was prepared to spend his entire life in prison if that were necessary for the good of his motherland.[4] To a political comrade he reiterated that his ideal of service was to give away and

[2] Subhas Chandra Bose to Sarat Chandra Bose, August 13, 1926; September 1, 1926; September 3, 1926; October 9, 1926; November 6, 1926; November 13, 1926; Sarat Chandra Bose to Subhas Chandra Bose, August 6, 1926; August 21, 1926; August 27, 1926; September 2, 1926; September 8, 1926; September 15, 1926; October 2, 1926; October 11, 1926; October 18, 1926; November 1, 1926.

[3] Sisir Kumar Bose, *Bosubari* (Calcutta: Ananda Publishers, 1985), p. 33.

[4] Subhas Chandra Bose to Basanti Devi, December 20, 1926; December 30, 1926.

ask for nothing in return. "You have asked about myself, what can I say?" he wrote. "One of Rabindranath's poems I like very much. Will it sound impertinent if I replied to you in the poet's words?

Who knows when shall I be able
To declare with all my heart:
I have reached my Realization,
Come all, follow me,
The Master is calling you all,
May my life bring forth new life in you all
And thus may my country awake."[5]

He could only pray, once again in Tagore's words, for strength:

Give unto your chosen one
The strength to carry your banner.[6]

Subhas' physical strength, however, was steadily dissipating during the course of 1926. Low-grade fever was a routine occurrence and matters came to a head with a serious attack of broncho-pneumonia with the onset of winter. On February 9, 1927, he was sent to Rangoon central jail to be examined by a medical board. The doctors, including those approved by the government, recommended against holding the sick prisoner any longer in Burmese jails, but the powers that be refused to relent.[7] On March 25 he was transferred to Insein

[5] *Kabe pran khuli balite paribo*
Peyechhi amaar shesh.
Tomra sakale esho mor pichhe
Guru tomader sabare dakichhe,
Amaar jibane labhiya jiban
Jagore sakal desh.

Subhas Chandra Bose to Bhubendranath Bandyopadhyay, 1926.

[6] *Tomar pataka jare dao*
Tare bahibare dao shakti.

Subhas Chandra Bose to Gopal Lal Sanyal, April 5, 1927.

[7] Subhas Chandra Bose to the governor of Burma, March 19, 1927; March 21, 1927; to the inspector general of prisons, March 21, 1927.

Jail where a friendly jailor, Major Findlay, who had known Subhas in Mandalay, was aghast to see him in his emaciated state. After receiving Findlay's report on the poor state of his prisoner's health, the government made an offer through a statement in the Bengal legislative council to release Subhas if he went straight from Rangoon to Switzerland at his own expense to recoup his health.

Subhas contemptuously rejected this offer of indefinite European exile. In a long letter to Sarat on April 4, 1927, he explained why he was going to reject the government's proposal. If he had "the remotest intention of becoming a Bolshevik agent," he would have jumped at it and "joined the gay band who trot from Paris to Leningrad talking of world revolution and emitting blood and thunder in their utterances." He was not inclined in that direction. The government seemed to have forgotten the suffering they had inflicted with no justification for two and a half years and that he was "the aggrieved party," not they. He could not persuade himself that permanent exile from his homeland "would be better than life in a Jail leading to the sepulchre." "I do not quail before this cheerless prospect," he wrote, "for I believe as the poet does, that 'the paths of glory lead but to the grave'." He asked Sarat to console their dear parents, but more suffering was in store before "the priceless treasure of freedom" could be secured.[8]

Sarat replied that the sentiments Subhas had expressed were worthy of him, but did not stop negotiating with the government for his brother's transfer from Burma. He wanted the government to move him in detention to the north Indian hill resort of Almora, where he could meet his relatives and recover his strength.[9] On April 11, 1927, Subhas went ahead and formally snubbed the authorities. "Much as I value my life—I love honour more," he wrote to the superintendent of Insein jail, "and I cannot for the life of me barter away those sacred and inviolable rights which will form the future

[8] Subhas Chandra Bose to Sarat Chandra Bose, April 4, 1927.

[9] Sarat Chandra Bose to Subhas Chandra Bose, April 16, 1927; A.N. Moberly to Sarat Chandra Bose, April 15, 1927; O.M. Martin to Sarat Chandra Bose, April 16, 1927.

body politic of India."[10] On May 6 he reaffirmed this attitude, which he explained to Sarat flowed from his general outlook on life. "Ideas are the stuff of which human movements are made," he passionately proclaimed to Sarat, "and they are not static but dynamic and militant. They are as dynamic as the Absolute Idea of Hegel, the Blind Will of Hartmann and Schopenhauer, the *élan vital* of Henri Bergson." A life consecrated to ideas was "bound to fulfill itself". He then invoked St Paul's famous words: "We wrestle not against flesh and blood but against principalities, against powers, against the rulers of the darkness of this world, against spiritual wickedness in high places."[11] Subhas had unflinching faith in the ultimate triumph of the ideas for which he stood.

Their offer of European exile having been rejected, the government ordered their prisoner's transfer to Almora jail. On May 11, 1927, Subhas was taken from Insein jail to a boat departing from Rangoon. In mid-May he was suddenly released. Bose inferred that the new governor Stanley Jackson had arrived with "an open mind" and with "the unerring instinct of a trained politician he had sensed the grievance of the people."[12]

Despite his rigorous apprenticeship in prison, Subhas was initially reluctant to assume the mantle of leadership upon his return from Burma. He pleaded with Basanti Devi to lead Bengal in place of her late husband C.R. Das. "The spiritual quest of Bengal," he wrote to her, "has always been voiced through the cult of the Mother." The "pack of vagabonds" he represented was importuning her not due to any lack of self-confidence but because "no worship is complete if we leave the mother out." He held up the examples of Madame Zaghlul Pasha and Madame Sun-Yat-Sen who had responded to the call of the Egyptian and Chinese nations after the death of their illustrious husbands. Basanti Devi, however, wanted to avoid being in the public limelight. She was prepared to stay in the background

[10] Subhas Chandra Bose to the superintendent, Insein jail, April 11, 1927.

[11] Subhas Chandra Bose to Sarat Chandra Bose, May 6, 1927.

[12] Bose, *The Indian Struggle*, p. 155.

and offer her adopted son emotional support. "May my life not wither away in the desolation of *sannyasa* (renunciation)," Subhas wrote to her, "may my life blossom forth in beneficent fulfilment with the touch of the inspiration that is behind this desolation—I crave for this blessing."[13]

The hill resort of Shillong in India's north-east was chosen as the most suitable place for the ailing Subhas during the months of summer and monsoon rains in 1927. Several family members accompanied him to the hills. Subhas spent the days playing with the children on the mountainside and the nights reading, writing letters, and preparing questions to be posed in the legislature. The eminent doctor Bidhan Chandra Roy came to treat him and his seven-year-old nephew Sisir, who was suffering from fever.[14] After some time his sister-in-law Bivabati and her children had to return to Calcutta. Sarat, a leading light of the Calcutta bar, was then building a new palatial home at 1, Woodburn Park, round the corner from his father's house at 38/2 Elgin Road. Bivabati had to be in charge of the Calcutta domestic scene and prepare to move house. "I felt rather uncomfortable after you all left suddenly," Subhas wrote to Bivabati. "The empty house gave a forlorn feeling—the mind became restive—I seemed to have lost for a while the moorings of my daily life—it will be no exaggeration to say that I felt a pang in my heart." He had imagined that he had transcended worldly attachments, but now had been given a stern reminder that he was not wholly unattached. Basanti Devi and Bivabati were the two significant women in his life at this stage, both of whom he had elevated to a motherly status. He blamed the long lectures he inflicted on them through his letters on the colonial masters. Arguing with the English, "even a shy and diffident person" like him had "become garrulous". It took some time to readjust to his quiet surroundings. "The azure sky, green fields, the mountain ranges all around, the play of light and shade in the forests, the continuous

[13] Subhas Chandra Bose to Basanti Devi, July 17, 1927; July 30, 1927; October 15, 1927.

[14] Sisir Kumar Bose, *Bosubari*, pp. 33–4.

roar of the waterfall," he wrote to his sister-in-law reassuringly, "all this keep me contented." When the rains cleared he would go out to commune with nature as he had done as a child in Cuttack and be reminded of Shakespeare's lines:

> And this our life, exempt from public haunt
> Finds tongues in trees, books in running brooks
> Sermons in stones, and good in everything.[15]

The exemption from public haunt did not last long. No sooner had he descended from the hills to the plains that Subhas was elected president of the Bengal Provincial Congress Committee. In December 1927, at the annual session of the Indian National Congress held at Madras, he along with Jawaharlal Nehru and Shuaib Qureshi was appointed a general secretary of the All India Congress Committee. As he criss-crossed the length and breadth of India addressing gatherings of youth, he wrote a few letters, far fewer than the huge number he wrote from prisons. "I have been shy by nature since my boyhood," he confessed in one private letter, "and I continue to be so until today—in spite of the fact that I go about making speeches at public meetings."[16]

"Jawaharlal has now given up Independence at the instance of the Mahatma," Subhas informed Basanti Devi in another letter.[17] The context for this criticism was the viceroy Lord Irwin's October 1929 announcement that he had been authorized by the Labour government in London to state that dominion status was the logical culmination of India's constitutional progress and that a round table conference would be convened after the Simon commission's report was published. A majority of the Congress leaders signed a manifesto in response to this overture, looking forward to the framing of a dominion constitution for India. Jawaharlal Nehru had initially hesitated to do so, but eventually fell in line as he had been selected by Gandhi to preside over the Lahore session of the Indian

[15] Subhas Chandra Bose to Bivabati Bose, [August] 1927.
[16] Subhas Chandra Bose to Kalyani Devi, October 26, 1929.
[17] Subhas Chandra Bose to Basanti Devi, November 5, 1929.

National Congress in December. Subhas Chandra Bose and two others, Saifuddin Kitchlew of Lahore and Abdul Bari of Patna, issued a separate manifesto calling for complete independence and rejecting the round table conference.

Subhas Chandra Bose's speeches and writings between 1928 and 1931 have been published in volumes 5 and 6 of the *Collected Works*. The letter-writing resumed in true earnest while spending time in British prisons during 1932.

Subhas was naturally among the Congress leaders to be arrested as soon as Mahatma Gandhi resumed civil disobedience and he was sent to a rather remote sub-jail in a place called Seoni in the Central Provinces. The only saving grace on this occasion was that he soon had his brother Sarat as his companion in prison. Sarat had suspended his legal practice to join the civil disobedience movement and now paid the price by being put away for four long years in British jails.

In prison Subhas kept himself busy reading Henri Bergson's *Creative Evolution* and other philosophical works. He asked a friend to send him recent biographies of Lenin and Trotsky, the four-volume memoirs of Alexander Herzen and literature on Thoreau. From late February 1932 he began to experience severe abdominal pain and by mid-May had suffered a weight loss of twenty-eight pounds. The civil surgeon of Chindwara thought there was something wrong with his gall bladder, but the doctors could offer no definite diagnosis.[18] As both brothers' health deteriorated—Sarat had early diabetes—they were transferred to Jubbulpore Central Jail. Subhas was subsequently shifted to the Madras Penitentiary, the Bhowali sanatorium, and Lucknow jail in quick succession, keeping him far removed from Bengal. With Sarat languishing in jail as well, it fell upon Bivabati to express concerns to the authorities about her brother-in-law's illness in detention.

In a letter to his nephews and nieces on August 29, 1932, Subhas described his living quarters in the Madras Penitentiary: "The local jail is smaller than that in Jubbulpore but the buildings are better,"

[18] Subhas Chandra Bose to a friend, February 27, 1932; April 22, 1932; April 29, 1932; May 14, 1932.

he wrote. "I live on the first-floor. The rooms are very small—just enough for one person—what they call 'cells' in English." In another letter to his sister-in-law Bivabati on October 1, 1932, he wrote: "I am very happy to know Neru's [Sisir's] examination results, but he must occupy the first place."[19] Sisir had stood second in class. A decade later he would choose this nephew to help him in his great escape from India in January 1941.

In early 1933 the government agreed to allow Subhas to travel at his own expense to Europe for treatment. The British would not set Subhas free on Indian soil or allow him to go to Bengal to see his parents before his departure for Europe. He would not see his father again. The government permitted him some time to be spent together with Sarat in Jubbulpore Central Jail where the brothers had a visit from Basanti Devi, Bivabati, and her children.[20] On February 13, 1933, Subhas was carried in an ambulance to the port in Bombay and released from detention only after he was put on board the Italian ship *S.S. Gange* sailing for Europe.

[19] Subhas Chandra Bose to Bivabati Bose and her children, August 29, 1932, and October 1, 1932.

[20] Ibid., pp. 49–51.

CORRESPONDENCE

1926—1932

1. *From Anil Chandra Biswas**

8/1/A, Devendra Ghosh Rd.
Bhawanipur.
1.8.26

My dear Subhasbabu,

I got your letter dated 9.7.26 on 17.7.26, and I am happy to learn that you received the report. I sent another copy of the report attached to the letter I wrote to you previously under the impression that, as I didn't get a letter from you for a long time most probably the report which I sent you before could not reach you. There has been many deficiencies in the list of books of the library, and I am also responsible for that.

....Illegible. More money was spent than was proper for us to spend and the amount of money spent would have been less had we cared to print the list in the way we printed the programme of variety entertainment. In the list, you will find that the name of the same book has been printed more than once, the reason being the library has more than one copy of that particular book and the library has quite a few books with three or four copies. The names of all such books have been printed more than once. You must tell us what we should do in such cases. The list of Bengali books has not yet been printed and I am going to send you a hand-written list very soon. You have asked whether it is possible to send books to you from the library. Please send the names of the books you want to have as soon as possible, and immediately after getting your letter we will arrange to send you books—two or three books at a time or whatever you like.

At present the journal *Atmasakti* is under the management of *Forward*, and it can be counted as a Bengali Weekly of the English journal *Forward*. *Atmasakti* is

* Translated from the original Bengali.

having a good circulation. Gopalbabu (Gopal Sanyal) is the editor and Upenbabu (Upendranath Banerjee) and quite a few others contribute to it. We get full sympathy for our Samity from such papers as *Forward, Bengalee, Atmasakti* etc.

I am really happy that you have sent me a detailed list of criticisms which have been made in regard to the Samity by outsiders. No harm really follows from such criticisms, though criticisms should be free from malice. Undoubtedly, criticism is never identical with slander or false allegations and a critic before making his criticism should know whether what he is saying is based on truth. If anybody who cares to criticise fails to follow this principle and indulges in criticism by accepting somebody's words as gospel truth and out of his enthusiasm for party spirit then he can't be called a real critic by any means. Anyway, I am going to answer to all the points of this criticism made by outsiders which you have come to know by now :—

1) Regarding house rent—In my previous letter I informed you that the Samity has to pay now twenty-two rupees more for the house rent than before. I made no secret of it and the present house rented by us was selected by all of us and before renting this house I informed you in detail about it. You too gave your consent and said that there was no fault in renting this house even if we were to pay Rs. 20 or 22 more. Now let us see whether by spending Rs. 22 more the Samity is really mis-spending the money out of its fund. Now according to me—probably you should agree—the spending of Rs. 22 more doesn't amount to mis-spending the money because this house with nine rooms is a very convenient place for the Samity and it is pretty difficult to have a house of this kind with the rent we pay for it. It is essential for the Samity to have quite a large number of rooms for its different departments. There are two rooms on the roof of this house and one of the rooms has been sub-rented, so we have just one room in our control on the roof. Don't you think that at least one room should be at our disposal if not for the members at least for the workers of the Samity such as Haricharan and others ? The critics

might say that the workers can jolly well use the reading room as their bedroom. But if any worker falls ill, should he be driven out of the house ? I also wrote to you before that a few members of the Samity wanted to have a members' room exclusively. They proposed that the room which had been sub-rented should be brought under our control again and the loss of money it would incur would be made good by them by increasing the number of members of the Samity or failing that by increasing the amount of money they contribute to the Samity as members. As a matter of fact quite a few of them could recruit new members. But unfortunately the person who took the initiative in this matter is in difficulty now, because his daughter has been suffering from typhoid for more than two months. As a matter of fact, it is essential for us to have a members' room where members can come and meet. So the spare room on the roof can serve a double purpose. For example the members can come there in the evening and meet, and at night the workers can sleep there. By allowing the members to use that room as their meeting place if the Samity can secure a donation of Rs. 10 from them, then the Samity will by no means be a loser. Recently we have decided that—and probably have informed you too by a previous letter—the members who are eager to keep that room and are ready to pay Rs. 15 for that fail to keep their promise then after waiting for a month we will sub-rent that room too. Of course, it will mean a great deal of difficulty for the workers of the Samity. But the Samity will be able to cut down expenses for house-rent by at least Rs. 13 a month and thereby the Samity will have to spend only Rs. 7 more for the house-rent than it used to spend before. Anyway whether we can keep apart a members' room or not, the Samity will at least be able to save money and pay only Rs. 7 more as house-rent. The house which the Samity rented and used before was not at all a convenient place and it had to face many difficulties there. As a matter of fact, there was not room enough for it there. The house the Samity is using at present is infinitely better than the former house. Jagubabu's bazar is very near to the Samity office and the house is practically situated on Russa Road. Quite a large number of people come regularly to the reading room of the library of the Samity in the morning and in the evening but the case was otherwise in the former house as practically none turned up to read sitting at the library. Under such circumstances, spending of Rs. 7 more in no way can be considered as wastage. Even if we fail to let out the members' room and lose some money thereby and continue to pay Rs. 22 more as house-rent, that also should not be considered as wastage of money because by being able to intensify and extend the works of the Samity we will have to spend more for house-rent. For example, at present, we use only one room for holding meetings of the Samity but if our activities go on increasing we will certainly require more rooms for holding meetings. Then, not to speak of letting out a room and earning money for the Samity, we will on the contrary have to spend more money on house-rent. Will it be then proper to say that the Samity is wasting money unnecessarily ?

2) It has been alleged that those who work for the Samity most dedicatedly sacrificing everything are not paid well for their labour. I do not want to know from you who has made this allegation but please ask him to furnish you with the names of such workers. Of course, at present, the Samity has workers who labour hard for it but neither do they get nor do they ask for any remuneration and certainly I am not going to say that workers who are paid allowances, get really good allowances. The Samity stands really on the loyalty and sincerity of its workers and it is undoubtedly true to say that the Samity should look after them. On this issue previously I had differences of opinion with Bhupen and others—specially regarding the remuneration of Haricharan. Those who work in the evening department of the Samity have no fixed pay. For weaving a yard of dhoti or Sari they get four annas and for starching two hunderd yards they get Rs. 5. For dressing a bundle of yarns they get four annas and for rolling up a bundle of yarns they get 10 paise per bundle. Well, this is the rate, and this has been so for a pretty long time. Pulin who has

been working as the tailor of the tailoring department of the Samity since the time of Samabaya Bhandar, takes voluntarily as his remuneration Rs. 16 a month—though it was decided that he would be paid Rs. 20 a month. Pulin only asked for a little amount of commission out of the profit made by the Samity and Pulin told us that if the tailoring department prospered then only he would ask for Rs. 20 as his monthly remuneration. Regarding paying some commission to Pulin nobody objects though what will be the rate of that commission has not yet been fixed. Haricharan teaches at school and does different types of works for the Samity (realising the fees, raising funds etc.) and he gets Rs. 30 a month as his remuneration. There is a worker called Nagen who opens the library in the evening and gets Rs. 10 as his remuneration. Nagen also works in the evening department of the Samity. At present Nagen is in difficulty because his mother has fallen ill. Formerly a gentleman named Priyanath Nandan was the librarian, but as he could land a good job he had to give up the work of the library for want of time and so Nagen was appointed for working in the library. To spare Nagen from renting a room for himself I allowed him to use a room of my own house in the ground-floor. There is another worker who teaches at another school during the evening and he is also in charge of such works as preparing cotton for making yarns, receiving paper containers made by others and arranging for their sale etc. and he gets a remuneration of Rs. 20 a month. I have something more to say about this particular worker about which I will tell you later. Apart from these workers there are many others in the Samity who work in its department of public service and also teach at school, but they do not get any remuneration. As a matter of fact their work can be counted as a labour of love for the Samity and they do work for it because of the love of it, and they really labour hard for it. Anyway, this is a full report of the Samity I have placed before you and if you think that allowances should be increased even after taking into consideration the present state of the Samity please write to that effect to me. The Samity as a whole is of the opinion that those workers who are given allowances, should be given more and it is also of the opinion that for the better efficiency of the Samity a few more workers should also be paid allowances (specially workers teaching at the school). Now I can say this with full confidence and emphatically that neither those workers who are paid nor those who are unpaid are aggrieved or sorry—the first group who are paid do not cry for more allowances and the second group for not being paid at all. As a matter of fact the workers of the Samity never lodged any complaint against it with anybody, never told anybody any word against it. So, the person who wrote to you bringing some charges against the Samity did so without having any proper knowledge about its inner working and its real condition. Please ask that person to provide you with a list of the names of the aggrieved workers of the Samity who have complaints of injustice being done to them etc., and then I think you will be able to understand whether I am telling you the truth or not. The person who wrote you that letter is closely connected with some institution and the workers who labour very hard "even at the cost of their lives" in that institution —what amount of money they are given as their allowance there—regarding that if you make enquiries I shall be very happy. Maybe, I ought not to have made the above comments and if it is deemed improper, I beg to be excused.

3) The charge that not enough efforts are made to sell the product of the Samity (khaddar cloths, paper bags etc.) is entirely false. As a matter of fact, khaddar cloths are sold at the shop and not only they are sold at the shop but also whenever Pulin goes out for canvassing tailored goods (i.e. dresses prepared at the tailoring dept.) he takes along with him khaddar cloths produced by the Samity and by Abhoy Ashram. We get khaddar pieces from Abhoy Ashram on loan and clear the loan after selling the goods and never keep the loan unpaid for more than Rs. 50. Besides Pulin, Haricharan too while raising funds also canvasses for the products of our weaving and tailoring departments. So, it is not the case that the khaddar pieces

which are produced by the Samity stock-pile without being sold—on the contrary our products are sold almost immediately after being produced. That the Samity cannot produce enough khaddar pieces is a fact and there are reasons for it. The person who wrote to you about this was neither aware of these facts nor ever tried to know them. The person who is in charge of making paper-containers and other items gets an allowance of Rs. 10 a month and he teaches at a school in the evening and earns altogether Rs. 20. This worker was told that if he could bring profit to the cottage industry department he would be given commissions on the profit. It is true that due to his negligence paper-containers and other products of the cottage industry department did not sell well but that does not necessarily mean that the Seva Bibhag of the Samity did not exert itself to sell the other products of the Samity. It is alleged that only for public display we have increased the number of persons who get monetary help from the Samity by decreasing the amount of money they are given as help. It is also alleged that even after cutting down the amount of help the Samity contemplates that anybody having help from any other source will be debarred from getting help from the Samity. Regarding this, I have asked the leading man of the Seva Bibhag of the Samity to submit a full statement. I am going to send the statement to you along with my next letter and from it you will come to know everything. It is true that the amount of help given to some of the persons seeking relief has been cut down and in some cases we have also stopped giving relief. Maybe, due to this the number of persons who get relief has gone up but this is not for public demonstration because we have never followed any such policy, the policy of making an image of the Samity by such unfair means. Had we resorted to such a policy we could have managed to get from the Corporation more money. I am giving an example of how we work. Whenever we go to the Councillors for seeking grant for the library we ask them firstly to come and examine our activities and whenever and wherever we go seeking for donation we don't ask for money, on the contrary we ask the would-be donors to come and visit our Samity and to examine its activities thoroughly. We went to Mr. T. C. Goswami. As soon as we met him he gave us Rs. 50. We of course at the very start asked him to visit the Samity and he said that he would and then he wrote in his own hand on the subscription book "1st instalment" and gave us Rs. 50. After that he, as he was a very busy man, could not manage to visit the Samity, though we went to his place so many times to bring him to the Samity. We did not take any money from him which we could have merely for the asking as the 2nd or further instalments. Believe me, I am telling you the truth, that even those who love the Samity very much and can spare money for it as donations are never pressed by us to contribute more money to the Samity. This I remember very clearly and will remember for ever that the day you were arrested—a Saturday—that day you wanted to give us some money to meet some of the liabilities of the Samity such as house-rent etc. I did not get the news of your arrest in the morning and only when I was back home in the afternoon, I got a copy of extraordinary edition of *Forward* on Russa Road and came to know of your arrest. You can easily guess how worried I became then about the Samity and when such was the situation the most respected Sarat Chandra Bose, after coming back to Calcutta told me, "I assure you that the Samity will never suffer from any want of money. Submit to me a detailed report on it mentioning specifically its different departments, what is their financial position and how much money every department requires and how all the deficiencies can be made up." I know that Sarat Chandra Bose is extremely generous in his donations and helps so many persons and organisations with money. When I realised that he took up the burden of helping those poor boys and those organisations you used to help, then I could have taken the opportunity of placing on his shoulder the financial burden of our Samity too, which I never did. From that day on when we saw him prepared to help our Samity, our respect for him increased hundredfold, and now we seek his advice regarding every affair of our Samity. This is true that now he is one of the greatest patrons of our Samity and not only a patron, but a guide. Yet we do not take from him more than Rs. 10 a month as donation which he used to pay us before your arrest. It goes without saying that had we so desired we could have got from him quite a big sum as our monthly donation, but we have not done so. As a matter of fact, after your arrest the Samity is only dependent on the money it could secure by arranging charity performances. Now our present plan is to extend the work of the tailoring department and gradually to switch over to other kinds of businesses and all these to make the Samity self-sufficient. I am telling you all these just to show that the Samity never resorted to any tricky policy to collect money for it. If I appear to be garrulous, talking a lot of nonsense, please excuse me. The Samity has of course cut down the amount of money given to some as financial help and even has stopped giving help to a few, but certainly not for artificially increasing merely the number of persons getting help from it. Some workers of the Samity never deny that they told some donors that if some of the workers of the Samity sought help from other sources for securing money then they would be given no more help. But this was necessary otherwise, the workers of the Samity would have neglected doing such works as spinning yarns etc. and would have concentrated only on going from door to door for securing money for themselves. So, I think just to stop them from concentrating on begging and to make them work hard for the Samity, they must be told that they should not spend their time and effort only to collect money and to drive this point home sometimes it is necessary even to stop giving them financial help or cutting the amount of money they get. Anyway, I have asked the leading worker of the Seva Bibhag to give a detailed statement about this and from that you will come to know everything.

4) The charge that the workers do not get their pay in time and that only some individuals get their pay and not others is not only entirely false but also indicates the person who brought this charge in his letter. We faced a great deal of difficulty after your arrest and found it difficult to pay the workers etc.—though, at that time there was no primary

school attached to the Samity and for doing work for the library none was paid—it was just an honorary work. At that time only Haricharan and the weavers used to get their allowance and even so it was difficult to pay them their allowances. Unfortunately, the writer of the letter never refers to that period, long in the past. The period he is specially referring to is not a period when it can be alleged that the workers did not get their pay in time or were not simply given any pay. Let me explain, why ? It was decided after the first variety entertainments arranged by us in December 1924 for collecting money that the money collected first be deposited with the man in charge of the cash of the Samity. Later, at the beginning of a new month, every department of the Samity should send a detailed statement to the Secretary of the Samity and then the Secretary, after going through those statements, would prepare bills for its different departments, and send them to the cashier and then the cashier would start paying different departments of the Samity. It was also decided that payments should be made on the 15th of every month and this policy was followed so the workers of the Samity used to get their pay in time. In last October, it was found that the Samity was failing in collecting enough money and drawing money from its bank-deposit to meet all these expenses of the Samity. This brought the Samity to such a situation that only a few hundred rupees were left in its bank account. Now if, instead of collecting more money for the Samity by arranging charity performances, the Samity went on drawing on its bank account, it would have gone bankrupt. So, we just suspended this policy of drawing money from the bank for a few months. For this reason, the workers of the Samity were told that the money needed for running it must be collected and earned and only a marginal amount if necessary would be drawn from the bank. The workers were also told that as before, they should submit monthly statement regularly. As this policy was followed no worker really remained unpaid because, whenever there was need for drawing the marginal amount from the bank we did so. By following this policy we could steer clear somehow and kept the Samity running. Now, we have decided to follow the old policy again—that is all collections and earnings should be deposited with the cashier and at the beginning of a new month he will start paying at a fixed date. As I have told above, for some time this policy was disregarded under the pressure of necessity which produced good results—we could realise money which was payable to us and neither the weaving nor the tailoring department had to do business on loans. We might have deviated from the former policy but that does not necessarily mean that only some individual workers were paid and not others. Regarding this, please write a letter to Sarat Babu (Sarat Chandra Bose) and then I think you will be given the true picture of the whole thing.

5) The so-called leaders of the Samity are responsible for the split in the Samity and making its Lansdowne Centre an entirely separate organisation. According to their statement it is not they who wanted to be separated voluntarily—they were forced to do so. Those who by casting their votes in the meeting managed to separate the Lansdowne Centre came only to cast their votes and nothing else because as a matter of fact quite a large number of them had practically no active interest in the workings of the Samity. I did not feel like writing to you regarding this Lansdowne Centre before because none of us felt happy on this issue of separation. I am bound to say that there was no way out other than separation because of the behaviour of this person and I am sure that you too would have preferred separation under such circumstances. I tried my utmost to fully co-operate with the Lansdowne Centre but when I found that the persons of the Lansdowne Centre were quarrelling with the workers of the Samity childishly on petty issues then I and others realised that this state of affairs should not be allowed to continue any longer and it was better to have a split and only then, the Lansdowne Centre was separated. I do not really like to write about all this in detail. Let me tell you that the charge that we brought a lot of persons to the meeting not interested in the Samity only to get their votes is not true. As a matter

of fact, we never went to any member of the Samity for vote-canvassing. On the contrary, Bhupen and others went to Mr. Haldar again and again but Mr. Haldar came to the meeting and spoke not in favour of them but against them. They went to Mr. Lalit Mohan Sen everyday for a week, with the motive that Mr. Sen would come to the meeting and fight for them. But when Lalit Babu was asked by Sarat Babu about his true opinion he said, "I cannot simply support Bhupen Babu and others." Later, all agreed to separate the Lansdowne Centre from our organisation. Their (Bhupenbabu and others) real motive was to dislodge some old members from the Committee and to push some persons chosen by their group. If we remember, Bhupen has all along been an assistant secretary himself though he never cared to carry out the duty of assistant secretary which led to a funny situation. Many workers and probably you too forgot that there was an assistant secretary called Bhupen, yet Bhupen is bent on holding some office here, there and everywhere, disregarding whether he is capable of doing any work or not. I am happy that now he has realised that it is not proper for him to hold so many offices at the same time. As a matter of fact, a few persons of this group were members of the Committee, but they were not satisfied with this and they wanted to occupy the whole Committee and turn it into a committee of their group and so they tried to dislodge other members of the Committee who did not belong to their group. Previously, they came into conflict with the workers of the Samity on very petty issues. We tried always then to settle these quarrels amicably, so that all could work in good co-operation. We were not ready to put up with this capturing policy of their group. Anyway, we even tried to come to some sort of understanding with them even on this issue. After the death of Deshbandhu, the workers of the Committee wanted to raise money for setting up a memorial to Deshbandhu. We organised a procession with this purpose and also decided to hold a variety performance. The members of the capturing group discouraged us in the matter of organising a procession, their reason being—as they would be busy with other things, they would not be able to join the procession which according to them would make the procession a failure. We tried to convince them that for their failure to join the procession they would not be blamed, and even if the procession failed to raise much money that would not be very harmful and we said, "Let us try our utmost". We failed to convince them and Bhupen afterwards went to the extent of seeing Mahatmaji to ask him whether a procession should be organised and Mahatmaji immediately recommended it and himself went to the Samity and contributed the first instalment to encourage others. Even after that they did not participate in that procession. In the beginning Bhupen joined the procession but later he was prevented by his group from joining it and then they started collecting money separately and publishing statements in the newspapers saying that the money was being raised by them for the cause of national library and Bhupen, Paritosh etc. were named as persons to whom the money should be sent. After all this we organised the variety performance. On the eve of that performance just a day before, Bhupen came to our place in the evening and wanted to know how many volunteers would be recruited from their group or centre. We said that the man who was in charge should be consulted regarding how many volunteers should be recruited and from where etc., because he had been given that power and none else. We also told him that previously when we organised a charity performance for raising money for the Samity which was held in Russa Theatre, many unwanted persons went inside the auditorium and occupied the seats for which a large number of people who wanted to buy tickets had to go back and on that occasion persons came with the whole family to see the performance. Despite all these talks, Bhupen repeatedly wanted to know whether a few from their group could be recruited as volunteers or not, and then we too were compelled to say that at least seven or eight of their boys would be enrolled as volunteers. After that Bhupen came to our place at 11 o'clock at night and told us that not a single person of their group would like to be a volunteer. On the day of the performance only Bhupen and two or three persons from his group came and none else and of course we also did not take the trouble of going to them and asking them to come. After that, they started a "systematic campaign of vilification and misrepresentation of facts." They also started a library in their centre and named it as National Library, and they demanded a grant of Rs. 5 per month for the library. By holding a meeting of the Samity it was decided then that they should formally apply for this grant and then their application would be considered. They did not like the idea and started saying that the Samity was not in favour of giving that grant. Then to pacify them I almost went against the decision of the committee and told them, "You better take a grant of Rs. 3 per month for your library. But as desired by the committee you should better send an application." Before setting up that library they were asked to agree to some conditions namely, 1) the library should be named the National Library, 2) if the National Library ever closes down then the original books donated to the library by patrons should go back to them and if they refuse to take those books, all the books should be consigned to the main library of the Samity i.e. National Seal library. They agreed to all these conditions and admitted that they would send an application as soon as possible. I had this confidence that they would, according to their promise, send their application and then the conditions being fulfilled nobody of the Samity would disagree to grant them Rs. 3 per month. I personally approached the members of the Samity and made them agree to the giving of this grant but even after getting this monthly grant for over a year they did not care to send that application despite my repeated request. Later after the death of Deshbandhu when the feud took the most severe turn they were specially requested to send that application. They sent an application all right, duly asking us to recognise their organisation as a branch of our Samity. In this application, they put down some conditions which were rather remarkable namely, (1) the executive committee of the Samity should consider 40% of the members of their organisation as members of the committee too (except Bhupen and others who are the direct members of the committee now), (2) if any feud arises inside the Samity, the executive committee will have no full power to judge about and give verdict on that feud. On the contrary, a board of members should be formed for that and the board should be open to anybody and everybody. They notified us that if the Samity failed to abide by these demands and recognise their organisation as a branch then they would be at liberty to follow their own path. After this their application was rejected and their organisation was separated from ours. We did not bring persons who would cast their votes in our favour. They on the contrary brought Lalit Babu to the meeting by persuading him, with the purpose of having his vote in their favour. Lalit Babu on the other hand, came and voted against them. For this, they vilified Lalit Babu as a traitor. We expected that they would accept their defeat in a sportsmanlike spirit and with this spirit they would agree to come to an understanding with others and then everything would be all right and the two groups, after burying the hatchet, would co-operate wholeheartedly and then everybody would mind his own business. We even were ready to welcome a healthy competition between these two groups. Belying this hope they just indulged all the more in false propaganda and vilification. They were not even satisfied with such activities and in the long run some of them took the trouble of writing letters to you directly. I don't know whether you believe it or not, even a few persons of that group tried their utmost to take away by cunning talks a few workers of our Samity. They even tried to stop the students from coming to school run by us and even asked them to leave our school. I wrote it before that I did not feel like writing all these again and whenever I remember all these I feel so dispirited that I wish to give up all work and retire. If you want I can give you a very detailed report about their activities to verify the truth of all these. You can contact Bhupen and ask him whether the report is true or false. You can also ask him whether any workers of our Samity ever indulged in any sort of false propaganda against them. As a matter of fact we are in no need of any kind of false propaganda. We are in such a positiion that we can do a great deal of harm to their group simply by telling the truth but no member of our Samity ever liked to do so. But what about the members of that group ? Is it not a fact that, not to speak of others, even Bhupen did never hesitate to bring false charges against the Samity and even to give bad names personally to Sarat Chandra Bose ? Bhupen is now a little bit wise and has stopped his campaign of slander. But a person called Sanat—a gentleman belonging to that group—is still now suffering from bad temper, which has not decreased even a little, and from the so-called criticisms which had been put down in the letter sent to you I can clearly see that this gentleman is the person who took the trouble to write that letter to you. You may remember that a young man called Bharati came to work for the weaving department of the Samity, a long time ago, in January 1924. It was Sanat who brought him. Before Bharati started working for us I told him, "Everyone has a right to improve his own conditions and should do it, and so if anybody has the good luck of landing a better job somewhere else we should be happy to allow him to leave us and join the other organisation." I also told him, "Before accepting any job anywhere one should consider carefully how long one will be able to stick to that job." I told all this because of the fact that it is rather difficult to recruit a man who really knows weaving, and also due to the fact that we had at that time another man who knew weaving. Bharati promised that he would not leave the job soon and join some other organisation. Just ten or fifteen days after, Bharati was sent to the provincial Congress office at the request of Nikunjababu to help them in setting up things for weaving. He stayed there for a few days, came back and told us that he had been able to get a better job somewhere else and that he would leave within a few days. I tried to persuade him to stay at least for one month but he was not ready to budge an inch from his decision. I told all this to you before, though I am not sure whether you remember them or not. Anyway, when I found that he was not even prepared to stay with us for at least a month, I took him to task and said some hard words. He too said things to me in an insulting tone and then left us. This chap Bharati even during his short stay with us, quarrelled with other workers of our Samity—Haricharan etc. He almost came to blows with Gopal, another worker and about Gopal, this can be said that he is really a good worker. Regarding no other worker we made such a comment before. I told you previously that Bharati happened to be a friend of Sanat and was well-known to him. So when Bharati left us Sanat became angry with me and when we had a feud with the Lansdowne Centre, Sanat left us and joined their group. Today when the feud has come to an end and some settlements have been reached, Sanat is not satisfied and even now is full of revenge. There was a worker called Sukhamoy who used to teach at our school and was also in charge of the cottage industry. Sanat happened to be a friend of Sukhamoy. Maybe, under Sanat's influence or for some other reason Shukhamoy was totally ignoring the cottage industry department and even was showing lack of interest in teaching at school which he used to do very enthusiastically. Sukhamoy failed to submit monthly statements regularly and did not care to see whether the boys were attending the classes regularly or not. Instead of himself teaching at the classes he deputed somebody else to do so—at least seven or eight days a month. He used to leave the school and go somewhere else and even to close the school at his own sweet will. Over and above, he was completely negligent about selling the stuffs produced by the cottage industry department. Though he was shown all these derelictions again and again and also was warned, he simply displayed a spirit of disobedience. As a result I asked Haricharan to stop paying him. Of course, when afterwards he submitted collectively the statements due for months, he was paid up all he was entitled to. When he wanted to visit his ancestral home in the countryside I asked him to write an application for leave stating how long he would stay there. This I did because once before, this man, on the plea of joining a conference, instead went to his country house and stayed there two months, though he was not supposed to be on leave for more than eight days for attending the conference. He submitted an application for leave all right but simply ignored to mention there how long he would be off from duty and be on leave. On the contrary, he just mentioned the name of a gentleman in that application saying that the said gentleman would act as his substitute for teaching at the school—though we came to know that he never consulted that gentleman before mentioning his name in the application. This particular gentleman was teaching at the school for quite a long time and when I told him about this he said, "I shall go on teaching here as I have been doing for such a long time but I am not ready to act as a substitute for anybody, and unfortunately Sukhamoy-babu did not care to consult with me before mentioning my name in the application." About a month later, this gentleman came to me and said, "After a week I shall not be in a position to devote so much time to the school because I shall have to attend to other works. So you should better appoint somebody else in my place." Meanwhile, we got no information from Sukhamoy whether he would be back or not and in his application, I have told you previously, he never mentioned the time he was going to spend outside. Under such circumstances, we were compelled to appoint a worker on a temporary basis. Sukhamoy came back a few days after. I had to send a letter to him asking him to see me. When he met me I tried to make the whole situation clear to him and also told him that if he wanted to continue in his work, he must abide by the rules of the Samity, that he should take care of the attendance of the boys, that he should not depute anybody else as his substitute to teach the classes whenever he felt like it etc. I gave him four or five days' time to consider the whole thing carefully and then to submit his answer. He did not care to see me after the expiry of that time and then I had to write two more letters requesting him to see me. Then he came to meet me and when I asked about his opinion he simply started disputing with me, saying such things as—he was once the headmaster of a school and he knew school management better than anybody else. After this encounter he stopped teaching at the school and stopped working for the cottage industry department. And, he started a propaganda against our school with the motive to prevent the boys from coming to school and in this matter he was helped by Sanat and few others. I am not ready to bring a definite allegation against this group called Tarun family group. All of them participated in this vilification campaign of Sukhamoy—but, Bhupen and others were against this act of Sukhamoy. It has been alleged that the weavers in our employment were grumbling as they were not paid their remuneration regularly. This is false because except Bharati none in the weaving department ever expressed such a sentiment, and apart from Bharati, Sukhamoy too was paid the remuneration not in time because of the reasons given above but his payments were never stopped wholly. I have reasons to believe that none other than Sanat did ever write to you bringing all these charges against us.

Weaving department—As a matter of fact our weaving department is not really in a happy state but, that does not mean that the charges brought against us by the writer of the letter is justifiable. Previously it was difficult to recruit weavers for our weaving department and at present it has become all the more difficult. The reason is—those who are weavers by caste, can earn a lot by doing their work staying at home. Marwaris and big businessmen come to them, place orders with them and provide them with loan of capital etc. and thus they collect the goods produced by the weavers. Boys coming from *bhadrolok* families usually do not show any enthusiasm for learning weaving and even those *bhadrolok* boys who learnt it before usually try to get jobs somewhere else. After buying yarns from outside at a high price (Rs. 2 and eight annas to Rs. 3 per bundle) the khaddar made out of them does not fetch any profit for us when sold at the market. It is not surprising that the workers of the Samity would feel dispirited if they find that the khaddar produced by them is not selling well. Moreover the present political situation of the country is such that the workers have lost their former zeal and enthusiasm, because formerly, though Khaddar was costlier than other cotton goods, yet so many people used to buy khaddar with hopes in their hearts, and the workers too used to think that by dedicating themselves to the cause of khaddar they were pursuing a great goal which made them forget their narrow self-interest. Just immediately after your arrest the work of the weavers had to suffer a bit for lack of yarn but that did not stop them working creditably well. We too never stopped their payment even at the time of their forced idleness due to lack of yarn because, we used to pay them on the basis of their average work-performance. So we have been trying all these days to run the weaving department well despite many difficulties. About these difficulties we are not secretive and we, as a matter of fact, publicly admit them and I am going to write more about all these problems later. I would like to ask you a question—if we use mill-made yarns while weaving towels, *gamchha,* duster etc. just on the borders of these products, will that appear objectionable to you?

Now let me tell you something about the World Health Association. Ramaprasadbabu is the spirit behind this organisation and he is also the secretary of this organisation. Our Samity helped this organisation by contributing some furniture to it and is also helping it now by bearing the burden of paying the rent for the room which holds its dispensary. A worker of the Samity goes about from bustee to bustee on behalf of the Health Association to render service to the bustee people, especially to arrange medical treatment for the poor of the bustees. This worker also has another duty—that is to look after the sanitation of the bustees and whenever he finds any part of the bustee insanitary he reports it to the district health officer. As a remuneration for this kind of work he is given Rs. 20 a month. The World Health Association has a doctor and a compounder attached to it and the doctor is paid an allowance of Rs. 50 a month and the compounder Rs. 20. All of them get the money from the Corporation. There are a lot of things which should be done collectively by the Samity and the Health

Association. But unfortunately this kind of work is not progressing happily. Though Ward No. 21 has no dispensary run by the Health Association yet Mr. J. N. Dutta the Secretary (your maternal uncle) is doing a lot, and is labouring very hard. Unfortunately, the Health Association in Ward No. 22 lacks good workers. I am not aware of any definite scheme which this Health Association has. Ramaprasadbabu is a very busy man and has not much time to devote to the work of the Health Association. Please prepare a scheme for the Health Association and send it to us and then I will try my utmost to make Ramaprasadbabu agree to this scheme, put it into practice and also see to it that the Samity be co-operative in this field. A Health Committee has been organised by the Samity with a view to co-operating with the Health Association in its activities. Of course, uptill now nothing much has been done. With the help of Bengal Social Service League and Calcutta Corporation the Samity is organising in different localities lantern lectures. Very soon we are going to publish the report of the year 1332 (Bengali Era). The publication is being delayed, as I am so very busy with other things and also due to lack of mental peace, caused by so many factors. The writing of the report has been finished and we have decided to secure advertisements for the printed report-book and it has also been decided that the constitution of the Samity should be given in the printed report as an appendix. We are going to send you a copy of the report by the next post—as a matter of fact the copy which we intended to send to you has not yet been typed.

A report regarding the financial position of the weaving and the tailoring departments will also be sent to you which will show the credit and debit side of the departments.

Mr. J. C. Mukherjee has arranged Hazra Park to be used by our workers as their playground. It was written by you in your letter that the boys of the National School did not have a ground to play and so I approached the Secretary of the National School and asked him whether he was ready to allow his boys to play together with the young boy-workers of our school. He told me that he would deliberate over it and then give his final answer. Then I came to know that you had written a letter to Santosh Babu asking him to arrange Hazra Park for the boys of National School as their playground and that Santosh Babu approached Mr. Mukherjee regarding this and Mr. Mukherjee was prepared to arrange it in such a way that the boys of the two organisations could play there alternately. As yet Mr. Mukherjee has not done anything of that nature and he only wanted to know our opinion. If such an arrangement is made, that will really be inconvenient for our workers. I admit that the National School requires a playground for its boys but as there is a big compound within the premises of the National School it can be used as the playground (assuming that they have no access to Hazra Park) but we have no such facilities and so feel badly the need of a playground. Our workers are really boys from local schools. So what is the harm if they play with the boys of the National School? After all, we could arrange Hazra Park as the playground after undergoing a lot of trouble, and if our workers are deprived of sports that will not be good for the organisation. We are in need of a magic-lantern apparatus of our own and so we have asked Mr. J. C. Mukherjee to arrange some money for it. Mr. Mukherjee promised that he would himself contribute something and would collect some money for us too. If you write to Mr. Mukherjee regarding this then I am sure Mr. Mukherjee himself will be able to provide us the whole amount of money required for buying the apparatus.

We have a catalogue of the books in our library and we are sending you this catalogue. I am also sending you the catalogue of the Bengali books in our library. From these two catalogues you will come to know what books are there in our library, and we expect suggestions from you regarding books. If we already have the books suggested by you we will not buy them again but we will certainly buy other books suggested by you which are not there in the library. I have prepared a complete list of the books of our library. You know our library is frequented by a lot of college boys and our library also contains books useful for them but still it will be better to buy more books for them. We are not going to buy any book till we get the suggestions from you. So please send the suggestions as soon as possible.

Yours sincerely
ANIL

PS. I am sending an album containing the photographs of the boys and workers of the school. These photographs were taken by. . . . (illegible) and we had to spend some money for it. I made enquiries regarding Haricharan and a few of his closest friends remarked like that and I have tried to persuade them. Bhupen and Kulada came today to see me and they said that they had no objection against the boys of the National School playing with the workers of our Samity. So the boys of the National School and the workers of our Samity are going to play together using Hazra Park as their playground. Send a list of the books you want to borrow from the library and as soon as we get the list the books will be sent to you.

ANIL

2. *From Sarat Chandra Bose*
Censored and Passed
Illegible
7/8/26
for D.I.G., I.B., C.I.D.
Bengal

38/1, Elgin Road
6th Aug. 1926
Friday 8 p.m.

My dear Subhas,

My last letter to you was on the 31st July.

I received your message yesterday. The reason why

I asked you whether you were willing to contest North Calcutta was this : Mr. J. N. Basu (the sitting member) is desirous of contesting again and uptill now, the only rival candidate in the field is Rai Lalit Kumar Mitra of Shambazar. You know Rai Lalit Kumar Mitra and I believe you will agree with me when I say that he is absolutely no good. Srijut Upendra Nath Banerji has withdrawn his candidature. The body which he represents viz. the Karmi Sangha, have practically decided not to go into the Council. In the circumstances I thought that you might be asked to contest the seat. If you contest, I doubt if Mr. J. N. Basu has any chance. Influential residents of North Calcutta would also like to have you. A seat in the Bengal Legislative Council would not interfere with your work as C.E.O. Please give the matter a thought and if you revise your decision, please send me a telegram.

As for my going into the Council, I have decided to contest if I am given the University seat. In the present state of my health, I cannot think of contesting 24 Parganas or Diamond Harbour. To do so would mean my spending the whole of the long vacation here. I must have at least a month and a half's rest.

I do not understand why Srijut Satyendra Ch. Mitra preferred the Assembly to the Bengal Council. Noakhali may not be a safe seat for any one except Satyendra Babu. Indu Bhusan Dutt might be sent to the Assembly.

Please remember me to Satyendra Babu with my love and kindest regards.

Khuku's marriage was celebrated on Tuesday last. The bridegroom's father is a perfect gentleman. He created a most favourable impression on all.

I haven't had news of you for quite a long time. Possibly the fault is mine—I am so irregular in my correspondence. Hope you don't mind it.

With love,

Yours affly

SARAT

Subhas C. Bose Esq.

3. *To Sarat Chandra Bose*
Censored and Passed
Illegible
25/8/26
for D.I.G., I.B., C.I.D.
Bengal

Mandalay
13.8.26

My dear brother,

Your letter of the 6th reached me on the 11th inst. I have considered the matter as coolly as I could and I would like you to consider the following points :—

I. I am getting disgusted with the Councils because I find that people who go there do not mean to do any tangible work for the country. It is time for the pendulum to swing back in an anti-Council direction.

II. If it is considered necessary for me to stand, would not my election to the Assembly, say from the City of Calcutta or the Presidency Division, have a greater significance ? If my name is not on the electoral role, I may be authorised to vote on behalf of some limited company or Corporation.

III. If my election is going to cost a lot of money, I do not want the luxury of being an M.L.C.

IV. It is more important that you should be in the next Council, rather than I. If you think you have a good chance, I shall be glad if you stand from North Calcutta, failing a better constituency.

V. I cannot think of any reliable man on whom I can depend for the success of my election campaign. All would-be M.L.C.s will be busy with their own fight, and in the absence of reliable and capable election agents, I may come to grief.

VI. Your health is much more important than my election to the Council. I am afraid that if I stand, the burden will ultimately come down on your shoulders and you may be prevented from taking your annual rest. This I consider to be disastrous in the present state of your health.

VII. What guarantee is there that Kiron Babu and Company would like me to stand? Uptill now they have not shown any anxiety about having me. Will there not be a repetition of the Council of State Election?

VIII. Last but not least, I cannot contest North Calcutta as long as there is any possibility that Upen Babu or any other representative of his party will be a candidate. I cannot even stand for the Council or the Assembly, if the leaders of the Karmi Sangha view my candidature with displeasure.

These are the considerations which are weighing with me at the moment. Please consider them and if you think that my election will be in the public interest or of public importance, please advise me accordingly and I shall abide by your decision. I am not aware of what is happening outside and that is why I leave the last word with you. Your argument that work in the Council will not interfere with my work as C.E.O. seems to me to be unnecessary. My C.E.O.-ship will cease in May next and you can rest assured that till then I shall be here.

If after considering the above points you think it necessary for me to stand, please send me a wire. Otherwise I shall take it that the matter has been dropped once for all.

I shall write more about Maymyo in my next letter. Hope this will find you all quite well.

Yours v. affly
SUBHAS

S. C. Bose Esq.
38/1, Elgin Road
Calcutta.

4. *From Sarat Chandra Bose*
Censored and Passed
Illegible
27/8/26
for D.I.G., I.B., C.I.D.
Bengal

38/1, Elgin Road
27th Aug. 1926

My dear Subhas,

Your letter of the 13th was to hand yesterday. I trust you have got my message by now saying that it is my view that you should contest North Calcutta. Let me deal with your points in the order in which you have stated them :—

I. It is true that members of the Council have uptill now done very little work for the country. The reason is that we haven't got the right type of men there. If Mr. Das had been alive, we could have sent any number of nonentities to the Council. But as he is no more, we should see that the Council is not only strong in number, (I mean the Congress group) but also in talent.

II. I could have chosen some other constituency for you but that would mean more work for me and others. In North Calcutta, I expect you will have a walkover. Mr. J. N. Basu might even give up the fight, though he has great influence in that quarter. Further to beat Mr. Basu would have a great significance.

III. The election will not cost a lot of money.

IV. I have decided to contest the University seat. I might not be opposed there.

V. Plenty of *reliable* men have already offered their services for your election campaign. They will not take up other work.

VI. You needn't feel concerned about my health. I am all right now and I shall have at least a month's rest. I intend to leave for Burma on the 12th September (if not earlier) after making the necessary arrangements here.

VII. Mr. J. M. Sengupta (which expression includes

Kiron Babu & Co.) is most anxious that you should contest. Rai Lalit Kumar Mitra (who sought Congress nomination) cannot really be thought of, so far as Council seat is concerned. As regards your apprehension of repetition of the Council of State election muddle, you can depend upon it that I would not have consented on your behalf if I was not sure that there was no such apprehension this time.

VIII. Upen Babu had finally decided not to stand before I consented on your behalf subject of course to your approval. There were various considerations which led him to withdraw and financial considerations were not the least important among them. The leaders of the Karmi Sangha welcome your candidature. I had a talk with Upen Babu last night and he said that that was so. I had also a talk with Amar Babu day before yesterday in the High Court and that was his view also. Amar Babu further thinks that Mr. J. N. Basu will withdraw.

Taking everything into consideration, I have come to the conclusion that you should contest. If I had not felt in my mind that the situation demanded your services in the Council, I would never have consented. I know that my decision will not be very palatable to you; but as you have left it to me, I shall go ahead.

I shall not write any more today as I am anxious to catch tomorrow's (Sunday's) mail.

Please let me know if the climate of Maymyo is good now. Some people here were saying that plague breaks out occasionally there.

Hope you are better.

Yours very affly

SARAT

5. *To Sarat Chandra Bose*
Censored and Passed
Illegible
for D.I.G., I.B., C.I.D.
Bengal

Mandalay Jail
3.9.26

My dear brother,

I was in receipt of your letter of the 27th August yesterday. Your pointed reply has thoroughly satisfied and re-assured me. The reason why I favoured an Assembly seat, particularly a constituency like Calcutta City was two-fold. Firstly, I thought it would be of greater significance and secondly it would cost us less trouble and money. I did not think that the fight in North Calcutta would be so easy though I had not the least doubt about the issue. However the matter is now in your hands.

I am happy to learn that you expect to be returned unopposed. But there is no knowing—somebody might pop in at the last moment and cause anxiety. I do not think Sir Nilratan Sircar would desire to contest ; if he does Dr. Bidhan Roy might be able to dissuade him. But I feel almost certain that Prof. Devaprasad Ghosh will enter the arena, if for no other reason, at least with the intention of putting you to some amount of trouble and expenditure. The Responsive Co-operation Party, as far as I can judge, will not allow the seat to go uncontested. But if you can tackle Mr. I. B. Sen (who will be responsible for setting up candidates) and Mr. B. Chakravarti and if some one else could influence Prof. Devaprasad through Sj. Hirendra Nath Dutta or Sj. Shyam Sundar Chakravarti or Sir P. C. Roy—there may not be any trouble from that quarter. I believe Sir P. C. Roy has great influence over Prof. Devaprasad and I think Sj. Lalit Mohon Das of the B.P.C.C. to some extent. (Both Lalit Babu and Devaprasad Babu hail from Barisal). If Rai Bahadur Jogendra Ghosh stands, no one will take him seriously.

At first I did not realise how you could think it possible

to stay out of Bengal for over a month at this juncture with two elections hanging over your head, as it were,—but now I understand. I am glad that you are so hopeful about the Mahomedan candidates—but the point is—will they remain loyal after they enter the Council Chamber ? However, I suppose one has to choose the lesser of two evils and make the best of a bad situation. I am only anxious that there should be no attempt at unity on false or unreal issues—for such attempts will prove futile. We should rather build our "mansion", to use Deshbandhu's expression, on solid rock—even if the immediate future does not appear to be rosy and a falling off in numbers proves to be inevitable.

I agree with your estimate of Rai Lalit Kumar Mitra—or rather with what I think to be your estimate of him. I really do not know what will happen to him when he adds a few more letters to the tail end of his name. I find from the papers that he has started using the title F.R.E.S. which one can purchase by paying a subscription and which, in worth and importance, vies with the dignified title M.R.A.S. I am afraid a too rapid ascent may prove his ruin. He has a clever knack of anticipating his nomination by announcing his candidature in advance.

I hope you will put up a good candidate for the Calcutta seat in the Assembly. Failing a better candidate you may set up Sj. Satcowripati Roy.

In fixing up your future programme, please bear in mind the nomination and polling dates.

Maymyo is a healthy place, no doubt. There is no plague there. Between Maymyo and Mandalay the Governor and his staff spend the greater part of the year and they do not give more than a month to Mandalay. There is no hotel there, worth the name and the officers mostly live in bungalows. In your last message you have asked me not to engage a house at Maymyo till the end of this month. This letter will reach you about the middle of this month at the very latest. If your coming to Maymyo about the end of this month is finally settled, I shall expect a message from you about the middle of this month instructing me to engage a house. One of our non-official visitors, Mr. Jamnadas Umechand Jhaveri, has offered his services in this connection. He is a highly respected gentleman and is the premier pearl merchant of this city. I have found him to be a decent and straightforward man though he is an Honorary Magistrate and has intimate relations with the big Government officials. Though I have got other offers, I shall probably depend on him in the matter of fixing up accommodation for you. His telegraphic address is "Osval", Mandalay.

What have you done about the grants to the Ayurvedic Colleges? Has the Health Com. reported again about the matter which was referred back to it viz. the enhanced grant to the Ashtanga?

Hope this will find you all quite well. I am so so. When is father going to Kurseong? Where is he now?

Yours v. affly
SUBHAS

S. C. Bose Esq.
38/1, Elgin Road
Calcutta.

7. *From Sarat Chandra Bose*
Censored and Passed
Illegible
16/9/26
for D.I.G., I.B., C.I.D.
Bengal

Giddapahar
Kurseong, 15.9.26
Wednesday

My dear Subhas,

I got your letter of the 3rd on the 12th.

The latest news from Calcutta is that Jatin Bose has decided to put up a big fight. Well, we are determined to put up a bigger fight and let us see whom the Lord favours. I enclose two letters I have received from Babu Nripendra

Ch. Mitra (of North Calcutta) who is one of our staunchest workers.

Pravash Bose (brother of Sarat Bose of Burdwan) has purchased a second hand Ford car for us for Rs. 600/-. I am told that the car is in excellent condition. The car has been placed at the disposal of North Calcutta for election purposes.

Prof. Devaprasad Ghosh has entered the lists and is going to fight me over the University seat. I shall therefore have to work harder than I had expected it would be necessary. When I heard from Dr. Bidhan Roy that neither Sir Nil Ratan nor Devaprasad was going to contest, I thought there was chance of my being returned unopposed. However, I don't mind a fight. It will mean of course, that I shall have to visit important mofussil stations.

When I go down to Calcutta, I shall see Sir P. C. Roy and ascertain if he is supporting Prof. Devaprasad Ghosh.

I find now, contrary to my previous expectations, that the chances of my going out of Bengal are rather remote. I can only do so, if Jatin Bose backs out. I cannot decide one way or the other before the 4th Oct. the date fixed for the nominations.

I have asked Dada to see Pandit Pasupati Nath Shastri and request him to prevent Rai Lalit Kumar Mitra from doing any mischief. Pandit Amar Nath was Rai Lalit's Guru and Pandit Pasupati Nath may be able to dissuade him from joining hands with Jatin Bose. Rai Lalit Kumar is very sore on account of his application for the North Calcutta seat being rejected by the B.P.C.C. executive and his 'Moshaib' S. K. Banerji (late of the Bombay Chronicle) may egg him on to do mischief.

Nirmal Chunder is going to contest the Assembly seat. I don't think any one will be able to contest him successfully. Satcowri Babu is not contesting this time. Prabhudyal is contesting Burrabazar and has very good chances there.

Please don't delay in writing to the persons named in my last letter for support of your candidature, particularly to the Cossipore-Chitpore representatives in the Corporation. I shall also see them as soon as I am in Calcutta.

I don't know yet when father is expected in Calcutta. Probably he will come early next month.

I am going down to Calcutta by the Darjeeling Mail today and shall send this letter by messenger to 13 Elysium Row.

I am leaving wife and children here as I intend to come up here from time to time, whenever I can snatch a few days' rest.

This leaves us well. Hope you are feeling all right.

Yours very affly

SARAT

Subhas C. Bose Esq.

8. *To Sarat Chandra Bose*

Censored and Passed
Illegible
2.9.26
for D.I.G., I.B., C.I.D.
Bengal

Mandalay
26.8.26
Thursday

My dear brother,

I have not had any further news about Maymyo since I wrote to you on Monday last. I am making the necessary enquiries and shall have someone sent down there this weekend. I shall probably be able to send you a wire on Monday or Tuesday next. As I have already written to you, all these arrangements notwithstanding, you should reconsider the whole matter in the light of what I have said. I shall be sorry if you put yourself to inconvenience or sacrifice public work in coming over to Maymyo. What will happen to the *Forward* case in your absence ? If an adverse judgement is delivered before the Puja, arrangements will have to be made to fill up the vacancy in the editorial staff. There are so many other things of importance which will demand your attention during the long vacation and if you remain at Kurseong or Darjeeling you will be able to do justice to them. Even if the house is engaged in the meantime, you should not hesitate to alter your plans at the last moment, if you find it necessary for your own convenience or in the public interest.

So Mr. Jadunath Sarkar has been appointed Vice-Chancellor after all. I was interested to read an extract from his famous letter translated into Bengali and reprinted in the *Charumihir,* a Bengali weekly of Mymensingh.

I was very much surprised to learn that Mr. Sasmal's election as Chairman of the District Board of Midnapore had been set aside by the Government and that Mr. Debendra Lal Khan had been appointed in his place. This is a bad precedent for all local bodies and is against the spirit of local self-government. Have Government given any reasons for acting thus ?

How is the Chittaranjan Seva Sadan working ? Who are in-charge of the institution ? Is the management in the hands of the trustees or of a smaller group ?

One of the reasons why there is so much trouble in the Mofussil is that the Mofussil has been almost forgotten by the Calcutta leaders. They seldom stir out and there is no living relationship between them and the Mofussilites. The only people who are working among the Mofussilites are those who are out to create communal trouble and strife and the consequences are therefore disastrous. Members of the Council too hardly consider it necessary to nurse their constituencies. I am afraid this can hardly be remedied if the leaders are not able to devote more time and energy to their public work.

How is the Deshbandhu Village Reorganization Committee working ? How many centres are they now managing ? Are they drawing money from the capital or are they simply spending the interest ?

I am strongly of opinion that communal franchise and communal electorate should go. I am glad that public opinion in England is gradually coming round to this point of view. I have with me a cutting from a Rangoon paper giving an extract from the *Manchester Guardian's* leader on this subject. The *M. Guardian's* view is thoroughly sound. Further, if a fixed number of seats is set apart for Mahomedans, there can be no apprehension that Mahomedan interests will suffer and we can expect reasonable Mahomedans to support a scheme for the establishment of mixed electorates. I hope Muslim opinion on this point will gradually veer round when the evil consequences of communal strife are fully realised. I am sending you the cutting referred to above along with this.

Do you know how the *Atmasakti* is getting on ? Who is the editor now and what policy is it following ? Is the paper improving financially or gaining in influence ?

A fellow detenu here has recently written Nalini Babu a letter regarding my candidature. If Nalini Babu happens to refer to it, you may tell him that I have not had any hand in it and that I was definitely against his writing it—though I do not think any one can doubt the truth of its contents.

If you ultimately decide on Maymyo, you may ask Goswami or Nalini Babu or other friends to come up for a change for a week or fortnight at Maymyo. They can easily afford the expenditure and it would give us great pleasure to meet them. By the way, before you start, you may get a permit from the Bengal Government to interview Satyen Babu, Suren Babu (Mohan Ghosh) and other fellow-detenus here.

You probably know that according to the existing rules we are entitled to at least one interview a week. With the special sanction of the Government we can have any number and you probably remember that when I was in Calcutta, I used to have interviews daily. In view of the fact that ordinarily we do not avail ourselves of this right, it is only fair for me to expect that if you decide to come up to Maymyo, the Bengal Government will make a special concession regarding the number of interviews which I shall be allowed. I do not think the local Government (Burma) will have any objection to granting me as many interviews as possible, if Bengal do not object. Anyway you should settle this matter with the Bengal Government before you leave Calcutta. Please do not forget to get special permits for all the members of your party to interview me.

Please send me a wire if you want any special arrangements to be made for you e.g. engaging cooks or servants, engaging a whole-time taxi etc. I believe you will be bringing all your crockery etc. with you.

You may bring some Darjeeling tea with you and some *Sandesh.* We can arrange to have a Jailor or warder sent to the Mandalay Station to meet you when you arrive, on your way to Maymyo—if you have any parcels for us like tea or *Sandesh.* I do not think you will get a through train to Maymyo—you will have to change at Mandalay station where there will be an hour's halt.

Have you been able to send the money to Cambridge for the M.A. degree ?

I hope you will not forget about the Baidyasastrapith. I am sorry that Jamini Babu expired so suddenly—no one expected it, as he was quite young when he died. It is natural that people will think kindly of him now and his friends may utilise this feeling for securing a better grant for the Ashtanga School. Under the circumstances, the Health Committee may reaffirm their former recommendation for a total grant of Rs. 23,000/- for the Ashtanga or may even enhance the grant recommended. If the recommendation comes up before the Corporation while the emotion lasts, it may be accepted by the house. Personally I think that the question of amalgamation should be raised once more. There can be only one first-grade Ayurveda College in Calcutta and this is possible only when all efforts are combined and amalgamation takes place in some form. We can pay a real and tangible tribute to the memory of Jamini Babu only by erecting first-grade Ayurveda College in Calcutta and it would therefore be in the fitness of things to raise the question of amalgamation once again. If there is no amalgamation, all my sympathy goes to the Baidyasastrapith.

Have you been able to find Mr. S. K. Sen's certificates ? If so, please return them to him.

I understand that Mr. Bhaskar Mukherji was appointed Assistant Secretary but that in the meantime he got an attack of brain disease. Are you going to give him leave or will you appoint someone else in his place ? What is the matter with Bhaskar and how is he keeping ?

Where and how is Mrs. Das now ? Bhaskar's illness coming on the top of Bhombal's sad death is another blow for her. I wonder where and when this chain of misfortunes is going to end. May God grant her strength !

I hope *Rangamamababu* is seeing to it that his concern is improving financially from day to day. A paper is first and foremost a business concern and its politics must be subservient to its financial interests. I hope the paper is sailing with the tide of popular opinion without unduly offending the feelings of any section or party. By-the-by, how is the Patrika doing financially ? Has the *Bengalee* been able to improve its circulation since Mr. I. B. Sen took over charge ?

I have received the following communication from the Revising Authority, Calcutta University Constituency :—

"Mr. Subhas Chandra Bose obtained his first degree of (Calcutta University) in 1919 and is therefore not qualified under Rule eleven of Schedule II of the Electoral Rules (quoted in the margin) as an elector for the Calcutta University constituency of the Bengal Legislative Council."

"A person shall be qualified as an elector for the Calcutta University Constituency who has a place of residence in Bengal and is a member of the Senate or an Honorary Fellow of the University or a graduate of the University of not less than 7 years' standing."

I have the honour to be Sir
Your most obedient servant
Sd/Ahsanullah
Revising Authority

According to my calculation, I am entitled to be a voter this year, having completed 7 years after graduation. What do you think ? Though I am not standing at the coming election, it is advisable to have my name in the electoral roll. If you think that the Revising Authority's interpretation is wrong, the Courts may provide a remedy—otherwise the dicision of the Revising Authority is final.

How are you keeping now ? I am so so.

Yours v. affly
SUBHAS

P.S.

Will father be going to Patna ? How long will he be staying there ?

S. C. B.

P.P.S.

Bipin has been promoted to the 4th year class of the National Medical Institute. He will be requiring some medical books and instruments. I have asked him to see you regarding the matter. If you think it necessary, you may introduce him to friends who may be inclined to help a promising and needy student.

S. C. B.

Enclosure—a cutting from the Rangoon Gazette—

SEPARATE MAHOMEDAN ELECTORATES
DANGER OF EXTENSION OF COMMUNAL PRINCIPLE

July 17.

In an editorial on the communal riots in India, the Manchester Guardian, after referring to Sir Tej Bahadur Sapru's proposal to disfranchise districs where communal rioting occurs as deserving of attention, expresses the opinion that the contention that the abolition of communal representation will tend to soothe inter-communal feeling is sound, but there is no evidence to show that Mahomedans have yet changed their minds with regard to the insistence on separate Mahomedan electorates.

The paper says : We cannot override the will of 60,000,000 Mahomedans when we set about building up India's new constitution, but possibly, in three years, communal riots made some alteration in the view-point of the Mahomedan rank and file. The question will require the serious attention of the Royal Commission, to be appointed under the Government of India Act, for it is disquieting to observe the principle of communal representation extending from the Legislatures to the Civil Service. If it is admitted in the Civil Service, can it be excluded in the Army, and, if the army of Swaraj India is officered on the communal principle, would it not soon be distracted by Hindu-Moslem feud ? The truth is, if the Mahomedan community persists in its present attitude towards Hindus, it will be impossible to think of Swaraj except as a beautiful dream or nightmare.

Rangoon Gazette
July 19, 1926

9. *From Sarat Chandra Bose*
Censored and Passed
Illegible
3/9
for D.I.G., I.B., C.I.D.
Bengal

38/1, Elgin Road
Calcutta
2nd September,
1926

My dear Subhas,

In my letter of the 27th Aug. I acknowledged your letter of the 13th Aug. Since then, I have received two letters from you—one letter dated 11.8.26 which I received on 27.8.26 and another letter dated 16.8.26 and posted on 23.8.26.

Practically the whole of the second page (numbered 255) of your letter of the 11th Aug. was deleted. In the first page you began discussing Jones's letter to Ray Knight.

Now as regards the Council elections, I have been nominated candidate for the Calcutta University.

No one is contesting Mr. Surendra Nath Roy of Behala because he has signed the Congress creed.

Your telegram from Mandalay regarding nominating Mr. Satish Chakravarty for the Khulna constituency was duly placed before the B.P.C.C. Executive. Before receipt of that telegram, Srijut Sailajanath had been selected for that seat. However on receipt of your telegram, the matter was reconsidered and the opinion of all (including Sj. Amarendra Nath Chatterji & others) was that it would not be right to change after accepting Sj. Sailajanath. Amar Babu further said that the principle for which we are fighting will be sufficiently vindicated by setting you up for the Council and Sj. Satyendra Nath Mitra for the Assembly.

I have received the telegram sent by you. I think I had better not decide definitely about my movements until the end of this month. I believe hotel accommodation is available at Maymyo and you can make some arrangements for my stay there if I give you seven days' notice.

The publication of your name as candidate for North Calcutta has set Jatin Babu a-thinking. I don't think he will withdraw ; but if I am not very much mistaken in my calculations, he will have to suffer a defeat.

The *Forward* case has been fixed for the 15th.

I am leaving for Kurseong on Saturday next and shall be back here again on the 14th or the 15th.

I must stop here today. Hope you are well.

Yours very affly

SARAT

Subhas C. Bose Esq.

10. From Sarat Chandra Bose

Censored and Passed (posted on 4/9)
F. J. Lowman
D.I.G. of Police, I.B.
4/9

38/1, Elgin Road
4th September, 1926

My dear Subhas,

Your letter of the 26th August was to hand yesterday.

As regards my coming to Maymyo during the holidays,

I have finally decided not to arrange anything until the end of this month. Towards the end of this month, I shall know whether my presence will be needed in Calcutta either for our election campaign or for any other public work. If I come, I think it would be better to stay in a Hotel at Maymyo, (if there be one).

I am leaving for Kurseong tonight by the Darjeeling Mail and shall be back here either on the 15th or the 16th instant. The *Forward* case has been adjourned till the 16th. On that day, I shall cross-examine the prosecution witnesses and after cross-examination is over, I believe the case will be adjourned for some time for calling defence witnesses.

I believe I shall be going to Noakhali on the 18th to appear for the defence in *Desher Bani* Sedition case.

No reasons have been given for setting aside the election of Mr. Sasmal as Chairman of the District Board of Midnapore. One is left to speculate.

The Seva Sadan is doing very good work under the direction of Dr. Bidhan Roy.

The Village Reorganisation work is proceeding very slowly, I am sorry to say. There is not sufficient money to do work on a large scale. We are now spending the interest. Some portion of the capital was touched during Deshbandhu's lifetime. I shall ask Nalini Babu to send you a complete statement of the work done uptill now.

Our own centre at Kodalia is doing fairly good work.

As regards the *Atmasakti,* haven't I told you before this that the Forward Publishing Ltd. has taken it over ? I kept it going till Chaitra last and from Baisakh, made it over to the *Forward.* Since Baisakh, the sale of *Atmasakti* has gone up about 10 times. Advertisements are rather dull because of the general slackness in business. Gopal is continuing as Editor and there is a big list of contributors. The paper is gaining in influence daily.

Nalini Babu was referring to a letter received by him recently from a fellow detenu of yours there. I have told him that you were against writing a letter like that.

If I come to Maymyo, I shall apply for permission regarding interviews etc. mentioned by you. If I come, of course I shall want a cook and some local servants and a furnished house (including crockery, cutlery etc.).

No, I am sorry I have not been able yet to send money for your M.A. degree. I think it will have to stand over till next year.

I shall bear in mind all you have written about the Baidyasastrapith. Unfortunately on account of my absence from the Corporation for several weeks, I have been unable to do anything for Baidyasastrapith.

Mrs. Das left for Purulia last week with her daughters and daughter-in-law. She will stay there for a couple of months certain.

Bhaskar is all right now. He has applied for the Assistant Secretaryship of the Corporation but I don't think he acted wisely in doing so. I doubt very much if his health can stand so much strain.

Rangamamababu's concern is improving financially. Last year it made a profit of Rs. 12,000/- half of which was however put to machinery depreciation a/c. He has improved the business side of it very much with Harish's help—though of course, that means a certain amount of unpopularity with people whom he has to deal strictly with.

I don't think either the *Patrika* or the *Bengalee* is doing well.

I was rather surprised to hear about the decision of the University Revising Authority against your case.

I went to see Mr. Durga Ch. Banerji this morning. He has promised me the fullest support to your candidature and he has already begun making the arrangements. I had also a talk with Sj. Rajendra Ch. Deb and some members of the North Calcutta Committee this morning regarding the plan of campaign and have no doubt that they will throw themselves heart and soul into the work. Election work will begin in right earnest from the 9th instant and as soon as I am back here, I shall direct it myself.

I am fairly well. Hope you are better. So long today.

Yours very affly

S. C. Bose

11. From Amrita Lal Chatterjee *

83, Lansdowne Road
9.8.26

Dear Subhas,

I am not going to write anything to you before having a talk with Hemendrababu. For this reason I have not written to you so long. As Hemendrababu was ill, he could not go to the Court for quite some time and so we could not meet. Anyway, recently we had a talk between us regarding Sevashram, and he requested me to work for this institution. Tomorrow on Sunday I shall go to the Sevashram with Hemendrababu and shall choose the nature of work for which I am fit. There is no need of appointing me the second Assistant Secretary. Yet if I am not included in the Working Committee as a member then probably I shall be deprived of the opportunity of doing work with proper authority in many fields. You wanted to know whether I shall be able to co-operate with Hemendrababu in a fitting manner and do the works for the Samity. It goes without saying that I have not even a little bit of animosity against Hemendrababu. I cannot simply think that I maintain any grudge against anybody not to speak of Hemendrababu. So, why should I not be able to work with anybody ? Yet it must be admitted that one cannot simply escape having honest differences of opinion with others in the field of work. That does not necessarily mean the existence of bad blood between them who are working together. But allow me to point out that if anybody, however big or important he may be, proves himself to be a nuisance and a hindrance to the work then it will be imperative on our part to remove that person from the organisation. I think in such a case, there is no scope for compromise.

I read the letter which you wrote to Bhupen. Don't you think that the letter rather betrayed a pessimistic spirit ? After going through that letter it just struck me that many persons try to keep you misinformed regarding many things. Of course, you yourself are quite aware of

* Translated from the original Bengali.

it. I have nothing more to add at present. I would like to write to you a big letter in which I shall deal in detail about the affairs of this Sevashram. Don't forget to inform me about the state of your health at present.

Accept our love.

Yours very sincerely,
AMRITA

12. *To Sarat Chandra Bose*
Censored, deleted and Passed
Illegible
21.8.28
for D.I.G., I.B., C.I.D.
Bengal

Mandalay
11.8.26
Wednesday

My dear brother,

In my letter of 7.8.26 I have replied briefly to your last three letters. I now intend to deal elaborately with some points mentioned in your letters.

I have read carefully the papers, letters etc. sent by Jones to Ray Knight. I wonder if *The Englishman* and *The Statesman* approached the Bengal Govt. for help as suggested by Mr. Dunne. It is interesting to note that Mr. Rattigan quoted the precedent of the Panjab Govt. in order to get the active assistance of Mr. Hose and of the India Office and he was not altogether unsuccessful. I wonder also, if Lord Birkenhead did approve of the draft telegram to the Bengal Govt. written out by Mr. Hose and order its despatch. The whole thing is so very interesting in as much as it reveals the intimate relations between the India Office and the Anglo-Indian Press.

Who is this Lord Evans who supplied copies of the Ordinance and the Regulation ? Is he the Under-Secretary ?

Jones' remark that "some Indian Judges are scarcely to be trusted more than Indian jurors" is worthy of note.

The statement that "there was no documentary evidence against Bose but only the testimony of highly credible witness etc." is full of significance.

I am sure that on the whole these papers will be of valuable help to us in more ways than one, in the suit that is pending against *The Statesman.*

Some portion deleted—by D.I.G., I.B., C.I.D. Bengal.

Are you going to stand for the Bengal Council ? If so from where ? Is anyone going to contest Mr. Surendranath Roy of Behala ? I believe he is at present representing the Municipalities of Sadar, Barasat and Basirhat Sub-divisions of the 24 Parganas.

I hope you will not forget the Baidyasastrapith when the question of an annual grant comes up again. Please speak to Santosh Babu and others beforehand while there is time.

Yes, it is a pity that Chakravarti signed the bond. Satya Babu is now on his trial. If he acquits himself manfully he will have made his future. May God grant him strength on the occasion. Your appearance in the case as well as the novel line you took up must have caused some sensation there. It has attracted notice here also—since the Deputy Commissioner, who is the official visitor under the Regulation, was referring to it, when he was here a few days ago. It is time for you to look out for a substitute for Satya Babu.

There is no reason why you should not take up important criminal cases now and again in future. The High Court Bar has become so weak on the Criminal side that a fresh influx of talent is badly needed.

Mr. Brown the Deputy Commissioner has been transferred to Arakan as Commissioner. He was dutiful as an officer and his manners were excellent. Both he and the Superintendent helped to have the lock-up rule dispensed with and but for their backing, the Local Govt. may not have agreed. The present incumbent also seems to be decent in his behaviour.

What is Dr. J. M. Das Gupta doing nowadays besides his professional work ? Has he given up Politics ? Is he not going to stand for the Council ? Is Bijoy Kaka going to stand for the University constituency ? Who is going to stand from the Diamond Harbour sub-division ?

It would be advisable to preserve the letters that I write to you. They may be useful later on.

I was surprised to find in the papers that Govt. had refused to confirm the election of Mr. Sasmal as Chairman of the Midnapore District Board. If Govt. interfere in the case of one District Board, there is nothing to prevent them from interfering in the case of other district boards and municipalities.

I want to have some news of Nadumama when Chotodada is back. What is the former doing now ? Is Chotodada going to join Belgatchia on his return ?

Is there any news of Gywe ? Has he got his admission into any medical college ?

Maymyo is a healthy place with an elevation of 3500 ft. above the sea level. It is the summer seat of the Local Govt. The climate is bracing, I am told, and the water is good, as there are waterworks there. It is in many respects like Darjeeling. Living is dear no doubt, but house-rent is on the whole cheap. Strawberries grow there and cauliflowers, cabbages etc. can be had all the year round. There is a cart road from Mandalay to Maymyo and people are constantly knocking up and down in their cars. Taxis are available, I am told, and can be engaged at a monthly or daily rate.

Govt. offices have removed to Rangoon by now but all the big pots come up for the "Maymyo week" in October when all Maymyo will be astir. There is no Puja season in Burma and Maymyo will be quiet in September and October, except for a week or ten days in October.

Maymyo is divided into two parts—the Civil lines—which constitute the fashionable quarter and the town proper which is about a mile off. The bazaar is in the town. Cooks and servants will, I think, be available locally. The leading advocate of the place in one Mr. Ganguli who is also the Chairman of the Municipal Committee. Some of the other leading pleaders are also Bengalis and the Upper Burma Tennis Champions are two Bengali gentlemen of Maymyo known as the Moitra Brothers.

If your proposed trip to Ceylon does not materialize

and if you decide to come to Maymyo, please send me a wire and I shall make the necessary arrangements. Furnished bungalows will be available. If you give me a fortnight's time I hope to be able to make the necessary arrangements. I shall have to depend entirely on others and that is why I want a sufficient margin of time. Before you decide about coming to Maymyo, it would be advisable to ask Govt. what facilities would be given you in interviewing me frequently. Under the ordinary rules we are entitled to one interview a week. Since we hardly avail ourselves of this right, it is only fair that special concessions should be made in case you come up to Maymyo. I don't think the Burma Govt. will have any objection to any arrangement which the Bengal Govt. may sanction in the matter of interviews.

If I am able to gather some more information about Maymyo, I shall write to you again on Friday next—as Friday is a mail day.

I take it Mejobowdidi and the children will accompany you if you decide to come up to Maymyo. In that case the steamer fare will be a pretty expensive item and will have to be taken into account. I do not know if your professional services will be in requisition while you are here.

I am surprised to learn from Santosh Babu's letter that the Health Committee recommended in the case of the Astanga a grant of Rs. 5000/- for indoor work, Rs. 3000/- for outdoor work and Rs. 15000/- as a capital grant—while in the case of the Baidyasastrapith the total grant recommended was Rs. 3200/-. Last year the grant for the Astanga was Rs. 3500/- and for the Baidyasastrapith Rs. 2500/-. The Corporation did well in referring the increases back to the Health Com. for reconsideration. I think the E.G.P. Com. should step in at this stage and turn down the proposals for increase put forward by the Health Com. In any case, if you want to foil the tactics of Jamini Babu's group, prompt action is necessary. It is simply monstrous that the Health Com. should show such favouritism for one College. I am afraid the Health Com. may confirm their first recommendation and the matter may come up before the Corporation in a thin house when the Puja is near and be consequently passed. So you should deal with the matter finally before you leave Calcutta.

I shall stop here. More in my next.

Yours v. affly.,
SUBHAS

13. From Janakinath Bose

Censored and Passed
Illegible
16/8/26
For D.I.G., I.B., C.I.D.

38/2, Elgin Road
Calcutta
15th Aug. 1926

My dear Subhas,

I have received your letter of the 30th July; I am rather anxious to hear that dyspesia is troubling you. All that I can suggest from a distance is that you ought to be very strict in your diet and see that nothing you take, is adulterated. In your next letter I hope to get a better account about your health.

I am doing well at present. Yes, I shall go to Kurseong or some other healthy place during the Puja holidays. Your mother is just now at Puri and doing well ; Dolly and Kanak will be going to spend a few days there.

Sunil will return either this month or the next, but I am not sure. Nadu will not be coming as he got plucked in the Final Examination.

The products of Suresh's factory are selling well, but as yet the outturn has not been large.

Gopal Babu's son Charu has given up practice and has been appointed a munsiff.

I am not aware that there is any book or manuscript about our family history.

Babu Nagendra Nath Basu of *Vishwa-Kosh* fame may know, and I shall consult him. I expect to get some useful information from him.

I did not know that our ancestors originally lived at Kulingram but this much I know—that Purandar Khan was a prince amongst men and settled at Mahinagar, a village close to ours ; hence we are called *Basus of Mahinagar*. The remains of his palatial house can be found even now and there is a দীঘি (tank) there which is called after him. Nagendra Babu has written a leaflet about him.

I have read somewhere that a Basu of Kulingram (a *sishya* of Bijoy Krishna Goswami) was asked to continue the supply of the rope to Jagannath.

Your letter is very interesting ; I shall preserve it and try to give you more information.

We are doing pretty well. Trust this will find you in better health.

With love and blessings,

Yours v. affly
J. N. Bose

14. To Sarat Chandra Bose

Censored and Passed
Illegible
for D.I.G., I.B., C.I.D.
Bengal.

Mandalay
16.8.26

My dear brother,

I had a talk with Capt. Smith the other day regarding Maymyo and this is what I gathered from him. Maymyo is not as bracing as Darjeeling. It is wet in September but dry in October, especially in the latter half, and in November. The Government come up to Maymyo in October and stay on for a month and a half (not for a week, as I said in my former letter). The water is not very good. People get colitis (called Maymiyitis by many people) now and again. Nevertheless on the whole it is a nice place and one gets a good appetite there. Capt. Smith himself is very fond of Maymyo and goes there pretty often for a weekend. He is of opinion that places further up—i.e. to the north—are more bracing than Maymyo, though a little out of the way.

The great advantage of Maymyo is that you can make that your base and travel from there up or down the Irrawady—up towards Bhamo and down towards Prome. I must mention here that there is a regular river-steamer service in Burma especially along the Irrawady and river-trips are exceedingly beneficial.

Personally I find it difficult to make up my mind regarding your trip to Maymyo. That Maymyo is on the whole a healthy place—is beyond question. It is also true that the sea voyage, to and from Burma may do some good as also the river trips along the Irrawady. You may also find new scenery, new faces and new experiences to interest you. When Maymyo gets dull—if at all—you can take trips to places of interest not far off. Nevertheless I feel that in coming to a decision you will have to consult your present engagements and commitments. The great advantage in choosing Kurseong or Darjeeling is that you can easily go down to Calcutta for a day or two when anything urgent crops up. Moreover while you are there you can be in touch with what is going on in Calcutta. If you decide to stand for the Council, I don't think you can leave Bengal.

I am glad to know that you all like Khuku's new relations. Mejdidi has been very lucky in the marriage of her daughters.

I have with me here a letter from Deshbandhu written from Patna. This is probably the only letter I possess and I want to preserve it as a memento. It consists of one sheet only, written on both sides. I am thinking of sending it to Calcutta to have photographs taken. We can then have the photos bound in decent frames and preserved. Please let me have your opinion as to what I should do with the letter. I am also anxious to preserve the original—so that the ink may not fade with the lapse of time. Capt. Smith communicated to me your telegram to him which he received yesterday.

23/8/26
Monday
10 a.m.

I had a further talk with him this morning regarding

Maymyo—especially regarding the climate in September and October. He is of opinion that there will not be many showers during the latter half of September and there is hardly any danger of getting colitis if one stays only for a month or two. On the whole, I have been reassured regarding the place and I am trying to arrange about a furnished bunglow from the 15th September. I am going to send a telegram through the Superintendent just now saying that I am trying to make the necessary arrangements. Probably the rent will have to be paid in advance and I shall have to pay the expenses in connection with sending someone to Maymyo to fix up a house. I shall again wire to you as soon as the arrangements are complete and if necessary shall ask for money.

Please reconsider the matter once again and in doing so please consult your engagements. If you go up to Kurseong or Darjeeling you can remain in touch with Calcutta and can even go down occasionally on urgent work. Here you will be out of touch, owing to the delay in getting letters. Moreover I can never be sure that you will be comfortable in a strange place—especially when I cannot make any arrangements myself. There is no such risk in the case of Darjeeling or Kurseong. There has been a serious breach in the Mandalay-Rangoon line and our mails are being held up and that is why I did not post this letter so long. I am however going to post it today and take my chance. I am told it will take about a week to renew the passenger service. If for any reason, you think it necessary or desirable to abandon your Maymyo trip, please do not hesitate to do so. I am exceedingly anxious that you should not inconvenience yourself in any way or sacrifice your public engagements in order to come up to Maymyo. In fact I shall be sorry if you arrange your Maymyo trip at that cost. There is no reason to feel panicky or anxious about me.

All arrangements notwithstanding, I shall not consider your Maymyo trip as "pucca" arrangement until you reconsider the question after perusing this letter.

If you have to alter your plans suddenly, the forfeiture of advance house rent should not matter at all.

Yours v. affly
SUBHAS

15. From Sarat Chandra Bose

Censored and Passed
Illegible
23/8
for D.I.G., I.B., C.I.D.
Bengal

38/1, Elgin Road
21st Aug. 1926

My dear Subhas,

I received your letter dated 7.8.26 (despatched on 9.8.26) on the 18th instant. Your silence for about three weeks made me rather anxious.

I find from your letter that you have not even regained your weight at the time of the hungerstrike. The net loss is 40 lbs. That is not a state of things which one can put up with equanimity. I do not wish to force you to take any action; but I still think you ought to apply for transfer to some hill-station in Upper India.

Re—the talk of compromise of *The Statesman* case the gentleman who approached us on behalf of *The Statesman* has not yet made us a definite offer. He told us some time ago that *The Statesman* people have written 'Home' for instructions.

Mrs. Das is staying at Beltola Road (Sudhir's house). She is most anxious to go and stay at Purulia for a few months in peace and quiet and will probably be leaving next week. I am glad to tell you that she has pulled herself up considerably. The strength of mind she is showing is very rare indeed. We go to see her off and on and I believe she likes our company more than that of most of her relatives and so-called friends.

Sunil and Ranen arrived here yesterday. Ranen's home coming was a surprise. He got plucked in his Final Examination—and that was his last chance. I haven't yet spoken to him about his future plans but I understand he intends to go back again and try for a job in a Chartered Accountants firm there.

I am glad the lockup has been dispensed with. It was a most unnecessary precaution to take and I am glad that better counsels have prevailed at last.

You needn't be at all anxious for me. Kaviraji medicines have done me good and I am digesting better. If I get 1½ months or a month's rest, I shall be all right.

I am yet undecided as to where I shall spend the long vacation. The choice lies between Mussoorie and Maymyo. I shall decide when I hear from you next. By the way, is there any good hotel at Maymyo ? We can't take a house at Maymyo as that means the bother of housekeeping.

Now as regards your contesting the North Calcutta seat in the coming elections. You must have realised that when the suggestion came from me there was good reason behind it. I can well imagine the reasons which prompted you to decide not to contest—and they are good and valid reasons. I was of the same opinion as you are, until lately. But I feel now that the country demands your services in that direction and that you cannot very well refuse. North Calcutta is enthusiastically in your favour and I think you will have a walkover, Mr. Jatin Bose notwithstanding.

I am happy to tell you that we have now a good chance of having the majority of Mahomedan Councillors with us in the Bengal Legislative Council. I have been working quietly for it and I believe I shall succeed.

Do please give the matter of your contesting further consideration and let me know your decision.

The matter of appointment of Assistant Secretary will, I believe, come up for consideration by the E.G.P. Committee next week. Your remarks regarding the two candidates named by me will be most helpful. I haven't yet received the complete list of candidates and hence can't make up my mind. I think the tie eventually will be between Biren

Babu and Suren Babu. Personally I prefer the former.

Mr. Sen's is a hard case, specially after Bhombal's death. Sujata requested me the other day to consider her father's case. I really don't know what to do.

So long today.

Yours v. affly
SARAT

Subhas Chandra Bose Esq.

16. To Sarat Chandra Bose

Censored and Passed
Illegible
1.9.26.
for D.I.G., I.B., C.I.D.
Bengal

Mandalay
1.9.26

My dear brother,

Your letter of the 21st August reached me yesterday. I am eagerly awaiting your final decision regarding my constituency. I shall be glad to know what arrangements you intend to make regarding my election campaign. Who will be the chief organiser ?

I find from *The Statesman* of the 27th August that in the Swarajist papers of the 26th, my name was announced as the candidate for North Calcutta. In my telegram of the 27th I have had my last say and I now depend entirely on your decision, *whatever that may be.* I would like to know what the attitude of Mr. Durga Charan Banerji, Solicitor, is ? At the last election he was the chief agent of Mr. Jatin Bose and Babu Hari Sankar Pal was the Chief agent of Mr. Krishnalal Dutta. Babu Jogesh Chandra Sen's people were warm supporters of Mr. Jatin Bose—particularly his brother. I am afraid Babu Manmatha Nath Sen, Solicitor, and his relations will put their whole weight on the side of Mr. Bose, as on the last occasion. But I wonder if we could influence Babu Mani Mohon Sen, our Ex-Solicitor, through Sarat Babu (Mitra) his son-in-law. Dr. Sasi Kumar Sengupta will, I think, be able to give us the tips as to who the people were who gave him trouble last time. Babu Jatindra Nath Pal (a merchant I think) of Hari Ghosh's Street was also another strong supporter of Mr. Jatin Bose. Even if we can't win over these gentlemen, it would be a great gain for us if we could count on their neutrality.

It would be desirable to start and keep up a vigorous campaign. If Mr. Jatin Bose realises the strength of the opposition he will have to encounter and if he finds that defeat is sure, it is not unlikely that he may beat an honourable retreat. He may not mind an honourable defeat but after his last success, he may not feel like facing a bad defeat, if that could be guaranteed. So, even if you think that we shall have a walkover, a vigorous campaign will be necessary.

I would like to have the voters' lists of your constituency and mine as soon as they are published. They may be sent to the C.I.D. office with a request for early despatch. Regarding your constituency it is most important to have the support of the libraries and Associations throughout the province. Each Bar Library is a place where you can get so many solid votes, if only the members could be approached. Every district and sub-divisional bar library will have to be requested to support your candidature and at least one person should be made responsible for the votes of each Bar Library. All things being equal, pleaders are bound to support a lawyer and any one who gets the solid support of the pleaders of the province is bound to be returned as the University representative. Next in importance to the pleaders are the teachers. There are two teachers' unions as far as I know, one belonging to the Govt. school teachers and the other to the private school teachers. Their support has also to be courted. Last time Babu Ishan Chandra Ghosh, late Headmaster of the Hare School, had a resolution passed by the Teachers' Union supporting his candidature. But he retired from the field when the campaign started and his withdrawal helped the other candidates.

If the Teachers' Unions cannot for any reason support your candidature as a body, they may at least refrain from passing any resolution in favour of a rival candidate. I do not know who the rival candidates are likely to be, but I expect that Babu Devaprasad Ghosh, who stood last time, will be in the field. As he can hardly expect any support from the lawyer class, he will leave no stone unturned in his efforts to enlist the support of the teachers. It is therefore necessary to forestall him. Unfortunately Bijoy Kaka hardly did anything during the last three years to further the interests of the teachers or to placate them. Otherwise they would probably have started with a predisposition in favour of the Swarajist candidate. You will have to employ some itinerant agents whose business it will be to appoint local agents wherever there are votes. If possible you may pay visits later on to big centres like Dacca & Mymensingh where there are likely to be many votes.

I have already wired to you about the Khulna constituency. If you have not already announced the candidate for the seat, you consider the case of Satish Babu (Chandra Chakravarti) who is here. Whatever Calcutta people may be inclined to think he stands a very good chance. His people have so far been Sailaja Babu's supporters and his (Sailaja Babu's) success has in no small measure been to that. I know Haren Babu (Chowdhury) will press for Sailaja Babu's nomination but there are so many things to be said against Sailaja Babu. I do not know why men like Sailaja Babu and Babu Surendra Nath Roy should be made candidates when they can be unseated. Last time we failed to unseat Sailaja Babu because we had a particularly bad candidate.

I have not so far made any enquiries about hotel accommodation at Maymyo. I shall do so as you prefer that and shall wire the result. Re—Maymyo too, I have given my opinion. Please consult your convenience and do not let your public work suffer as a consequence of your Maymyo trip. The coming months are so important for a public man ! I would of course like to meet you once, as also Messrs Goswami & Nalini Ranjan Sarkar. If you come, please try to bring them with you and please try to get permission for yourself to interview other inmates here. I have already written to you that if you finally decide to come up to Maymyo, you should try to get the permission of the Bengal Govt. to interview me as often as possible. After arranging with Bengal, you may write to the Burma Govt. or to the I.G. of Prisons, Burma. It often happens that the Rangoon people are not informed about these interviews till the last moment and that is inconvenient for them.

I am not writing to the Bengal Govt. now about my transfer. I shall do so, if necessary, after I meet you.

Why did not uncle Ranen become an Incorporated Accountant at least ? That would have been something.

I received the following books on Saturday last :—

1. Corporate life in Ancient India
2. Dravidian India
3. Kshatriya Tribes of Ancient India
4. Asoka
5. History of the Deccan
6. Evolution of Indian Polity
7. Indo-Aryan Races

I have already written to you about the Revising Officer, Calcutta University constituency. Please take legal action if you think that I am entitled to have my name in the roll. He has also raised objections about the inclusion of the names of Messrs Satyendra C. Mitra and Satish Chandra Chakravarti in the electoral roll. Both of these gentlemen were University voters at the last election—but in spite of that, objections have been raised.

I am concerned to read about the developments in the Sevak Samity in the papers. I hope everything will be done to ensure a good defence for the accused.

Who will be accompanying Mrs. Das to Purulia ?

I would like to know definitely if you are coming to Maymyo in any case—whether you get any hotel accommodation or not. Your telegram of the 30th has made it clear that after spending a few days at Kurseong you intend to leave for Burma about the end of this month (September) and to spend the whole of October at Maymyo. Re—

accommodation you have not said anything and I therefore take it that what you have written on the 21st Aug. holds good—namely that you would prefer living in a hotel to keeping a house.

We have started making our image and are trying to get ready for the Durga Pujah.

Hope this will find you all quite well. I am so so.

Yours v. affly

SUBHAS

S. C. Bose Esq.
38/1, Elgin Road
Calcutta

P.S.
What about M.S. Gywe ? Has he found a seat in any Medical College ?

I have just had a talk with Capt. Smith. He says that there is no hotel worth the name at Myamyo.

P.P.S.

I understand from the papers that you have come to a compromise with the workers. You have done the right thing.

S.C.B.

17. *From Sarat Chandra Bose*
Censored and Passed
Illegible
13.9.26
for D.I.G., I.B., C.I.D.
Bengal

Giddapahar
Kurseong
11.9.26
Saturday

My dear Subhas,

I received your letter of the 1st this afternoon.

As regards your election campaign, it is now in charge

of the Chief Agent of Mr. Jatin Bose at the last election, the Chief Agent of Mr. Krishna Lal Dutta at the last election, Sriyut Rajendra Chandra Deb (President, North Calcutta Congress Committee), Sriyut Baren Dutt of Garpar (Jatin Bose's relative), Sriyut Nripendra Chandra Mitra (Attorney-at-law) and the office bearers and members of the North Calcutta Congress Committee. I haven't yet decided as to who is to be 'installed' as Chief Organiser, but possibly the Chief Agent of Mr. Jatin Bose at the last election will have to be given that position. He has great influence in North Calcuta and knows how to organise the thing. I think Rajen Babu will agree to that.

Before I left Calcutta, I went to the office of the North Calcutta Congress Committee, and met the workers of North Calcutta. I also met Sriyut Pulin Mitra who was one of the principal workers of Mr. K. L. Dutta and he assured me that he would throw his heart and soul into the work.

At Durga Charan Babu's place last Saturday morning, I met Jogesh Sen's brother. He explained to me the difficulty of his position—he said he and his family were very much indebted to Mr. Jatin Bose in more respects than one. I don't think it would be possible to get round Jogesh Sen and his brother to support us actively but possibly we might succeed in inducing them to be neutral. Jogesh Sen is out of town. I shall see him as soon as he is back.

Bhabanath Sen's family will go against us, including Moni Lal Sen. The latter was never well disposed towards you—at any rate, that was my impression—and was reported to have said that he would not work in the Swarajist Corporation. I have however, asked Dada to see Sarat Babu and request the latter to try and influence his father-in-law.

I have not been able to see Dr. Sashi Sengupta yet but shall do so on my return to Calcutta.

Day before yesterday I wrote to Babu Phanindra Nath Bose (Solicitor of Babu Jatindra Nath Pal) to see his client and induce him to support us. Jatin Pal is also a client of mine and I shall personally see him. I have also written to Babu Panna Lal De Solicitor to see Jatin Pal.

I shall be back in Calcutta on the 16th and shall start

a vigorous campaign immediately. The present position will appear from a letter of the late Chief agent of Mr. Jatin Bose a copy of which I enclose herewith.

I think you ought to write personally to a few gentlemen of North Calcutta asking for their support. The names that occur to me are set out below :—

(1) Mr. Durga Charan Banerjee, Solicitor, Kasi Mitter Ghat Street
(2) Mr. Hari Sankar Paul
(3) Rai Bahadur Debendra Ballabh
(4) Kaviraj Shyamadas Bachaspati (*If you know him*)
(5) Mr. Jitendriya Bose, Councillor, Corporation
(6) Mr. Nalini Mohan Chatterji, Councillor, Corporation
(7) Mr. Girindra Nath Banerji, Councillor, Corporation

(He has promised his support)

(8) Mr. Nripendra Nath Bose, Councillor, Corporation
(9) Mr. Rajendra Ch. Dev and the members of the North Calcutta Congress Committee.
(10) Kumar Manmatha Nath Mitra, Shampukur Street, (who, I understand, told you at the time of the last election that if you had contested Jatin Bose, he would have supported you).
(11) Jyotindra Nath Mitra, Solicitor, Shampukur Street.

(If you know him)

Also please write to such other persons as you can think of.

Though I think you will have a walkover, that does not mean that we shall not carry on a sustained and *vigorous* campaign.

I have asked Khuro to purchase Electoral Rolls of North Calcutta and the University constituencies as soon as they are published and send a copy of each to you.

I wanted to place a car at the disposal of North Calcutta for election campaign before I left Calcutta but was not able to secure a suitable one. I heard from *Dada* yesterday that he had seen a private car and that he could get it on certain terms. I asked him by wire last night to close with the owner and place it at the disposal of North Calcutta.

I don't think Jatin Bose will retire from the contest. As soon as your name was announced he began thinking whether he would contest or retire, eventually made up his mind to contest.

Bijoy Kaka is mighty angry with me for having ousted him from the University seat. But I am afraid if he had been set up as our candidate for the University we would have lost the seat. He has become rather unpopular for many reasons and if we had forced him on the University electorate either Ramaprasad or his brother-in-law Pramatha would have contested him. The Responsivist and/or National and/or liberal parties have not yet announced their nominee for the University seat. The rumour is that they are going to put up Sasi Sekhar Bose (Alipore Dt. Board man). Devaprasad Ghosh may also contest.

I don't think the teachers will go against me—at any rate that was what Sukumar Ranjan Das assured me. I also wrote to Girish Babu (G. C. Bose of Bangabasi College) as soon as it was settled that I would be put up as the Congress candidate and though I have not heard from him I believe he will support me. I shall see him as soon as I go back to Calcutta. As regards the Khulna constituency your suggestion came too late. Still we discussed the matter and I have already informed you of the decision of the B.P.C.C. Executive.

Suren Roy's signing the Congress pledge created great sensation in non-Congress circles.

Do not trust the reports regarding withdrawals from the B.P.C.C. Executive that have appeared in the papers. Some people no doubt sent in their resignations but most of them will withdraw, if not all, except of course, Sasmal, Basanta Majumder and Ashrafuddin Choudhury (Comilla).

I am becoming more and more doubtful as to whether I shall be able to leave Bengal during the Puja vacation. In any case, I am not leaving before the 4th Oct. the date fixed for sending in nomination papers. If, however, Jatin Bose withdraws (which is unlikely), I shall be free to go anywhere I like.

I made a mistake in saying that Nadu had no further chances to take. I don't remember who gave me that impression, but I got it. I asked him on his return if that was correct and he said *no*. He could take the Chartered Accountant Examination as many times he liked.

I think I told you in my last letter that I had written to the Revising Authority Calcutta University Constituency about entering your name in the Roll. I received his reply day before yesterday and I enclose same herewith. He seems to be right, so long as the University notification holds good. But I have doubts if the University notification is legal and valid—it seems to conflict with the rule that graduates of seven years' standing are qualified to vote. I shall discuss this matter with Ramaprasad when I go down.

I must stop here today. I shall post this tomorrow (Sunday) so that I may avail myself of next Tuesday's boat.

Hope you are taking good care of yourself. This leaves us well.

Yours very affly

SARAT

Subhas C. Bose Esq.

18. From Sarat Chandra Bose

Censored and Passed
Illegible
10/9
for D.I.G., I.B., C.I.D.
Bengal

Giddapahar
Kurseong
8.9.26

My dear Subhas,

We arrived here on Sunday last. The weather has been fairly good since then though it has been raining off and on. Asoke and Ami are in Calcutta as their school is open.

There are some points in your letter of the 26th August (which I received on the 3rd September) which I did not touch in my last letter to you. The first is about communal electorate. Shortly after the B.P.C.C. meeting of the 13th June last, *Forward* declared itself boldly against communal electorate, anything to the contrary in the Bengal Hindu-Muslim Pact notwithstanding. Of course, Sengupta did not approve of this step, as he thought it might arouse Mahomedan hostility. We took the view that before the Royal Commission came out, we must educate the country on right lines, and so far as Mahomedans are concerned we were and still are hopeful that a large section of Mahomedans—I mean nationalist Mahomedans—would support our view. Since the 13th June last, we have written several articles against communal representation and I think on the whole, they have been well-received. After the coming elections are over, we shall revert to the subject and start an educative propaganda all over Bengal.

I do not quite remember if I told you in my last letter that the *Atmasakti* also is being prosecuted for sedition. The only offence that *Atmasakti* has committed, to my mind, is that it is being directed by Forward Publishing Ltd. The case has been fixed for the 28th and very probably I shall have to appear for the defence in that case also. So I am fast becoming a criminal lawyer—though much against my will.

Goswami has gone to Kashmir for a change. He will be back in Calcutta by the first week of October and will be very busy then with election propaganda. I don't think either he or Nalini Babu can be spared from Bengal either in October or November.

If I come to Maymyo, I shall apply in time for permission to see you often and also to see Satyen Babu and others. How is Satyen Babu ? Please remember me to him with my affectionate regards.

When I go back to Calcutta I shall see what I can do for Baidyasastrapith. I don't think there is much (if any) chance of an amalgamated Ayurvedic College.

Satya Babu is doing very well as Editor of *Forward.* He

has developed into a powerful writer and it is only the truth to say that for the last two years most of the well written articles have emanated from his pen. In fact, Chakravarti did not prove to be anything better than a figurehead. I feel sorry to have to make this confession, because I took in Chakravarti against Deshbandhu's wishes.

Won't Government revise their decision not to allow *Forward* to you ? How silly !

The day I left Calcutta I wrote to the Revising Authority of the Calcutta University Constituency requesting him to enter your name in the Electoral Roll and at the same time I forwarded a copy of my letter to him to Babu Ramaprasad Mukherji with a request to the latter to do the needful in the matter. I really don't see how they can refuse to enter your name, you having completed 7 years in June last.

As regards the letter of Deshbandhu you have with you, you can send it through the person who sees you next at Mandalay. I might be coming next month. Somebody will have to be sent about the middle of this month to get nomination papers signed by you and you can send it through him. I shall have it photographed and mounted on frames. It would be risky to send it by post.

I am enclosing a copy of my election manifesto herewith. To sign about 9000 letters is a job—I have finished signing about 2500 only.

I think you should issue your election manifesto. It ought to be in Bengali. If you draft one and send it on to me, I shall do the needful. I shall also request Mrs. Das to issue an appeal to North Calcutta.

I must stop here today. This leaves us fairly well. Please let me know how you are keeping. With love,

Yours very affly

SARAT

Subhas Chandra Bose Esq.

Enclosure : the Printed Letter to Electors of Calcutta University constituency.

38/1, Elgin Road
Calcutta, the 9th September, 1926

Dear friend,

Allow me to introduce myself as a candidate for election to the Bengal Legislative Council from the Calcutta University constituency.

As a Congressman and a humble camp-follower of our late leader Deshbandhu Chittaranjan Das, I realise that the Council and the elections are part of a much larger issue, the issue of our country's freedom. To this sacred struggle, the University has a large share to contribute, for it is not only the repository of our ancient heritage of culture and traditions but is also the fountain of our thoughts, hopes and aspirations.

As to the principle that should govern the relations between the University and the Government, I know of no other sentiment than the one uttered by the late lamented Sir Ashutosh Mookerjee—"Freedom first, Freedom second, Freedom always." As an individual and a member of a forward party I shall not spare myself in strengthening, perpetuating and extending that noble principle. I realise, of course, that in the prevailing atmosphere of distrust in the Council Chamber in a system that maintains an irrational divorce between power and responsibility, so far as the elective element is concerned, it will not be possible to do all or most of what we desire to do for our *Alma Mater*.

My *Alma Mater* has as its motto—"The Advancement of Learning'. I feel this is not the motto of the University alone, but a national motto, the battle-cry of our struggling militant nationalism seeking ever to express itself and to fulfil itself against the forces of injustice, oppression, squalor, poverty and ignorance. "Freedom and Advancement"—that is the problem for you and me ; and I can assure you in all humility that to the solution of that problem I shall direct all my thoughts and actions, and bend all the force of my education and understanding in even a larger measure than I have been able to do as Managing Director of

Forward and as an Alderman of the Corporation of Calcutta. This is the national problem and to its solution, the University, the lecture hall, the press, the platform and the Council Chamber must all co-ordinate their resources.

In the task to which I venture to address myself may I count upon your sympathy and support ?

Yours very truly

SARAT CHANDRA BOSE

19. *From Prabhabati Devi**

Puri
9.9.26.

Mother Durga Be With Us.

My dear Subhas,

After getting your letter full of reverence and learning that you are a bit better, I am feeling very happy. Baby and Nadu have come back from England on the 27th of August. Nadu will be back to England again on the 22nd of September. As a matter of fact he has his return-ticket with him. Both of them came here. Radhu, the daughter of Baby is now living with me. Only God knows when he will be here again. I so intensely feel like going to you and see you. Your father is well and comes here from time to time. I am well. How are you physically ? You must inform me by writing. Have you gained weight ?

Mejobowma has gone to Kurseong with the children. At present the weather in Calcutta is absolutely bad for health. Make me happy by letting me know about you and others who are with you there. Accept my blessing and kiss of affection.

Yours affectionately
MOTHER

*Translated from the original Bengali

20. *From Asoke Nath Bose (Nephew)**

38/1, Elgin Road.
14.9.26

My dear Uncle,

I got your letter. Do not mind for my delay in replying that letter.

I have come to know from newspaper report that you are not in a happy state of health. You probably are going to get winter there. Here it is no longer raining much. Father and mother have gone to Kurseong with Mira, Neru and Geeta. Most probably father will be back here on Wednesday morning and mother will be staying there with the children. Nowadays we are not quite good at spinning yarns. Mother has taken a spinning wheel with her and here there are two spinning wheels. I have to go to school regularly nowadays and though there is spare time on Saturdays and Sundays, yet due to laziness I fail to spin yarns. I have decided to spin more from now.

Probably during the Puja holidays, not much time will be left for spinning more yarn. Our Puja holidays will start most probably from the 5th of October. Professor Jadunath Sarkar is now the Vice-chancellor of Calcutta University. We were told that Professor Sarkar would bring about a radical change in the system of the University. Our matriculation examination will start from 7th February. Formerly the examination used to be held on the 7th of March. I have a mind to take science as my subject in my college days. I somehow feel that by choosing Arts I will not be much benefited. I feel like studying science and I am going to do so but I do not really know what benefit I can derive from studying science. I would like to have your advice in regard to this. I have the least liking for studying and practising law, and for a long time I have cherished the idea of studying science. It is not at all sure whether we will go

*Translated from the original Bengali

to Burma and the chance of our going there is almost nil. Accept our respectful *pronam*.

We are well.

Yours affectionately,
ASOKE

*21. From Tarubala Roy (elder sister)**

Puri.
Thursday.
14.9.26

Mother Durga be with us.

My dear brother Subhas,

A long time ago I got your letter full of reverence. I could not answer it because of so many difficulties and I think you will not mind it. I am here with children for the last twenty-four days and Kanak too has been living here for the last twenty-four days. I shall go back to Calcutta after visiting Bhubaneswar and Cuttack. When will you be back to Calcutta ?

You have most probably heard that Chotomamababu and Chotodada came back to Calcutta from England on the 27th of last month. Chotomamababu is going back to England on the 22nd of September. He came here just for one month to see his relations. He came here too to see us.

If Mejdada and others ever go to Mandalay they will certainly see you. When will we be able to see you again ? Sarada is very anxious and eager to see you. But somehow you have been replaced by Rabi in her mind. The children are not keeping quite well after coming here. We are well. How are you ? Write whether you have gained weight. Is summer very hot there ? Don't you feel like coming to Puri ? Accept my blessings full of affection.

Yours affectionately,
DIDI

*Translated from the original Bengali

22. *From Kulada Ranjan Sengupta**
South Calcutta National School
Affiliated to the National Council of Education
Jadavpur.

101, Harish Mukherjee Rd,
Kalighat P.O.
Calcutta, 21. 9. 1926

Subhasda,

I have not received any letter from you for a long time. From Newspapers I have come to know that you are in a bad state of health and that you have lost 25 seers of weight. Trailokya Babu too in his letter has intimated us about the deterioration of your health. This news keeps all of us full of anxiety. Please write a letter and let us know how you are at present. We are always praying to God expressing our desire that you be kept well under divine dispensation. We hope that by now your health must have improved and you have recovered. We have been permitted by the Acting Chief Executive Officer of Calcutta Corporation to use Hazra Park as the play-ground for the boys of our school on every alternate day. I have been asked by the Sevak Samity and the authorities of our school to convey to you their eternal sense of gratitude, because this privilege (of using Hazra Park as play-ground) given to us is undoubtedly due to you. The boys are so happy to have a play-ground like that and the boys wish your early release from the prison. We could secure the play-ground because of the letter you wrote to Santosh Babu. Santosh Babu took the initiative himself for getting the permission for the use of the ground and so we had it. As a matter of fact, it is admitted by all and sundry that what worked like magic was your request to the Corporation authorities, otherwise we would not have any access to the ground. We have started playing foot-ball there since Monday last—the 20th Sept.

*Translated from the original Bengali

The flood in Midnapore has taken a dangerous form and conditions there are really bad. It appears that our country is being subjected to disaster after disaster and who knows what will be the end of it ?

The news that a boy aged five or six talked to you all about religion inside the prison where you are, is really wonderful and pleasing. I had doubts whether such a thing was at all possible.

The Samity of our school is doing its work regularly according to routine. The boys want that by advising and guiding the Samity regarding further progress and improvement from time to time you will provide them with a source of encouragement. Nowadays we collect 3 maunds of rice on behalf of the School Committee. Nine families are helped by getting rice from us. Our monthly magazine is coming out regularly. A meeting of the boys is held once a week. There the boys discuss about national situation, about religious and moral themes etc. It is my intense desire to open a gymnasium in the school. There are many difficulties in doing so and we need a lot of money for it and at present it is pretty hard to raise funds by begging. People are in no mood to contribute. Yet we are going to try and you will be informed how we fare.

The general meeting of Tarun Samity was held and I was selected as a member of the Executive Committee. Tarun Samity is making progress day by day. The organisation has a lot of workers and good workers and good men at that.

Here all are more or less well. Give my *Pronam* to Satyen Babu, Trailokya Babu and other revered ones and you too accept my *Pronam*. The report and the prospectus of our school have been printed and we are going to send you a copy. I am all right.

Yours affectionately
KULADA

P.S.

I was glad to learn that you would celebrate Durga Puja inside the jail. Has the image been made ? Is it good to look at ? I wish I could be with you all and spend the Durga Puja days with you. After the Puja is celebrated you must inform us how you have all spent the Puja days. Our school will be closed for Puja holidays on 6th of October and the last day of the session will be the 5th of Oct.

KULADA

P.P.S.

Last Wednesday Apurba Krishna Mitra, the Vice-President of our school died. He spent substantial amount of money for the school and continued spending more until his death. His death is an irreparable loss to our school.

KULADA

23. To Sarat Chandra Bose

Censored and Passed
Illegible
9.X.26.
for D.I.G., I.B., C.I.D.
Bengal

Mandalay
30.9.26

My dear brother,

Your telegram to the Superintendent re-Sailesh's departure for Rangoon was received here on Friday last (the 24th inst.). On Monday the 27th Sailesh wired to the Superintendent intimating his arrival at Rangoon. This was followed by a telegram from you to the Superintendent which indicated that there was delay in informing the Burma Govt. that the interview had been granted by Bengal. This telegram was received at about 9 p.m. Thereupon we requested the Superintendent to wire express to the I.G. Prisons for official intimation of the interview and asking him to send the C.I.D. officer from Rangoon by the Tuesday noon train or to authorise the Supdt. to conduct the interview in the presence of a local officer. (Earlier in the day, on receipt of Sailesh's wire the Supdt. had wired to the I.G. Prisons for official instructions). According to our calculation, it would do if Sailesh took the Wednesday afternoon train from Mandalay and we expected that there would be time for an interview on Wednesday morning even if orders were received so late as 10 a.m. on Wednesday. But our expectations were upset when Sailesh brought the information that the train was running late and he would therefore have to catch the Tuesday night train at the latest, in order to avail himself of the Thursday boat from Rangoon. We had thus inadvertently put the I.G. Prisons on the wrong track by informing him that Sailesh would have to take the Wednesday afternoon train from Mandalay at the latest and requesting him to send the C.I.D. officer by the Tuesday afternoon train positively if he thought that a local officer would not do. However, Sailesh sent an express wire to the Deputy Secretary, Political Dept. requesting him to allow the interview in the absence of a C.I.D. officer, as he was going to discuss election matters exclusively and he would have to leave Mandalay by 8 p.m. at the very latest. A reply was received by 1-30 p.m. but the Supdt. was booked in the afternoon and the interview was fixed at 5-30 p.m. So I met Sailesh after all and had a hurried talk with him for about an hour. I need not recapitulate the details of the interview. Sailesh has noted down my instructions and they will be before you duly. I had a very anxious time till the interview took place particularly because I was afraid that Sailesh would feel helpless in a strange place under the above circumstances. The Jail staff did their best to help us out of the difficult situation. The Superintendent's advice to wire direct to the Dep. Secy. for permission stood us in good stead. By the by, I do not know if you are aware that the Govt. is now at Maymyo and the I.G. Prison's officer is at Rangoon. After we got the permission from the Dep. Secy. direct from Maymyo, we got a wire from the I.G. Prisons saying that he had no instructions from Maymyo till then but that he had sent the C.I.D. officer by the Tuesday afternoon train and had wired to Maymyo asking the Political Secy. to wire direct to the Jail his orders regarding the interview. So he evidently did his best under the circumstances. All this trouble could have been avoided if I or the Supdt. had been informed about the delay in informing the Burma Govt. I could then have got into touch with the Dep. Secy. direct and got his orders from Maymyo by the time Sailesh arrived. Even if Sailesh had mentioned in his wire from Rangoon that he would have to leave by Tuesday evening at the latest, I could have wired to the Dep. Secy. at Maymyo on Monday afternoon (instead of asking the Supdt. to wire to the I.G. Prisons at Rangoon) for official instructions. I was further misled because I expected Sailesh to bring a written permit with him from Calcutta and I also expected the C.I.D. officer to join him at Rangoon as on former occasions. When Rangamamababu came here in March last, the jail office did not receive any official instructions till after the interview—but there was no trouble because the C.I.D. officer joined him at Rangoon and both came with official permits in their pockets. However I hope the lessons of this experience will be useful in future. I am still eager to know why it was decided to send someone at the last moment. Sailesh could not satisfy me on this point, neither could your telegram to the Superintendent intimating Sailesh's departure for Rangoon. Now let me come to business :—

(1) From what I heard from Sailesh, I take it that the Maymyo trip has been dropped.

(2) ....(Deleted by Censor)..........

(3) I find from the University electoral roll that the names of Messrs Mitra and Chakravarti are in the original roll in spite of Khan Bahadur Ashanullah, the Revising Officer. Their nos. are 4221 and 1679 respectively. Please see to it that the ballot papers are *actually* despatched to Mandalay. We shall arrange for their attestation and return as expeditiously as possible. It would help us if you could send a wire advising us about the despatch of the ballot papers.

(4) Is Bijoy Kaka going to contest you? What about Devaprasad? Is he going to beat a gallant retreat or is he determined to beat the Returning officer hollow?

(5) I would like to repeat what I have written in a former letter about the importance of holding public meetings

and arranging processions. Durgacharan Babu may not realise the importance of these as his method of work is of a different kind. I do not belittle the effectiveness of his method but I want to add our modus operandi to his. The North Calcutta Congress Committee people should be able to arrange the meetings and processions. It is more desirable to hold meetings in Ward I than in any other part of the constituency. After you hold half a dozen successful meetings you will find that Mr. Basu's organization has gone to pieces. If we can storm Ward I successfully then only can (we) hope to make Mr. Basu realise the weakness of his position. As long as he gets a certain measure of solid support in his ward, he will go on hoping for the best.

(6) I am enclosing an analysis of the votes in my constituency. You will find therefrom that more than 50% of the total no. of votes belong to Ward I. So it is natural that Mr. Basu should feel that he is strongly entrenched there.

(7) I am glad that you have enlisted the support of Messrs Upendranath Bose of Baghbazar, Kumar Manmathanath Mitra and Satish Chowdhury—in addition to those you have already mentioned. Please do not neglect to try and commit the A. B. Patrika to supporting my candidature. I do not know if you will succeed—but it is worth trying. In spite of past events I do not think that Messrs Gopal Lal Ghosh and Mrinal Kanti Bose are altogether ill-disposed towards me. I hope you will be able to get the support of Babu Nandalal Bose's family through Mr. Nirmal Chunder. You are aware no doubt that Nalini's brother Billy has married into that family. I think Rai Bahadur Fanindra Lal De is as staunch a supporter of Mr. Basu as Mr. Manmatha Sen—but is it not possible to influence him at all ? I have already written to you about Mr. D. N. Roy M.L.C. Bar-at-law of Cossipore.

(8) I have already written to Messrs Nalinimohan Chatterji and Jitendriya Basu. I shall write to some more this week and shall continue to do so every week. Is it necessary for me to write to Mr. Jogesh Sen ?

(9) I want some money badly.

(10) Why has not Dr. Mohini Das, our only Namasudra M.L.C. been renominated this time ? I wired to Messrs J. M. Sengupta and N. R. Sarkar about him but have not heard in reply. I hope you all will see to it that the Maharaja of Nattore is able to beat Kumar Shibsekhareswar Roy this time. The nomination of Babu Amulya Dutta for the Hoogly Municipality Constituency appears to me to be a great blunder. I do not understand how the choice came to fall on him. The nomination of Babu Sailaja Ray has also been a mistake which will be realised by all as time goes on. Probably Rai Harendranath Chowdhury—himself an estimable gentleman— pressed his case.

(11) I am sorry to hear of the death of Dr. Crake our Health officer. I hope that the post will be widely advertised before it is filled up and that a suitable Indian will be appointed as Dr. Crake's successor. I shall write more about this later on. You may communicate my suggestion to Mr. Sengupta in good time.

(12) I understand from Sailesh that Girish Banerji wants to enter into a partnership with Sejdada in some business enterprise. Please ask Sejdada to avoid financial transaction with him.

(13) I would like to have a copy of the amendment to the written statement of *The Statesman*.

(14) I would like to draw your attention to the following points in connection with the elections :—

(a) As there should be one polling agent at every booth, there should be at least as many polling agents as there are booths. If the names of the polling agents are sent to me in time, I shall send the required number of letters authorising their presence at the booths.

(b) The election agent should keep details of expenditure together with vouchers.

(c) The election accounts should be submitted within 35 days of the publication of the result in the Gazette and should be affirmed on oath by the candidate and his election agent before they are submitted. It is therefore necessary to send the accounts to me (after they are affirmed by the election agent before a magistrate) as early as possible when the election is over. Both the successful and the defeated candidate have to submit accounts. Breach of the rules regarding the return of election expenses will disqualify both the candidate and his election agent from standing for a period of 5 years. If the election accounts are sent in good time there need be no anxiety about their timely return to Calcutta.

(d) Satyen Babu's address in the University electoral roll has been entered as 113/1 Bowbazar Street, the old address of the Congress office and Satish Babu's (Chakravarti) as C/o D.I.G. C.I.D. etc. It is necessary to see that Satyen Babu's ballot paper is sent on from Bowbazar Street. It is necessary to have a representative in every Bar Library and in every School and College, if possible, to see that the ballot papers are filled in and despatched to the Returning Officer in time.

Hope this will find you all quite well. Were you able to go to Noakhali ?

The Associated Press now give very meagre news of Bengal events in the Rangoon papers.

Yours v. affly
SUBHAS

Enclosure—1
S. C. B.
To
S. C. Bose Esq.
38/1 Elgin Road
Calcutta.

Enclosure to letter of 30.9.26

Analysis of votes

Ward	Male voters	Women voters	Total for the Ward	
1	2408	458	2,866	
2	1248	219	1,467	
30	283	56	339	827 (added areas)
31	123	23	146	
32	306	36	342	
Total no. of male voters 4368		Total no. of W.V. 792	Grand Total 5160	

24. *From Sarat Chandra Bose*

Censored and Passed
Illegible
12/10/26
for D.I.G., I.B., C.I.D.
Bengal

38/1, Elgin Road
11th October, 1926

My dear Subhas,

I got your long letter of the 30th Sept. last day before yesterday. I am sorry I can't reply in detail today.

Your election manifesto has been withheld and the reason assigned by the Deputy Secretary, Political Dept, for withholding is that political prisoners are not allowed to issue appeals to the public. More of that in my next letter.

I decided to send Sailesh as I was very doubtful if the blank papers sent by you previously were proper nomination papers. I couldn't send him earlier as the electoral roll was not published before the 20th Sept. and I had to get people to sign as proposers and seconders.

Parents have come here and are keeping well.

The election campaign is in full swing. Hope you are better.

Yours very affly
SARAT

Subhas C. Bose Esq.

25. *To Sarat Chandra Bose*
Censored and Passed
Illegible
3/11/26
For D.I.G., I.B., C.I.D.
Bengal

Mandalay
23.10.26

My dear brother,

Your letter of the 11th Oct. reached me yesterday. The delay was due to a breach in the railway line. This is the third or fourth breach this year and God only knows whether this is the last. It is lucky that Sailesh just managed to get through—there were breaches before he came and after he left. I believe the mail from Rangoon is now coming by steamer.

I have written to all the gentlemen whose names you sent me, with the exception of Rai Bahadur Debendra Ballav whom I do not know and Sj. Rajendra Ch. Dev, whose address I do not know. I have also written to Sj. Pulin Behari Sawoo, Councillor, who lives with the Rai Bahadur.

Where are father and mother going to spend the vacation ? Is Bardada going to be in Calcutta all along ? Will you be able to run up to Kurseong for a few days ? When will Mejobowdidi and the children be returning to Calcutta ?

I am afraid the Calcutta-Mandalay mail will be delayed until the breach is repaired.

Hope this will find you all quite well. My *Bijoya pronams* to all superiors and my love to the younger ones. I am continuing Ayurvedic medicine. I hope it will do me good. The office has received Rs. 100/- from Calcutta and placed it to my credit.

Yours very affly
SUBHAS

To
S. C. Bose Esq.
38/1, Elgin Road
Calcutta.

26. From Sarat Chandra Bose

Censored and Passed
Illegible
4/10/26
for D.I.G., I.B., C.I.D.
Bengal

38/1 Elgin Road
Calcutta
2/10/26

My dear Subhas,

Since returning to Calcutta I have received two letters from you dated 9.9.26 and 20.9.26 respectively—both enclosing nomination papers signed by you and also one cover enclosing letter from the University Revising Authority to Major Smith and some nomination papers. I have also received from Major Smith two letters (both under Registered covers) dated 22nd September and 20th Sept. and some nomination papers.

I received a message from Major Smith informing me that Sailesh had seen you on Tuesday last and had nomination papers signed by you. I also received a telegram from Sailesh from Rangoon saying that he is coming by the S.S. Angora. I find from the papers that the S. S. Angora is due tomorrow morning at 10 a.m. That will be all right.

The deposit money of Rs. 250/- has already been deposited and all that remains to be done is to file your nomination papers before 3 p.m. on Monday next. All the proposers and seconders will attend to present the nomination papers.

The election campaign is going on quite well. We are going to have a big meeting this afternoon at New Shyam Park which will support your candidature. Jatin Babu has felt that in spite of the last six months' hard canvassing he is going down. But he won't withdraw. God willing, we shall give him a damned hollow defeat.

I am afraid my letters to you from now till the election will be short. But I would welcome long letters from your side giving us suggestions regarding your election campaign.

Take good care of your health and we shall take care of your election campaign. This leaves us well.

Yours very affly

SARAT

Subhas Ch. Bose Esq.

27. *To Sarat Chandra Bose*

Censored and Passed
Illegible
18/10/26
for D.I.G., I.B., C.I.D.
Bengal

Mandalay Jail
(C/o. D.I.G., I.B., C.I.D.)
9.10.26

My dear brother,

Your letter of the 2nd Oct, is to hand. I find that you have received my letters of the 9th and 20th Sept. I have since written to you on the 22nd Sept., 24th Sept., 30th Sept. and 4th Oct. I am anxious to know whether you received these in time.

I have already informed you that my letter to you dated the 13th Sept. has been withheld. It was a long letter and as it contained important election matters I have wired and have also written to the D.I.G. asking him to delete anything he considers objectionable and pass the rest of the letter. I hope it will be possible for him to accede to my eminently reasonable request.

You also mention in your letter that you have received a cover containing a letter from the University Revising Authority and some nomination papers. I find from my record that these were enclosures to my letter of the 13th Sept.

I don't think it was necessary to send Sailesh with the nomination papers. My idea is—I am not sure that I am right—that it is immaterial *when* the candidate puts down his signature. What was the decision in Deshbandhu's election case?

I find that my foreboding has come out true and that you have had to take the burden on your shoulders. I doubt if you will now be able to go up to Kurseong at all. Is Bardada also going to remain in Calcutta till the election? I shall be glad if you could snatch a rest in the midst of your numerous engagements. Whom have you left in charge at Kurseong?

I do not expect Mr. Jatin Basu to withdraw though he would be well-advised to do so. His "moshaibs" will not allow him to do so, even if he feels inclined.

I am glad that you have begun to hold meetings. It would be advisable to hold them as frequently as possible. I cannot sufficiently emphasise the importance of this aspect of the election campaign.

I have been thinking of writing to Sj. Rajendra N. Dev but I have forgotten his address. I have glanced through the electoral roll of Wards I and II but I have not been able to find his name. I have also forgotten the address of the North Calcutta Congress Committee Office.

The Statesman of the fifth has given a brief account of the meeting at Shyam Park.

There are several small parks in Wards I and II and I think there is one park in front of Mr. Manmatha Sen's house. Meetings should be held there and Mr. Basu should be bearded in his den.

I am anxious to know if anyone is going to oppose you. I expect the Calcutta papers will bring me the information within a few days.

I have written to Santosh Babu about the Baidyasastrapith. I do not know what he has done—I have not had any reply from him.

Have you taken any action in order to have my name entered in the University electoral roll?

Please preserve the letter from Cambridge which gives the amount I shall have to send them for the M.A. degree. You need not bother about sending the money now—that can stand over till next year.

Sailesh writes to say that you will be going to Noakhali.

Where is Sati now?

Hope this will find you all quite well.

Yours v. affly
SUBHAS

S. C. Bose Esq.
38/1, Elgin Road
Calcutta.

28. To Sarat Chandra Bose

Illegible
11/10
for D.I.G., I.B., C.I.D.
Bengal

Mandalay
4.10.26

My dear brother,

I have written to you on *(1)* the 6th September *(2)* the 9th Sept. *(3)* the 13th Sept. *(4)* the 22nd Sept. *(5)* the 24th Sept. *(6)* the 30th Sept.

I have been informed by the D.I.G. that my letter of the 13th Sept. has been withheld. I do not know the reason yet, neither do I know what the fate of the subsequent letters has been. In the meantime I am anxious to know about the fate of the enclosures. During the month of September I have been enclosing nomination papers with every letter I have written to you. I am in a fix now as I do not know what will be considered as objectionable by the Censor.

I want some money badly. Please wire Rs. 50/- or Rs. 100/- to the Superintendent to my credit. I hope Sailesh has arrived safely in time and has delivered the nomination papers.

Trust this will find you all quite well. Please let me know the dates on which you have written to me during September and October. I am so so.

Yours v. affly
SUBHAS

S. C. Bose Esq.
38/1, Elgin Road
Calcutta.

29. From Sarat Chandra Bose

Censored and Passed
Illegible
for D.I.G., I.B., C.I.D.
Bengal
20/10/26

38/1, Elgin Road
18.10.26

My dear Subhas,

Your letter of the 4th was to hand on the 11th.

I believe I have acknowledged your letter of the 30th Sept. which I received on the 9th instant.

Have you asked the authorities to let you know why your letter of the 13th Sept. has been suppressed? I shall let you know in my next letter which of the letters you wrote to me last month have been received by me. At the present moment, I cannot lay hold on any except the letter of the 30th Sept.

Your election manifesto and the covering letter have been withheld. I shall write to the authorities on the subject tomorrow.

I have remitted to the Superintendent, Mandalay Jail the sum of Rs. 100/- for your expenses there.

The election campaign in North Calcutta is going on splendidly. Durga Charan Babu and others are working very hard and God willing we shall succeed.

Given below are the dates on which I wrote to you last month—2nd Sept., 4th Sept., 8th Sept., 11th Sept., 15th Sept., 2nd Oct., 11th Oct.

I received the nomination papers you sent me by post but did not use them. I used only those which Gopali brought back from Mandalay signed by you. Objection was taken by Jatin Bose even to those.

By next mail, I shall send you letters appointing polling agents for your signature.

Please let me know how you are keeping. Parents are going to Sijua (Dhanbad) tomorrow and will stay with Sudhir for a fortnight.

I am not leaving Calcutta until the elections are over. I shall have to look to the University also, as Sir Nil Ratan is opposing me. He has been set up by Chakravarti's party.

With *Bijoya asis* & love,

Yours very affly
SARAT

30. To Sarat Chandra Bose

Censored, deleted and Passed.
Illegible
For D.I.G., I.B., C.I.D.,
Bengal
30/10/26

Mandalay
16.10.26
Bijaya Dasami

My dear brother,

I wrote to you last on 4.10.26. Since then we have been busy with the preparations for the Durga Puja. Thank God, our arrangements have been satisfactory and the Puja has uptill now been a success. To one accustomed to an uneventful and monotonous life, an occasion like the Durga Puja has much more than its normal value. It is a source of aesthetic enjoyment, intellectual recreation and religious inspiration and affords abiding solace. Today is *Bijaya Dasami* and throughout Bengal relations, friends and even enemies—children of the same mother—will be soon embracing one another in fraternal love.
(......deleted by Censor......).

We have received the Puja *dhoties* and *chadars* in good time this year. Two extra sets have been sent through mistake, I think. I have been asked to convey the thanks of all—together with *Bijaya* greetings—for the present which has been warmly appreciated.

I find from the papers that you had been to Noakhali. I trust you are back now. I hope the election campaign is now in full swing. I do not expect either Mr. J. N. Basu or

Mr. Nilratan Sircar to withdraw.

Please accept my *Bijaya pronams* and convey same to superiors and my love to the younger ones.

Hope this will find you all quite well.

Yours v. affly
SUBHAS

To
S. C. Bose Esq.
38/1, Elgin Road
Calcutta.

*31. From Amrita Lal Chatterjee**

Cuttack
17th October, 1926

Dear Subhas,

I spent my Puja days in Cuttack. The citizens of Cuttack have got a lot of initiative indeed. I had the opportunity of seeing images of infinite varieties—in some places I found the image of Mahadev instead of Durga and in some places the image of Krishna too. It appears that the citizens of Cuttack enjoy absolute liberty in regard to the Puja and do whatever they like. Of course, I did not miss the image which was worshipped at your home in Cuttack. This was not my first visit to Cuttack and as a matter of fact about 25 years ago, I started my academic life as a student of Ravenshaw Collegiate School.

On 25th September last, a Committee meeting of the Sevashrama was held and I was enrolled as a member of the Committee. In that meeting, a resolution was passed to set up a sub-committee, and the sub-committee (with Babus L.M. Sen, A. Chatterjee and the Secy.) decided "to enquire into the wants of the orphanage and to suggest means for the better work of the institution." We have finished the enquiry and I have decided to prepare a report of it, sitting right here in Cuttack. When the report will be finish-

*Translated from the original Bengali

ed I shall send a copy to you. Meanwhile let me inform you that we have already decided to advertise in the newspapers seeking the service of an efficient superintendent for the institution. It is not at all advisable to leave the boys under the charge of them who are now running the institution, and there is a consensus of opinion regarding this. I think I should add a few more words. In the first letter which I wrote and sent to you regarding the orphanage, I rather gave vent to criticisms against Jatinbabu which were very bitter. I admit that by doing that I committed a great blunder and the criticism was not at all just. Whatever might be the nature of Jatinbabu as a person, it never appears to me that he has done anything which has harmed the orphanage very much. Here I am not going to point out the defect which has its source in his unwillingness to do any work. I admit that I wrote that letter to you by being influenced by outsiders and I was biased and so wrote that letter. Jatinbabu is rather fond of hatching conspiracy and forming factions. I have discovered that there is bad blood between Jatinbabu and Hemendrababu and Jatinbabu specially dislikes Hemendrababu.

Anyway, let us leave aside all these things at present. How did you celebrate the Puja there ? How are you keeping ?

Accept my affectionate *Bijoya* embrace. We do not know when you will be amongst us again but meanwhile if I can render even a little service to your Sevashram and bring about some improvements in it my mind would be satisfied.

Farewell today.

Yours very sincerely,
AMRITA

P.S.
I am going back to Calcutta at the end of this month.

32. *From Sarat Chandra Bose*

Censored and Passed
Illegible
1.11.26
Phone Cal. 4434
For D.I.G., I.B., C.I.D.
Bengal

38/1, Elgin Road
Calcutta
1.11.26

My dear Subhas,

Your letter of the 16th Oct. was to hand on the 30th. Very glad to learn that your Puja celebration has been a success. I was getting rather nervous about the parcel of *dhoties* and *chaddar*. Glad to learn that they reached in good time. I sent two extra sets on purpose as I was not sure that your number was the same as before. Please take the extra sets for your own use.

No, Mr. J. N. Basu will not withdraw nor will (name illegible). I think North Calcutta is all right and that Mr. J. N. Basu is daily losing ground. Durga Charan Babu had a dinner party at his house last night at which all our workers were present. Hari Sankar Babu is working *splendidly*.

Possibly I shall have to send the list of your polling agents by telegraph. As soon as you receive the telegraph, please write the letters appointing polling agents and send them in one packet to me.

I am afraid I must stop here. My letters to you until the election is over will be very short. You need not be nervous about the result. Your letters under reply came in a very mangled form—very badly deleted.

Please convey my *Bijoya* greetings and embraces to our comrades there and accept my love and good wishes yourself.

In haste.

Yours very affly
SARAT

33. To Sarat Chandra Bose

Censored and Passed
Illegible
25/11/26
for D.I.G., I.B., C.I.D.
Bengal

Mandalay
13.11.26
Saturday

My dear brother,

Your letter of 1/11/26 was to hand yesterday. I have already informed you that I have received all the letters you wrote in September as also your letters of the 2nd, 11th and 18th Oct. I do not know if you have written any letter between the 18th Oct. and the 1st Nov.—I have not received any such letter.

You say in your letter that my letter of the 16th Oct. has reached you though in a mangled form. You have not yet informed me as to whether you have received my letters of the 22nd Sept. and the 10th Oct., though I have been informed by the C.I.D. office that my letter of the 10th Oct. has been passed and forwarded. You have already informed me that my letters of the 13th Sept. and 24th Sept. have not reached you and I find from your letters that the remaining letters I have written up to 16.10.26 have all reached you duly. Since the 16th Oct., I have written to you on 23/10, 1/11, and 6/11. I have sent letters appointing polling agents as enclosures to my letter of the 1st Nov.

I have sent you the following message by wire earlier in the morning :—"Letters appointing polling agents despatched on first November through Intelligence."

I have written to all those gentlemen whose names you supplied me with. I have heard from Jitendriya Babu in reply but from none else. I believe they are too busy at the moment. I have written to Babu Pulin Behari Sawoo, Councillor, Calcutta Corporation in place of Rai Bahadur Debendra Ballav.

The Rangoon papers which came in yesterday gave a description of a novel form of electioneering introduced by our party in the North Calcutta election viz. distribution of coloured leaflets by means of rockets. Very ingenious indeed! Reminds one of the distribution of leaflets from flying aeroplanes in France & Flanders during the last war.

Please let me know Rajen Babu's (Dev) address if you happen to know it.

The Rangoon-Mandalay railway line is still out of order and through communication will not be resumed before the end of the month. At present the mail is coming from Rangoon partly by train and partly by steamer. There is a delay of two or three days owing to the longer route.

I have been informed that Govt. will not permit any electioneering to be done from inside the jail—this includes writing instructions re—the election campaign.

I would like to remind you again about the election expenses. Please try to be as prompt as possible in sending them. You should try to avoid sending a representative to Mandalay solely for this, especially in view of the railway breach.

Since I wrote to you last I have had another relapse of influenza. I had a remission on Saturday last but I was not feeling fresh and I had a relapse two or three days later. I have been feeling better since yesterday.

Hope this will find you all quite well. I am forwarding to you a letter which I have received from Babu Sabitri Prasanna Chatterji.

Yours v. affly

SUBHAS

P.S.

I sent a wire to you a few days ago asking you to send me copies of manifestoes, leaflets etc. published for Mr. Jatin Basu and myself. They would be interesting reading. You may also send me copies of ভোটরঙ্গ (voteranga) through the C.I.D.

S. C. B.

S. C. Bose Esq.
38/1, Elgin Road
Calcutta.

Enclosure : A letter from Sj. Sabitri Prasanna Chatterji to me.

S. C. B.
13/11

34. To Sarat Chandra Bose

Censored and Passed
Illegible
17/11/26
for D.I.G., I.B., C.I.D.
Bengal

Mandalay Jail
6.11.26
Saturday

My dear brother,

Your last letter dated the 18th Oct. said that you would be sending by the next mail a list of polling agents on behalf of whom I would issue letters authorising their presence at the polling stations. The mail came in day before yesterday but I did not get any letter from you. Another mail is due today. However, I anticipated delay due to some reason or other and I sent you along with my last letter, dated the 1st. Nov. a number of letters to the Returning Officer authorising the presence of my polling agents at the different polling stations in the constituency. I am sure this will reach you in time and will be of some service. Obviously you will not get all the polling agents you want in my list— because I do not know who are working on my behalf and that is why I asked you long ago to send me a list of the polling agents. It can be easily imagined what inconvenience there is likely to be if there are no polling agents to represent me inside the polling booths.

I have had an attack of influenza during the last week. The attack commenced on Saturday last and fever left me only yesterday. I am still very weak and have got a broken voice along with sore-throat and cough. It was rather painful when the attack was on especially as I could not sleep at all. However I am now on the road to recovery and hope to be fit before long. I think the attack was due to a sudden change of weather. It was raining even in the last week of October—a strange phenomenon in a place like Mandalay—and with the advent of this month there was a spell of cold weather. Even now, dark angry clouds are floating overhead and local soothsayers say that a fortnight's rain is still in store for us.

I am anxious that you should send me the election accounts within a week of the publication of the result in the Calcutta Gazette. You should leave a double fortnight for the election accounts to come and go—which means that you will have only a week within which to prepare the accounts. Breach of this rule regarding timely submission of election accounts entails a heavy penalty on both the candidate and his election agent. Delay in despatching the accounts will mean that a messenger will have to be sent at considerable expense.

Hope this will find you all quite well.

Yours v. affly
SUBHAS

P.S.
There is no letter in today's mail which has just arrived.

S. C. BOSE
6/11

To
S. C. Bose Esq.
38/1, Elgin Road
Calcutta.

P.P.S.

I have been informed that my letters dated the 13th Sept. and 22nd Sept. have been withheld. You have said that my letter of the 24th Sept. has also been withheld. I therefore take it that you have received the remaining letters of the 9th Sept., 20th Sept., 30th Sept., 4th Oct., 10th Oct., 18th Oct., 23rd Oct. and 1st Nov.

S. C. BOSE
6/11

35. From Janakinath Bose

Censored and Passed
Illegible
8/11/26
for D.I.G., I.B., C.I.D.
Bengal

38/2, Elgin Road
Calcutta
7th Nov. 1926

My dear Subhas,

I have duly received your letter of the 16th Oct. Very happy to hear that Durga Puja was smoothly and satisfactorily celebrated at Mandalay and the worship of the Mother has been a source of "solace, enjoyment and inspiration" to you.

The Puja was a success at Kodalia and Cuttack.

Your mother and I left Cuttack on the 9th Oct. ; I shall go back tonight but she will remain here.

We passed a week at Sijua with Sudhir, it is a pleasant place.

Sati has been sent to Cuttack to work in the Match Factory and it is likely Gopali will go in for Textile Industry.

I have not been able to go to Kurseong ; I think I am doing pretty well.

I very much regret I have not been able to see Sj. Nagendra Nath Basu ; I shall do so at the earliest opportunity.

Please accept our whole-hearted *Bijoya* blessings—we are all pretty well.

Trust this will find you in better health. Please continue the Kaviraji medicines.

Yours v. affectionately
J. N. Bose

*36. From Rajendra Chandra Dev**
Censored and Passed.

3, Muktaram Row
Calcutta
9th Nov. 1926.

Dear Subhas,

For long long days, I was feeling like writing a letter to you, yet I could not quite do it and why I do not myself know. Whenever I try to write a letter my mind is upset with emotion and grows nostalgic. I remember those days of friendship, companionship—we quarrelling within the B.P.C.C. and again working together and moving about in our accustomed ways and with our usual trends. The memories of the late lamented Deshbandhu come back to my mind and how after becoming a no-changer I quarrelled even with him and with Satyenbabu (Satyendranath Mitra) who is like my own brother. I remember how even after such quarrels I contacted you, Anil Babu, Sukumar and dedicated ourselves to the cause of Khaddar. Anyway, it is better not to remember those things. Now let me tell you brother why I am writing this letter. Whatever I did before, I am now in the twilight days of my life that is, I am in my fifties and being a Bengalee it means the twilight days of my life and my health is not quite good, rather I am in a broken state of physique and health, suffering from fever and I am not quite sure how long I will be alive. I am not sure whether I shall be able to see you amongst us released from jail within my lifetime and so I am writing this letter to you.

Please don't be vexed and try to put up patiently with irrelevant talks of an old man. The day when after carrying on the election campaign I won as a radical no-changer on the strength of using your name in my favour that day I was feeling highly pleased. But the pleasure was short-lived and I felt depressed. I told Sarat Babu (Sarat Chandra Bose) that unless and until Subhas is back again I shall not visit

* Translated from the original Bengali.

his (Sarat Babu's) home. I really did not go and cancelled the engagement and that was because my mind revolted and I remembered your handsome figure full of spirit and I thought, "where my younger brother Subhas is today and I do not know what kind of food he gets there and how can I have a sumptuous feast at his house in his absence. No, it is impossible."

When you were imprisoned I thought that I would write and again quite could not do it. One day I even came out to see you at the jail, but again I felt—was it due to weakness ?—You were then in a Calcutta Jail.

I often meet Sarat Babu and Satish Babu and enquire about you—I also get news from Suresh and others—yet my dear younger brother, my mind pines for seeing you personally.

If you have enough time please answer this letter. If you are quite well physically and otherwise then write a letter and inform me about the other brothers (other political prisoners) who are there. What is there to tell you about me—an old man whose days are numbered ? What pains me is that I shall have to leave this world without being able to render any real service to the world and before being able to make my motherland free from her sorrows. But, I shall depart from this world with this hope that I am leaving behind my worthy brothers wherever they might be—outside or inside jail. This is my blessing to you, "Be immortal and as a *Yogasiddha* person gather strength to put an end to the sorrows of our motherland."

Yours affectionately,
RAJENDRA CHANDRA DEV

37. From Tarubala Roy *

38/1, Elgin Road
Friday
12.11.26

Mother Durga be with us.

Dear Subhas,

I wrote you a letter but forgot to send it to you. I am ashamed of that and am now writing again.

Kanak is sending a *dhoti* and a *chaddar* on the occasion of *Bhatri-Dwitiya* and also I am sending a *dhoti*.

How are you nowadays ? Have you gained in weight ? Is winter quite severe there ?

Father has gone to Cuttack last Sunday. He is quite well.

How are your companions ? How are the fledglings of the peacock ? What do they take as their food ? Is there any cat there ? Sarada is mad for seeing you. When will God give us the day when we will see you again ?

I hope that you are quite well now.

Accept my affectionate blessings.

Yours affectionately,
SEJDIDI

38. To Sarat Chandra Bose

Censored and Passed
Illegible
24/11/26
for D.I.G., I.B., C.I.D.
Bengal

Mandalay Jail
15.11.26

My dear brother,

Your letter of 1.11.26 was to hand duly—I have already replied to it.

I was glad to learn day before yesterday that you had

*Translated from the original Bengali

received the letters appointing polling agents which I had sent some time ago and that my chances were very good. The news was very welcome indeed because the newspapers we receive do not disclose the real state of affairs re—the elections.

I have sent a message to the Editor Municipal Gazette as requested by him. I hope he will get it in time.

Could you please ask *Chotodada* if he could supply me the following information re—the L.R.C.P., M.R.C.S. examination of London :—

(1) What is the length of the course ?

(2) Will a student who has passed the State Medical Faculty examn. of an Indian University (Campbell School standard, for instance) be entitled to a concession re—the period of study in London ?

(3) If the above student has not passed either the B.A. or the I.A. examn. of an Indian University what examn., if any, will he have to pass before he can appear for the L.R.C.P., M.R.C.S. ?

(4) Which is the easiest examn. which qualifies one for the L.R.C.P., M.R.C.S. course ? Is it the London Matriculation or the Senior Cambridge ? Has this qualifying examination got to be taken in England or can anyone appear for it while in India ?

(5) Is any classical subject like Latin or Greek compulsory in any such qualifying examination ?

(6) What Indian subjects, if any, (like Sanskrit or Arabic or Persian) are substitutes for Latin or Greek or any European language ?

When is *The Statesman* libel suit coming up again before the High Court ? Please let me know in time if there is going to be a Commission.

I have lost about 6 lbs. as a result of influenza. I hope to make up the loss soon if I do not get a third attack. I do not feel quite fit yet but I hope I shall gradually recoup my health.

Has Durga Charan Babu got my letter which I wrote some time ago ? I have not had a reply yet.

Nripen Babu (N. Basu) has replied to my letter saying

that he has been supporting my cause.

Hope this will find you all quite well.

Please do not forget to expedite the preparation of the election accounts.

Yours v. affly
SUBHAS

S. C. Bose Esq.
Bar-at-law
38/1, Elgin Road
Calcutta

39. To Sarat Chandra Bose
Censored and Passed
Illegible
14/12
for D.I.G., I.B., C.I.D.
Bengal

Mandalay
22.11.26
Monday
Despatched on 23.11.26

My dear brother,

Your message regarding the result of the scrutiny reached me last night. Though I was confident about the result I did not expect such a big majority. I do not know how to express my feelings of gratitude towards those whose combined efforts have brought about this welcome result. May God make me worthy of their love and confidence.

I have sent you a wire this morning asking you to convey to all well-wishers, supporters and friends my deepest gratitude for their enthusiastic sympathy and support. For reasons which are apparent, it is not possible for me to write to them individually. Further, there are several kind gentlemen whom I never had the privilege of knowing who have come forward of their own accord to espouse our cause. To them it is not possible for me to write even if I could—as I do not know them. Being a worker myself my love and fraternal greetings are specially due to the workers whose indefatigable labour day and night has largely contributed to the present success.

I am gradually shaking off the after-effects of flu. The Civil Surgeon of Mandalay, Col. Brayne, was called in a few days ago to examine me carefully. He has said that I have been suffering from enteroptosis—which literally means dropping of the viscera. According to Col. Brayne this theory can successfully account for my several complaints viz. dyspepsia, constipation etc. I have been recommended a further and closer examination in Rangoon—including test-meal examination, X-ray examination etc. If I have to go to Rangoon, I shall send you a wire before I leave. My present weight is 139 lbs. This is probably the effect of flu.

The Rangoon—Mandalay line is still out of order. The mails come partly by rail and partly by steamer. Up to Mycirgyan the mails come by rail via Thazi and from Mycirgyan by a steamer. This causes a further delay of 2 days. The breach which has not yet been repaired is within 50 miles of Mandalay. Through running is expected by the first week of December.

I am anxious about the results but there is no help. Hope this will find you all quite well. Please let me know your public engagements in advance if possible. What about *The Statesman* Suit? When is it coming up again?

Please tell Dr. Law that owing to my illness I was not able to finish his books in time. I shall try to hurry up now.

Yours v. affly,

SUBHAS

To
S. C. Bose Esq.
38/1 Elgin Road
Calcutta

40. *From Amrita Lal Chatterjee**

83, Lansdowne Road
24.11.26

My dear Subhas,

Herewith I am sending you a copy of our report.[1] We could do very little work for the orphanage during these days as everybody was busy with the elections.

It is needless to write how we all feel at your success at the polls—only if you are now set free from this most unjust incarceration.

Yours very sincerely
AMRITA LAL CHATTERJEE

41. *To Sarat Chandra Bose*

Censored and Passed
14/12
for D.I.G., I.B., C.I.D.
Bengal

Mandalay
27.11.26

My dear brother,

I have not heard from you for some time past. You must have been too busy.

I saw in the papers that mother, Bowdidi and others had been to the polling station on the polling day. It must have been very exciting there. I wish some one had time to describe the election campaign for our entertainment. The papers give a fairly vivid description.

We are having very nasty and wet weather for the last few days. It is cloudy and drizzling all the day long. The weather is typical of the rainy season at its worst. Through railway communication up to Mandalay had been restored for a day or two but further rains have reopened the breach and the mails are again held up. There seems to

* Translated from the original Bengali.
[1] See Appendix.

be hardly any prospect of having the Rangoon-Mandalay communication restored at an early date.

I think I shall have to go to Rangoon by steamer for the medical examination. The Civil Surgeon has particularly recommended (in agreement with the Supdt.) an X-Ray examination for enteroptosis. But he has not yet diagnosed my trouble as due to enteroptosis. He thinks that the trouble is due to constipation causing intestinal toxaemia which can account for the slow fever and night sweats from which I have been suffering for a month or so. I thought at first that the slow fever and night sweats were a passing phase but they are persisting. Along with this the pain in the spine which had almost disappeared has reappeared. I got the attack of influenza on the 30th October but I was having a temperature a few days before that. I neglected it however thinking it to be of no significance. I am still convalescent and do not feel fit yet. The symptoms which are persisting are slow fever with night sweats and pain in the spine. There is however nothing which should cause any anxiety.

Before you post the election accounts please ascertain by wire my address at the time. If I happen to be in Rangoon, you may send the papers to the I.G. of Prisons, Rangoon, who will forward them to me.

Have you been able to find the testimonials of Mr. S. K. Sen who applied for the post of Asst. Secy ? If so, please return them to him. By the way, has Bhaskar taken up his job yet ?

The following books would be helpful to you in your work in the Council :—

(1) Erskine May's "Parliamentary Procedure".

(2) Hammond's "Electioneering in India" (I am not sure about the exact title of the book). The book deals among other things with election rules, case law etc. The recent enlarged edition costs about Rs. 20/-.

(3) "Speakers of the House of Commons". There are two books on the subject by two different authors—one of which is in the Council Library and the other with Mr. Nalini Sarkar.

I find from the papers that the application for a commission was abandoned by my counsel Mr. A. K. Roy and that consequently Mr. Langford James asked for costs. If the report of *The Statesman* is a full one, Mr. Roy did not meet the latter's arguments as successfully as he could have. However Buckland put off the matter for the present. The next hearing is on Dec. 6, I think, when Mr. Wilkinson will be in the witness box.

Hope this will find you all quite well.

Yours v. affly
SUBHAS

To

S. C. Bose Esq.
38/1, Elgin Road
Calcutta

42. *To Sarat Chandra Bose*

Censored and Passed
Illegible
11/12
for D.I.G., I.B., C.I.D.
Bengal

Mandalay
4.12.26

My dear brother,

I wrote to you last on 27.11.26. I hope you have received all my letters duly.

The weather has improved to a certain extent. The railway breach still continues and God only knows when it is likely to be repaired. It is taking the mails from Rangoon two or three days longer than before to reach us. The Governor of Burma usually spends the winter in Mandalay. He has had to abandon the trip owing to the railway breach.

I have not received the election accounts yet. I hope there will be no unnecessary delay. I sent a wire to you day before yesterday to the following effect :—"Anxious election accounts not received yet stop please expedite despatch as railway breach continues thereby delaying transmission stop before despatching ascertain my address from this jail owing possibility of my going Rangoon for medical examination." It would be desirable when you send the election accounts to obtain the approval of D.I.G., C.I.D. of sending the election accounts direct from Mandalay to Calcutta. The C.I.D. may communicate this to the Supdt. while forwarding the accounts.

I am hoping that some of my ailments (viz. daily afternoon rise in temperature, pain in the spine and night sweats) are the after-effects of influenza and will disappear in time.

The point is whether they will disappear without a change in environment. I have wired to Shyamadas Kaviraj yesterday enquiring whether there should be any changes in medicine owing to the after-influenza symptoms. There is nothing however which should cause any anxiety.

The question of grant of land to the Baidyasastrapith will come up before the Corporation (or the Finance etc. Com.) shortly. They will apply for the land near Upper Circular Road opposite Bose Institute used till recently as a *Dhobikhana.* I understand the *Dhobikhana* sub-committee has recommended the abolition of that *Dhobikhana* and the land will therefore be available. Please try to do your best and speak to Santosh Babu and other friends. The Baidyasastrapith people were disappointed last time.

There is a very interesting criticism of the Bengal Relief Committee in this month's *Prabasi.* Please make time to read it.

Hope this will find you all quite well.

Yours v. affly
SUBHAS

S. C. Bose Esq.
38/1, Elgin Road
Calcutta

43. To Sarat Chandra Bose

Censored and Passed
Illegible
24/12
for D.I.G., I.B., C.I.D.
Bengal

Mandalay
6.12.26
Monday

My dear brother,

I have just been informed by the I.G. of Prisons that my trip to Rangoon for medical examination has been sanctioned and that arrangements are being made. I shall be going during the course of this week and shall in all probability be going by steamer.

I wired to Shyamadas Kaviraj through Intelligence on the 3rd December asking him whether any changes in medicine should be made after my influenza attack. In the wire I mentioned the present symptoms viz. *afternoon rise in temperature with pain in the spine and night sweat.* Impaired digestion and lack of appetite are of course the symptoms that are persisting. I am expecting a reply by wire any moment. I am sending you along with this *my temperature chart from the 13th Nov. to the 5th Dec. for the use of Kaviraj Mahasay.* Please send it over to him. I am not writing to him this week. I shall send you a wire before I leave for Rangoon. Hope this will find you all quite well.

Yours v. affly
SUBHAS

To
S. C. Bose Esq.
38/1, Elgin Road
Calcutta

Enclosure :—My temperature chart from the 13th Nov. to the 5th Dec.

S. C. B.

44. To Sarat Chandra Bose

Censored and Passed
Illegible
17/12/26
for D.I.G., I.B., C.I.D.
Bengal.

Mandalay
10.12.26
Friday

My dear brother,

I have not heard from you for over a month I think and I am rather anxious for news. I believe you are having a very busy time now. On 7.12.26 I sent the following wire to you and I am expecting a reply every minute :—"Starting Rangoon shortly by steamer for medical examination stop interview more convenient and desirable there than Mandalay owing to railway breach stop you may come Rangoon if intending interviewing in near future stop shall wire again before leaving."

Since then through running between Mandalay and Rangoon has been suddenly resumed. I have now been informed that I can go by train—which is more convenient. I shall be leaving within 2 or 3 days at the outside and do not expect to be in Rangoon for more than 3 or 4 days—so that within a week of my leaving this place, I shall be back here. I hope to get the election accounts on my return from Rangoon. I am thinking of sending another wire to you before leaving, asking you not to attempt to see me in Rangoon owing to my altered programme.

I agree with what you have said about *The Statesman* suit. I do not expect a judgement in my favour from Mr. Justice Buckland.

I hope the appointment of the Health Officer will be made after due deliberation. It should be possible to find a capable Indian to fill the post. I hope you will not forget the Baidyasastrapith matter. They are going to apply for the land now used as a *Dhobikhana* which is going to be abandoned.

I wish arrangements could be made to start compulsory primary education within a select area during the next financial year and that necessary provision could be made in the Budget. Hope this will find you all quite well. I am so so.

Yours v. affly
SUBHAS

To
S. C. Bose Esq.
38/1, Elgin Road
Calcutta

45. *From Santosh Kumar Bose*
Censored and Passed
Illegible
22/12
for D.I.G., I.B., C.I.D.
Bengal

10A, Gopal Ghosh Lane
Kidderpore
10.12.26

My dear Mr. Bose,

Your short but very interesting letter reached me on the 17th November—the day of polling for the Council elections in Calcutta, when your name was being uttered by thousands of people in Calcutta. Your candidature had called forth the affectionate enthusiasm of the whole of Calcutta, and if silent sympathy, apart from the active propaganda of the workers, had any efficacy, you had it in an abundant degree from high and low, young and old alike. The actual results have justified the popular expectation. You will kindly accept my most heartfelt congratulations, which is only a poor attempt to express my joy. I know you will realise it full well, though my words cannot give it any adequate expression.

I find from your letter that you have recently undergone an attack of influenza. Following upon it comes the news that you will shortly proceed to Rangoon for medical examination. All this goes to show that your health is far from satisfactory. All that we can do is to pray to God that He might keep you in His protecting care and in perpetual health and spirits. We shall remain greatly anxious for the result of the medical examinations.

You have by this time seen the election results in Bengal. The province has worthily maintained Deshbandhu's traditions in the first election after his death. In the South Calcutta Election contest I have myself seen what an asset to all great causes is the sacred memory of Deshbandhu. It is inspiring, it is vivifying, it raises every Bengali to a high moral plane, far above all petty considerations of tinkering reforms or personal canvassing. The average voter, to my mind, has well realised the true meaning and inwardness of the situation in the country, and the election results are the effect of a deliberate and intelligent casting of votes.

Coming down to matters municipal, the conclusion of the Council Elections has given me the preliminary humming about the municipal elections.

You have no doubt seen the anniversary number of the *Municipal Gazette*. Has it not been a creditable performance from every point of view ? The paper has great possibilities, which could have been fully developed if it could receive your fostering care.

19.12.26

I have received your letter this morning, before I had completed my reply.

....

I spent the Puja holidays—about 25 days—at Jamshedpore, and thoroughly enjoyed the rest and change. I used to take long walks in the morning extending over 5 or 6 miles of fine undulating country. The weather was just getting cold, and those early morning rambles on lonely roads in direct view of the Chotanagpur hills, finishing very often on the wooded bank of the river Subarnarekha, were delightful indeed. I badly needed some rest and change, and had a lot of it there. But on return to Calcutta, the compensation came with compound interest.

I have heard about your visit to Rangoon for medical inspection. I earnestly hope that the examination has not shown anything bad. Kindly let me know all about it, and how you are doing now and what the trouble has been found to be.

I find that you have not had a steamer trip. That would have been very pleasant in this season.

I am very glad to learn that our Manasha Mela has interested you so much. I have been enquiring about the past history of the Goddess Manasha in this locality, but have not been able to get anything yet. There is no literature on the subject. But I may get something from old residents, of whom there are very few left. Last year I heard that the masons were working to repair the old and dilapidated room of the Goddess, which stands under a huge, old *Ashathwa* tree, which rises right from the middle of the room. It is said that as soon as the worn out roof was taken down, a huge cobra came threatening the masons, but retired somewhat inside the tree without making any further attack, when the mistries finished their work. The image which is of "eight metal" as it is called, is a very small one, and was found more than a century ago buried in the ground on the spot. The place was in the heart of the thickly populated *bustee,* which has now been cleared by the C.I. Trust, which has driven the 80ft. road by the side of the temple, connecting Circular Garden Reach and Diamond Harbour Roads.

Hoping to be excused for this exuberance of local patriotism, I pass on to the other items touched in your letter. Mr. S. C. Bose has moved in the E.G.P. Committee for the grant of the *Dhobikhana* land to Vaidyasastrapith. We have decided to have an inspection. Mr. L. M. Sen has also tabled a motion in the Committee for granting the land to the Widows' Home. I remember that about 2 years ago Lady Bose invited a few of us to tea, and while we were negotiating most tempting dishes of much more solid and substantial things, we had discussed the question of the grant to the *Bani Bhawan.* The appeal to our heads and hearts was very telling having come through the right channel. But since then nothing had been done as the *Dhobikhana* Sub-Committee had not finished their labours, and partly because the land was considered somewhat costly. We have also invited Mr. L. M. Sen to the inspection, and shall see what can be done. I shall let you know what we decide.

I am so glad to find that you have expressed your appreciation of the Gazette in identical language. I shall convey your congratulations to the Editor.

As regards free and compulsory education in a selected area, we have got it very prominently in view. I hope it will be possible to make some provision in the Budget. Compulsion in the whole city is mixed up with the question of cost. The Education Officer has circulated a note for the opinion of Councillors suggesting an education cess of ½ p.c., which is likely to bring about 8 lakhs. As you can well understand, Councillors have not exhibited too much eagerness to adopt the suggestion, and it rests there. The educational survey has been taken up.

As regards the gentleman in the Stores Department, I shall try my best for him when I get all the facts from him.

Regarding the District Engineers, the question of having B.E.'s in our district staff has come up very prominently now in connection with application for extension by retiring upper subordinates. The general view is to have qualified men in this most important department. The question of centralising the Roads Department was, I understand, taken up by the Re-organisation Committee after I resigned the membership after my illness in June. I am told by the Secretary that they have decided against centralisation. I intend to go into the matter before the Budget.

The Retrenchment Officer's report has been submitted and printed by instalments, and I am not sure that he has submitted the whole of it. He did make some valuable suggestions, but the Committee, I understand, have made other independent suggestions after dicussing the report.

I could not understand the reception accorded to the Deputy Mayor, when after a long absence, he put in appearance, on the third day of the debate on my Added Areas Bill resolution. There were some visitors sitting on the floor of the House, and perhaps the temptation to produce a spectacular effect proved too strong for some members. Some of us continued in our seats in spite of the overtures of the seceders from the corridor. A committee of enquiry and such public condemnation, did, to my mind, go ill together.

I am very much interested to know about your experiments in improving poultry breeds. It is a very good hobby —profitable as well as enjoyable. I take it that the experiments are completed at the dinner table.

Regarding the Social Hygiene Deputation, the Bengal Govt. are making arrangements and have invited the Corporation to co-operate. Miss Lloyd has been elected the Corporation representative and a small Committee has been appointed in a conference at the Writers' Buildings. I do not know what arrangements are being made. I think lectures and private talks will be arranged.

The statistics for Kala-azar and tuberculosis cases have been left to be collected by the Ward Health Associations. Every Association has got an M.O. and two assistants, whose duty it is to collect statistics. The Associations are expected to have as its members all the medical practitioners in the Ward, and their co-operation is expected.

In our vital statistics, columns for suicide and lunacy will be very useful. The difficulty seems to be in getting accurate information of such matters. Still an attempt should be made to collect statistics. I shall make the suggestion to the Health Officer.

It is our earnest desire to have a qualified Indian Health Officer. The post is a highly responsible one, and the choice seems to be difficult.

I do not think that any action has been taken on your report on fodder. I find, however, that this time it was the Chief Engineer and the new Supdt. of Gowkhana II who made the purchase of ponies. Supdt. of Gowkhana IV, I hear, makes a grievance, as he has always made regarding the purchases in the past.

The sweepers' stores in my Ward, which is for Dist.

IV, is going on well. There has been a satisfactory increase in the number of members. We get occasional complaints about the prices or the quality of articles, and they are promptly attended to.

It is now midnight, and I had better not carry this scribbling to tomorrow. As it is, the reply has been delayed long enough. The size of the papers gives this letter the look of a state despatch, but it gives me more room to fill with my words.

I hope and trust that this will find you doing much better. That indeed is our constant prayer. May the New Year bring you health, happiness and the best of spirits.

With kindest regards,

Yours fraternally
SANTOSH KUMAR BASU

46. To Santosh Kumar Basu

Censored and Passed
Illegible
12/2/27
for D.I.G., I.B., C.I.D.
Bengal

Mandalay Jail
4.2.27

My dear Mr. Basu,

I was delighted to receive your letter of 10/19.12.26 which was to hand duly. Your reference to the elections and the people's sympathy have touched a soft corner in my heart. I am human and love and hate are not, therefore, quite the same to me—in spite of the Bhagavad Gita. What more can one in my position either expect or get—next to the approbation of his own conscience ? Though it is so late, allow me to reciprocate the loving message you have so kindly sent me.

I hope you are offering yourself for re-election in order to continue the noble work you have been doing for the rate-payers of Calcutta during the last three years. I have no doubt that your constituency will re-affirm its confidence in you. Need I assure you of the regard and esteem which I have for you.

I am glad that you enjoyed your vacation trip to Jamshedpur. I have not been there but I have been to Ranchi and I can imagine what the scenery would be like.

I shall wait for further light on the past history of "Manasha" and "Manasha Mela" in Kidderpore. It would be worthwhile to put some young enthusiasts on to the work. They can approach the old residents, collect information and publish articles in periodicals or a pamphlet on the subject.

I do not think it would be advisable to split up the *Dhokhana* and that for two reasons. In the first place, the Baidyasastrapith should preferably have a big plot, in order to meet future requirements. In the second place the proximity of a Widow's Home would not be desirable for an educational institution. Please consider these two points seriously when the matter comes up before the Corporation. I have also written to Mejdada about this matter. I have every sympathy for the Widow's Home but it should not be difficult to find a decent plot for them elsewhere.

The Education Officer does not seem to be satisfied with the selection of the officer appointed for carrying out the educational survey.

It will not be an easy task to effect centralization in the Roads Department. Wholesale opposition from all the departments will have to be faced—but the task will have to be done nevertheless.

I am glad that we are in agreement over the treatment accorded to the Deputy Mayor. I am sorry that there was no one at the time who could check the desire to show discourtesy. I find in the Rangoon papers that the committee of enquiry are going to ask for the removal of the Deputy Mayor. I am pained to read this. I hope that the Corporation will turn down this recommendation if it is really submitted. Without entering into any controversy, the fact that the Corporation is shortly going to be dissolved should afford a sufficient reason for doing so.

Dr. T. N. Majumdar, acting H.O. wrote to me for a testimonial a few days ago. I felt very much embarrassed at first and did not know what to do. Ultimately I decided to give him one in general terms on the ground that if I had been in my office today, he would have been entitled to it. I do not think I would have been right in refusing it. I have however asked him not to make use of it officially if he can help doing so and I have suggested that it would be better if the Corporation officially asked me for my opinion.

You will be expecting some further information about my health but I have to disappoint you. My condition continues the same as before except that the temperature is tending to go higher up nowadays. You will get the details from Mejdada—you will excuse me for not giving you first-hand information. I do not feel up to writing long letters nowadays and get tired sooner than before. Thank God my spirits are all right and shall remain so. I have read the debate in the Corporation regarding my health, etc. in the Calcutta papers.

Hope this will find you all quite well ; with kindest regards,

Yours affectionately
SUBHAS C. BOSE

47. *To Sarat Chandra Bose**

Rangoon Central Jail
(C/o, D.I.G. I.B. C.I.D.
13, Elysium Row).
17.12.26

My dear brother,

I have not received any letter from you for a long time. I hope that all of you are well. I reached here last Tuesday and I do not know how long I shall have to stay here. I shall be medically examined by Colonel Kellsal tomorrow and on his report depends my staying or not staying here.

* Translated from the original Bengali.

Yet, most probably I haven't got to stay here more than three or four days. The plan was to bring us here by a steam-boat. But due to some mismanagement the plan was not carried out. Now probably we will go back by train because a journey by steamer takes eight or nine days. Had I not been pre-occupied with the thought of election accounts I would have tried to go back by a steam-boat.

An X-ray plate of my abdomen was taken but I have not yet come to know its report—probably I shall come to know of it tomorrow. If it is necessary X-ray plates of my chest and my back will also be taken. Even now, I am suffering daily from fever and like before I am still now suffering from dyspepsia without any radical change. The pain on my back is still there. All these facts are known to you and so there is nothing more to talk about. I have sent a letter to Kaviraj Mahashaya by today's post.

I have not received even now any news about the Council, when its session will take place, when the president will be elected etc. and if you have news about that please inform me. If your programme of this month and the month of January is fixed up please let me know about it. Are you going to Gauhati ? If you intend to go there then please inform me who are the persons going there and when you all will be back. In the newspaper it has been reported that Basanti Devi is not in good health, and I am very much worried about her.

In my previous letter, I enclosed a temperature chart to be studied by Kaviraj Mahashaya. I hope that has been sent to the Kaviraj Mahashaya in due course.

If due to any mismanagement connected with my journey to and from Rangoon the election accounts fail to reach me then the need might arise to send it by some messenger and so please make a copy of the accounts at the right time. If the need for having the account carried by a messenger arises I shall inform you to do so by sending a telegram.

Probably father and mother will stay in Calcutta during the Christmas holidays. I am sending a letter to father by today's post. How are they ?

A young man called Nagen Sinha was employed for working in the stores department of Calcutta Corporation. He has written that he has got to deposit money as security and that he is facing no end of trouble in collecting that money. He says that he will be much benefited if the amount of money to be deposited as security is reduced or if he is allowed to have an extension of the period for collecting that money.

There is nothing more to add. How are you all ? What is the state of health of Pandit Motilal now ?

Accept my *pronam.*

Yours affectionately,
SUBHAS

*48. To Sarat Chandra Bose**
Censored and Passed

Rangoon Central Jail
20-12-26
Monday.

My dear Brother,

The telegram you sent to the Inspector-General on 17th of December reached me on the 18th. On hearing that the election accounts have been sent I am now free from worries and I think, it will reach me today or tomorrow and as soon as it will be here I shall put down my signature on it before the magistrate and send it back. If it fails to catch tomorrow's that is Tuesday's post it will certainly be sent by Thursday's post and will reach Calcutta in the morning of Sunday.

From here, the paper bearing the election accounts will first go to the CID office and so it will be delayed for two or three days to be sent to you. If you do not stay in Calcutta at the end of December then please arrange it in this way that as soon as the Election Accounts come to you somebody will take the trouble of sending it to the proper place that is to the Returning Officer. I think, most

* Translated from the original Bengali.

probably, you will get this letter in the beginning of January.

I got that very day the telegram which you sent on the 16th to the Jail Superintendent. But as the medical examination was not finished then, I could not answer your telegram. Moreover, it is not possible to inform you in detail through a telegram and so I am doing this in this letter.

After examining the X-Ray photo, the doctor is of the opinion that there is no stomach trouble. Then, Colonel Kellsal after examining my chest diagnosed that my chest was also free from any trouble. Yet, as I am suffering from slow fever, Dr. Kellsal wants to keep me under observation for fourteen days more to ascertain the cause of it. Within this period, everyday my temperature will be checked and my urine and sputum will be examined. Once, my urine was analysed and nothing abnormal was found in it. Today again, my urine and sputum will be analysed. You will be informed in due time. After coming over here, my temperature is being checked everyday, and I am suffering from fever, running a temperature of 99°. The pain on my back is there as it was before.

I was asked by the Inspector-General that as I was to be under medical observation for eight or ten days more whether I would prefer to stay in Rangoon during that period or would like to go back to Mandalay immediately. As this place lacks good arrangements for staying I told him that I would prefer to go back without delay as soon as matters related to Election Accounts were settled. But to be sure whether there is any possibility of anybody coming from Calcutta, I sent a telegram to you through the Inspector-General. Most probably you will get that telegram from the CID office today and I shall also get the reply either today or tomorrow. If somebody from Calcutta comes here to see me then I shall wait here till his coming. Otherwise, I shall be back to Mandalay as soon as possible. When I shall be in Mandalay, I shall write to you.

I hope all of you are keeping well. Accept my *pronam* and give my *pronam* to mother and father. How is Mrs. Basanti Devi ?

I received in due time the *dhoti* and *chaddar* sent by Sejdidi and Kanak on the occasion of *Bhai-Phota.* I wrote you a letter before this one on the 17th and I hope you received it in due time.

Yours affectionately,
SUBHAS

S. C. Bose, Esq.
Bar-at-law
38/1, Elgin Road,
Calcutta.

49. From Sarat Chandra Bose
Censored and Passed
Illegible
30/12
for D.I.G., I.B., C.I.D.
Bengal

38/1, Elgin Road
30.XII.26

My dear Subhas,

I received your letters dated the 17th and 20th written at Rangoon yesterday. I received also the election accounts signed by you. Dada will affirm the same on the 3rd January and file them the same day.

I hope you have received by now my letter dated the 11th December.

I decided on the 24th to go to Gauhati and left the same afternoon. Before leaving, I wrote you a short letter which I expect will reach you in a day or two. We are not at all satisfied with the medical examination at Rangoon. It is poor consolation to learn that "Medical examination revealed no signs of organic disease"—I am quoting from the telegram sent by the Inspector General of Prisons to me on the 23rd. Surely a more serious attempt should be made to find out what the low fever, night sweat and pain in the spine are due to. I doubt if a correct diagnosis will or can be made unless you are brought down to Calcutta for treatment.

I showed your temperature chart to Dr. Bidhan Roy. He said he could not venture on an opinion unless and until he was given the opportunity to examine you. He suggested however an X-ray examination of your whole system. I have written accordingly to the Additional Deputy Secretary, Political Department, Government of Bengal and have received the usual laconic reply "the matter will receive due consideration".

Dada is going to Shyamadas Kaviraj this afternoon with your temperature chart and I shall let you know what he says in my next letter (which I intend to write on Saturday next.) Dada will request Shyamadas Kaviraj to send you medicines by next Sunday's boat.

Father is naturally anxious for you. It is not possible to keep back these things from him. He arrived in Calcutta on the 23rd with the intention of coming to Rangoon with me. He hadn't the time to go to Mandalay as he was wanted at Cuttack on the 23rd January.

I suppose you will get a copy of the Medical examination report. If and when you get it please send it on to me. I shall take medical opinion and if advised shall apply for your transfer to Bengal for treatment.

Have you received the summons to the Council meeting of the 10th January ? We haven't yet decided as to whether we should run a candidate for the Presidentship.

This leaves us fairly well. Please let me have full details about your health etc. in your letter.

With love,

Yours very affly

SARAT

Subhas Ch. Bose Esq.

*50. To Basanti Devi**

Censored and Passed
Illegible
11/27
for D.I.G., I.B., C.I.D.
Bengal

Rangoon Central Jail
20/12/26

Revered mother,

I felt comforted to receive your letter after a long time. I wrote to you on the 13th September and again on the 17th November. The latter, I expect, has reached you by now. Your letter of the 3rd December was to hand today. I was brought down here from Mandalay five or six days ago for medical examination. I shall most probably return to Mandalay in two or three days.

I often sit down with the intention of writing to you but I can hardly make any progress ; the result is that I give up after writing a few lines. You stand no risk of making the rigours of my prison life more difficult by writing to me. It will not be true to say that I am not suffering here. But, will the suffering be any the less if people do not write to me ? And, how can letters add to my suffering ? Not that I do not feel sorry to read letters from home. But do they bring me only sorrow ? Moreover, how can I live without the memories of joy and sorrow, even though for the present there is more of the latter ? Not having chosen the path of renunciation, how can I forget all the memories of the outside world, even if they are sorrowful ? In spite of the torment, one cannot but cling to such memories.

You wish to live in seclusion—but will that bring you peace ? Can one be sure ? If you had a limited mind, possibly you could find peace. When I first read in the papers about your health two or three days ago, I thought of sending a telegram for news. But then I thought that as I was to leave this place in one or two days, I should rather try to

* Translated from the original Bengali. This letter was left unfinished in Rangoon and completed in Mandalay on December 30, 1926.—Ed.

get some news on my return to Mandalay. And then your letter reached my hands.

God alone knows how long I shall have to be in prison. However long it may be—I am thankful that He has given me the strength to endure it all. I feel sometimes or rather quite often, that I am not yet ready in body and spirit to go out. The purpose for which Providence sent me here still remains unfulfilled and my apprenticeship in prison is yet incomplete. When I look at it calmly, I feel that for the present prison life is doing me good. Of course, my heart refuses to accept it under all circumstances. Not only my own kith and kin, but also Bengal and the whole of India shine in matchless beauty in my dreams. Reality has receded from my life—I am now clinging to my dreams. My soul yearns from time to time for the reality behind my dreams. It is possible for a strong-willed person like myself to suppress such transitory cravings of the heart; but, I have already said that I do not accept *sannyasa* and I have therefore no right not to recognise sorrow.

Mandalay Jail
30/12/26

Memories of the past which crowd into my mind and sustain me in this enforced leisure are not, by and large, painful memories. There are more of happy and peaceful elements in them; only when I judge them in the context of my present state of existence that I feel unhappy. But then, I cannot be sure that there is no happiness in this painful experience as well.

One of my friends wrote to me some time ago in the following terms: "We have the consolation of mingling our tears with those of our countrymen at large; but Providence has chosen to deny you this consolation." This is true indeed. To have to weep in silence and seclusion is extremely oppressive: it is no less painful to think that in this hour of calamity we did not have the chance to be of some service.

There is no reason to assume that, by keeping away from the humdrum of public activity, you will succeed in keeping others away from your personal sorrows ; on the contrary, the result may just be the opposite. You have said, "I do not know if I shall ever see you again." I am not so pessimistic although I am always prepared for all misfortune. I feel sure that I shall not recoil from the prospect of even life-long imprisonment if that be necessary for the good of my motherland.

I have accepted life as an adventure—success or failure of my mission is in God's hands. My only regret is that I have not been able to equip myself as much as I should have done during my confinement here. Even so, my life in prison has not been in vain. You have said very rightly, "God will take account of your tortured lives. . . all this will some day come to an end". We also have the same faith,—in your words again, "Some day and inevitably, fulfilment of your mission will bring glory to your lives". Your priceless words of encouragement are echoed in our hearts and will sustain us under all circumstances. I would only go a little further and say—even life-long confinement here will not make our lives worthless, because the measure of success in life is not external activity but inner fulfilment. I pray that your blessings may always protect me as a shield and that I may, by keeping always to the path of truth prove worthy of your love and blessings.

I have a desire to write his (Deshbandhu's) biography but I do not feel confident. I tried to write a few lines a number of times, but that made me even more diffident. I still think that not many people can claim to have had the close glimpse of his deep and many-faceted character that I had. So, I cannot but feel that I should share my experience with others. Satyen Babu tells me that he (Deshbandhu) used to say that Mr. Girija Prasanna Roy Chowdhury would be able to write his biography rightly and properly. Nevertheless, if you will let me have some material, I should like to make an attempt despite my limitations. I can assure you that there will never be any want of time for this work. The real obstacle is not lack of time but lack of ability and insight. I have another task in mind and that is to write a well-connected series of articles or a book on the basis of notes he made during his imprisonment.

I felt anxious to read about your health in a letter from *Mejdada* that I received a few days ago. Whatever may be the state of your mind, you should not raise objections to what doctors and others want to be done. You do not care for your health ; and it is not that we are completely oblivious of what is passing in your mind. But, you are probably not aware how we and your countrymen at large value your health.

I returned from Rangoon about a week ago and shall be here for the present. Please accept respectful *pronams* from all of us. There is no cause for anxiety about my health—that is the view of the Rangoon doctor. Let me stop here today.

Devotedly yours
SUBHAS

51. From Sarat Chandra Bose

Censored and Passed
Illegible
13/12
for D.I.G., I.B., C.I.D.
Bengal

38/1, Elgin Road
11th Dec. 1926

My dear Subhas,

I believe I last wrote to you on the 1st Nov. acknowledging your letter of the 16th Oct. Since then I have received from you letters dated 23rd October, 1st Nov., 6th Nov, and the 15th Nov. I also received the messages you sent from time to time through Intelligence, the last of which was on the 7th instant informing me that you were starting for Rangoon shortly by steamer for medical examination.

I am glad that after all the authorities have thought it right to have you medically examined. The repeated attacks of influenza were rather alarming and it seemed to me that a thorough examination and change to some other place was necessary. I shall anxiously wait for the result of your medical examination.

The temptation to come to Rangoon is very great but I cannot say exactly just now if I shall be able to come. One thing is certain—I am not going to Gauhati. I want to have a little rest—and Gauhati will give no rest.

The hearing of your libel action against *The Statesman* was over on Tuesday last. Justice Buckland seems to be of the opinion that *The Statesman* has not asserted *any facts* but has merely commented on the Governor's Maldah speech. How any one could possibly come to hold that opinion I fail to see. B. C. also thinks that the article states *facts*. It was conceded during the argument that if the article asserted facts, it amounted to libel.

I am expecting judgement to be delivered next Monday and whatever the result, I shall wire the result to you.

Mrs. Das is here. She has been in very poor health, ever since Bhombal's death. Doctors have advised a course of radium treatment and she is now under that treatment.

Your election accounts are being prepared and they will be sent to you shortly.

This leaves us fairly well. I trust this will find you better.

Natunmamababu has been in *poor health* for some time past. He is now confined to bed with pain all over the body. As you know, doctors have never been able to diagnose the case.

With love,

Yours very affly
SARAT

Subhas Ch. Bose Esq.

52. *To Sarat Chandra Bose*
Censored and Passed
Illegible
7/1/27
for D.I.G., I.B., C.I.D.
Bengal

Mandalay
31.12.26

My dear brother,

Your letter of 11.12.26 reached me yesterday. It had been redirected from here to Rangoon but did not catch me there—hence the delay.

During the months of November and December I have written to you on the following dates :—(1) 1st Nov. (2) 6th Nov. (3) 13th Nov. (4) 15th Nov. (5) 23rd Nov. (5) 27th Nov. (7) 4th Dec. (8) 6th Dec. (9) 10th Dec. (10) 17th Dec. from Rangoon (11) 20th Dec. from Rangoon (12) 24th Dec. from Mandalay. I have also written to Bardada on 21/12/26 from Rangoon while forwarding the election expenses. I hope you have duly received the above letters.

I sent the following telegraphic messages through Intelligence :—11/12/26—Wire whether election accounts sent if so when and what address (Reply prepaid Re. 1/-) 13/12/26—Starting Rangoon today train shall wire on arrival there regarding length of stay there please send messages care Rangoon Jail Superintendent through Intelligence.

I also sent a telegraphic message from Rangoon through Intelligence on 15/12/26 and I got a reply to that through the Inspector General of Prisons on 15/12/26. I got a telegram from you through Intelligence and Rangoon Jail Superintendent on 17/12/26. The telegram was dated 16/12/26. I do not think I sent any reply to that. On 19/12/26 the Inspector General informed you by wire that there was no special reason for detaining me there unless some one wanted to interview me there.

I hope you have received the telegraphic messages duly.

I arrived here from Rangoon on 23/12/26. The same day I sent you a telegraphic message through Intelligence saying that I had returned owing to inconvenience in staying at Rangoon and that you might reconsider your proposed trip to Rangoon for the purpose of interviewing me. Before I left Rangoon I asked the Inspector General of Prisons to inform you by wire about my departure.

My health continues the same as before. I did not have a temperature for two days after my return—but I have been getting it again for the last 5 or 6 days. The temperature goes up to 99° in the afternoon.

When I was in Rangoon Jail, Mr. Justice J. R. Das paid me a visit during the course of his official visit to the Jail.

My weight is 139 lbs. i.e. the same as before I left for Rangoon.

I am anxious to catch today's mail so I shall cut short my letter here. I shall write other details in my next.

Hope this will find you all quite well.

Yours v. affly

SUBHAS

S. C. Bose Esq.
38/1, Elgin Road
Calcutta

53. From Satish Chandra Bose

38/2, Elgin Road
Calcutta
16.12.26

My dear Subhas,

Enclosed you will find the form containing the return of election expenses incurred on your behalf. All items of expenses have been entered in the said return except the item regarding the costs of telegrams (despatched by you) which has got to be filled up by you.

This leaves us well.

Trusting this will find you in better health,

I remain

V. affectionately,

SATISH

Replied
SCB
21/11/26

54. *From Satyendra Kishore Ray**

42, Sitaram Ghosh St.
Calcutta.
22.12.26

Revered Sir,

Most respectfully I beg to bring to your notice that though I am completely unknown to you yet I hope that if I try to introduce myself to you, you will come to know me as a man who is most unfortunate. I am related to Surendra Mohan Ghosh who is now a political prisoner imprisoned in Mandalay Jail. Surendra Mohan Ghosh's sister happens to be the wife of my maternal uncle. I am an orphan and extremely indigent. Some time ago, my mother died and while she was alive we used to get an aid of Rs. 30 from the Government. With the help of that money and by getting a little more help in some way or other we could eke out existence with great difficulty. We did not even get the whole amount of money from the Govt. and usually we were paid only Rs. 18. Now I am in no end of trouble with my younger brothers and sisters dependent on me. Had uncle (Surendra Mohan Ghosh) been outside the jail he would have tried to help us in some way or other. In this state of dire difficulty I submit myself to you for securing your help. Now it is you who can rescue me because you have been endowed with the power to do so by God.

I have been living in Calcutta for a long time and I am now looking for a job. My younger brothers and sisters live in the town of Mymensingh and they attend their schools there. I can't stop them from going to school because that will simply ruin their future, yet I am incapable of spending money on their education. Under such circumstances I feel so helpless that I have been forced to write this letter to you and I appeal to you that if you write a letter to Jatish Babu the acting Chief Executive Officer of Calcutta Corporation asking him to provide me with a job in the Corporation with a salary of at least Rs. 80 a

* Translated from the original Bengali.

month then I can somehow get over my difficulties. It will be better to mention specifically the amount of money which should be paid as my salary. I appeared in the matriculation examination in the year 1924 but unfortunately I could not pass the examination. Such being the case I can't claim to be sufficiently qualified for this kind of a job, yet I know that your kind recommendation will be a qualification enough for me. Please put the letter you will write to Jatish Babu in the same envelope which will contain the letter written to me because I want to see personally Jatish Babu with your letter. I hope that realising my situation you will come to the rescue of this poor fellow and thereby make me ever grateful to you.

May God bless you. If anything not proper or objectionable has crept into this letter then I beg to be pardoned by you out of your great generosity.

We are keeping somehow. I hope you are keeping well. All of you accept my respectful *pronams* and extend my *pronam* to my uncle and inform me how he is keeping.

Yours most respectfully,
SATYEN

55. From Sarat Chandra Bose
Phone Cal. 4434
Censored and Passed
Illegible
27/12
for D.I.G., I.B., C.I.D.
Bengal

38/1, Elgin Road
24/12/26
Friday

My dear Subhas,

I was rather surprised to read in yesterday's papers that you had returned to Mandalay. What sort of accommodation did you have at Rangoon ? Were you put to great inconvenience ?

We had decided to leave for Rangoon this morning (wife, I and the three younger children) but yesterday's news upset the arrangement. On reading the papers I wired both to the Inspector General of Prisons, Rangoon and the Superintendent of Mandalay Jail for information. I got replies from both yesterday. I was also glad to learn that you had signed and affirmed the election accounts.

It is no use trying to go to Mandalay because I will hardly have a day and a half there.

I am going to Gauhati this afternoon and shall be back here on the 28th or 29th. More in my next.

Please let me have details of your medical examination.

Yours very affly

SARAT

Subhas C. Bose Esq.

56. To Sarat Chandra Bose

Censored and Passed
Illegible
3/1/27
for D.I.G., I.B., C.I.D.
Bengal

Mandalay
24.12.26

My dear brother,

I returned here yesterday morning. This must have surprised you. On Sunday last (19th Dec.) I asked the I.G. of Prisons to send you a wire through Intelligence re. the length of my stay here. As far as I can recollect he wrote to say that there was no special reason for detaining me but he could do so, if anyone came up to see me and I agreed with the draft. On Tuesday morning (i.e. 21st) I was informed that the I.G.P. had sent word to say that one of my brothers was expected to sail on Friday (i.e. today). The I.G.P. wanted to know if I would like to stay on in Rangoon or if I would go up to Mandalay in the meantime. I found that I would have to stay on in Rangoon for 8 or 9 days more if I had the interview there. The arrangements in Rangoon Jail being of a temporary nature were not satisfactory at all and I was feeling rather cramped and there was a feeling of mental pressure. Moreover my temperature was going up daily. In Mandalay it usually went up to 99° daily but in Rangoon it began to go up to 100°—as the following chart will show. So after considering the matter coolly, I sent word to say that I would rather return to Mandalay. I knew that you would be coming under the impression that you would find me in Rangoon. So on Wednesday morning (22nd Dec.) I asked the I.G. of Prisons whom I happened to meet before I left the Rangoon Jail to send you a wire saying that I was leaving for Mandalay. I impressed on him the importance of the wire and said that you might have occasion or reason to alter your programme if you knew that I was no longer in Rangoon. He said that he would send the wire the same afternoon positively. Mr. Bhattacharya (D.S.P., C.I.D.) came to the station to see me off and I also told him to remind the I.G. of Prisons about the wire which he said he would. I am sure that the I.G.P.'s wire must have reached you yesterday (i.e. Thursday the 23rd). However, to make sure, soon after my arrival here yesterday morning I sent another wire to you through Intelligence to the following effect :—

"Returned Mandalay owing inconvenience staying Rangoon stop please reconsider Burma trip if necessary stop election expenses leaving Rangoon todays boat."

I am sure this wire reached you by yesterday evening. The Supdt. told me that you had wired to him yesterday, enquiring if I had returned to Mandalay and saying that you would not be able to come to Mandalay during the X-mas vacation. I have already wired to you to reconsider your Burma trip now and I do not want you to upset your programme or to sacrifice your public engagements by coming here now. In fact I shall be sorry if you do.

About my health I shall write more in my next. I am anxious to catch today's mail and I am in haste. I am only sending herewith my temperature chart during my stay in Rangoon. During the first few days of my stay there, the temperature was not taken. I am writing to Kaviraj Mahasay this week—so please send him the chart. Please inform him also that I have received the last parcel of medicine which he sent after getting my telegram of the 3rd December.

The election expenses have been sent to Bardada as I thought that you would be away. I have not signed the last page in the expenses book as it is meant only for those who are out of India and cannot therefore submit their accounts in time.

Temperature chart

Saturday 18th Dec.	
10-30 a.m.	98.9°
3 p.m.	99°
7 p.m.	98.4°
Sunday—the 19th Dec.	
7 a.m.	97.6°
11 a.m.	99.2°
3 p.m.	98.6°
7 p.m.	98.4°
Monday—the 20th Dec.	
7-30 a.m.	98°
11-30 a.m.	99.6°
3-30 p.m.	98.8°
7 p.m.	98.8°
Tuesday 21st Dec.	
7-30 a.m.	98.2°
11-30 a.m.	99.6°
3 p.m.	100°
8-15 p.m.	98.2°
Wednesday 22nd Dec.	
7-30 a.m.	100°
11 a.m.	99.2°

My health remains unchanged. Hope this will find you all quite well.

Yours v. affly
SUBHAS

S. C. Bose Esq.
38/1, Elgin Road
Calcutta

57. *To Anath Bandhu Dutta**

Mandalay Jail
December, 1926

Dear Sir,

I duly received your letter of the 9th November. Please do not mind the delay in my replying to you. If I had my way, I would perhaps not write to you—because to have contacts with a State Prisoner is not a desirable thing. But I decided to write to you on the presumption that you will be expecting a reply and will be happy to hear from me.

I am sincerely grateful to you for having collectively remembered and prayed for my health and release and for your message of greetings. What greater reward can a servant of the country expect ? I need hardly add therefore that I felt happy to receive your letter and to read the report of your meeting in the newspapers. I do realise that such a feeling of satisfaction is not indicative of an elevated state of mind. But what can I do ? I claim to be a servant of the nation but I am also human. Who does not feel happy at the touch of love and sympathy ? Nothing can be better than if one can overcome or sublimate the desire for a return. A public worker of higher category should be able to conquer the desire for a return, but to me this is still an ideal. If I am true to myself I must confess that I also feel from time to time like Alexander Selkirk—

"My friends do they now and then
Send a wish or a thought after me ?"

I have now been in prison for exactly fourteen months. Of that I have spent eleven months in far-off Burma. Sometimes I feel as if these fourteen months passed by so quickly ; at other times fourteen months appear to me like ages. I feel as if this is my hearth and home, everything outside of prison appears to be like a dream or a mirage—as if iron-bars and stone-walls constitute the only truth in this world. Verily, this is a new and strange world ! I feel sometimes that one who has not been to prison has

* Translated from the original Bengali.

seen nothing of this world. And, he has been denied access to so many realities of this world. I have found out by analysing my own mind that this feeling is not just born of jealousy. Prison life has taught me a lot ; many realities which were vague and distant now appear clear to me ; many new experiences have strengthened and enriched my life. If, some day, Providence grants me the opportunity and the power of expression, I hope to be able to communicate them to my countrymen.

I am of course a prisoner—but there is nothing to be unhappy about. To suffer privation for the Mother is a matter of glory. You have to believe me when I say that there is joy in suffering. Otherwise, one would go mad, one could not laugh with his heart brimful with joy even in the midst of privation ! What to external appearance is suffering, appears to be a source of bliss when you go deep into it. Well, of course, I do not feel this way every day in the year or every hour in the day ; after all I can feel the fetters on my body. But there can be no doubt that one who has not got this feeling more or less, can neither enrich his life through suffering nor keep calm in suffering.

My only regret is that I have largely wasted these fourteen months. If I were in a Bengal prison, I would perhaps have made considerable progress on the road to self-realisation. But that was not to be. My only prayer now is :

"তোমার পতাকা যারে দাও তারে
বহিবারে দাও শকতি"[1]

When I imagine being free again, at heart I feel more nervous than happy. I feel nervous lest the call of duty should arrive before I am prepared for it. At such moments I wish that I may not be released before I am completely prepared. Today I am not prepared either in body or in spirit ; that is why the call of duty has not come yet. But, once I have attained the necessary preparedness, nobody will be able to hold me in bondage for a moment longer. All this is fancy ; I do not know if there is any objective truth in this. Continued imprisonment leads to a merger of subjective and

[1] "O Lord, give unto your chosen one the strength to bear the cross."

objective truth. Emotions and memories appear as realities. I am now in this particular state. So, for the present imagination is the only reality before me ; and in this feeling of oneness lies peace.

You said in your letter, "distance and time have made you even dearer to Bengal." On the other hand, I can hardly express in words how much dearer and truer has beloved Bengal become to me on account of the distance and time that separates us. The late Deshbandhu said in his book of Bengal lyrics, "An eternal truth is inherent in the waters and soil of Bengal". Had I not been away for this one year, I would not appreciate the truth of this saying. "The wavy, green rice-fields of Bengal, the blooming and sweet-smelling mango groves, the spectacle of evening prayer at the temples with the burning of incense, the picturesque courtyards of our village homes"—to see all this even with the mind's eye is a rare delight.

When I see patches of white clouds floating across the sky in the morning or afternoon, I momentarily feel—as the exiled Yaksha of Meghdut did—like sending through them some of my innermost feelings to Mother Bengal. I could at least tell her in the Vaishnavic strain—

"তোমারই লাগিয়া কলঙ্কের বোঝা,
বহিতে আমার সুখ"[1]

As darkness descends, the sun disappears behind the high ramparts of the fort of Mandalay and the western horizon is lit up with the rays of the setting sun and the crimson rays give the countless clouds a dazzling beauty,—I am reminded of Bengal's skies, the scene of Bengal's sunset. Who knew before that there was such charm even in the imagined scene ?

When the light and colour of morning pervade the sky and then hit my sleepy eyes and wake me up, I am reminded of another sunrise, the sunrise through which Bengal's poets and savants have realised Mother Bengal.

I am afraid I am getting pedantic. However, this is not pedantry—rather verbosity. This is merely an example of

[1] "To face calumny for your sake is to me a blessing."

what happens when free exchange of thoughts has been stopped for long. My condition is just like an engine that saves itself by letting out steam from time to time.

I was pleased to know that the work of the Sevak Samity was getting on well. There should not be any ill feelings between you and the Lansdowne branch. I hope they are doing good work. It will be very good if you can help the Orphanage of the Dakshin Kalikata Sevasram. It does not appear to be making any progress although the work is a very important one.

I had no difficulty in recognising you. I hope you are all well. Please accept my affectionate greetings.

*58. To Bhupendra Nath Bandopadhyay**

Mandalay Jail
1926

Dear Friend,

I was very happy to receive your letter of the 2nd May. You will please forgive me for the delay in replying to you. You can well realise that I am no longer the master of my affairs in very many ways. I could not help feeling happy and sorry at the same time at all the news you have given me about Bhowanipore. All over Bengal today there are only groupism and internecine quarrels ; and where there is less of work, there is more of quarrel. Some work is being done in Bhowanipore and so there is relatively less quarrel there ; even then, whatever trouble is there is enough to demoralise a neutral person. I only wonder, if so many people are available to take part in quarrels, why cannot we get a single person throughout Bengal who could compose differences and settle problems ? Thanks to factionalism Bengal has today lost a patriot like Anil Baran Roy—who knows how many more she will lose ? The Bengalis are today blinded, immersed in internecine fights and squabbles and are therefore unable to appreciate the situa-

* Translated from the original Bengali.

tion. I no longer hear of selflessness and sacrifice anywhere. So noble a life, having spent itself to the very end, merged with the Infinite ; it came before us like a ball of fire and the embodiment of sacrifice ; with the aid of that divine light the Bengalis had for a moment a glimpse of Heaven ; but, as the light went out, Bengalis again took refuge in their narrow selfish world. Throughout Bengal today, a scramble for power is in progress. Those who have power are much too occupied in holding on to it. Those who have none are determined to grab power. Both the sides say : "If salvation of the country is to be achieved, let the salvation come through me and me alone ; otherwise let there be no salvation at all". Is there no such worker in Bengal today who can offer silent self-immolation in disregard of the quarrels of the power-thirsty politicians ?

Is it any wonder that those who entered public life neglecting their own intellectual and spiritual advancement should retire from the political arena in sheer disgust when they see all the rest indulging only in utterly petty squabbles ? Can those who dedicated themselves to public welfare work without caring for their own intellectual and spiritual advancement afford to get mixed up in such sordid quarrels ? Can we blame them, if they thwarted in their desire to serve the people, turn their attention once again to their own spiritual advancement ? I can see clearly that if the present social conditions continue, a large number of Bengal's selfless workers will be compelled to follow in Anil Baran's footsteps.

Today many workers in Bengal have developed a strong business and traders' mentality. They have started saying : "Give me power—else I shall not work". I should like to ask—since when has service to the poor been converted into a business or a contract ? I always knew that the ideal of service was :—

"দাও দাও ফিরে নাহি চাও,
থাকে যদি হৃদয়ে সম্বল।"[1]

There is nothing surprising in that the Bengali who has

[1] 'If there is anything worthy in you, give away, give away—and ask for nothing in return.

already forgotten about Deshbandhu's sacrifice, should have forgotten Swami Vivekananda's 'Bir-Bani",[1] preached so many years ago.

All this is a matter of sorrow, a matter of shame—the heart bleeds to think of it. No solution is in sight—I am unable to help—I therefore often think of stopping writing letters and severing all contact with the outside world. We shall, if we can, do penance for our countrymen by pouring our life-blood bit by bit—unseen by the world outside. And then, if there is a God in heaven, if truth comes to prevail again in this world, our countrymen will someday realise our heart's desire. I had never imagined that I would be a witness to such a colossal farce enacted in the name of the country and to a new example in the twentieth century Bengal of "Nero is fiddling while Rome is burning".

I have said so much—I could not hold my emotions in check. I dared to say all this because I consider you all very much to be my kindred spirits. You are engaged in constructive work; I hope you will not be drawn into the quagmire of group politics.

I was particularly pleased to learn about the school. Of course I could not help feeling sorry on account of the building. I anticipated this development since the beginning and I had already warned Chandi Babu and other friends about the fate of the house. I always felt that the school authorities took the land on lease and started construction in an unbusiness-like manner with the result that the landlord was the gainer in the long run. Anyway, now what is done is done. That you have not lost hope but taken a firm decision to launch a "Building Fund" is very encouraging news. I have no doubt that your efforts will be successful because—

"নহি কল্যাণকৃত কশ্চিৎ দুর্গতিং তাত! গচ্ছতি"[2]

I was very happy to have all news of the Samity. It will indeed be very good if you can open a school for children of sweepers, cobblers, etc., the so-called lower caste. Please consult with Amrita in this regard; I received his

[1] The Gospel of the Brave.

[2] One who is doing good to others is never thwarted.

letter a long time ago but unfortunately was unable to reply. I wrote to Kulada today ; I expect to be able to write to Amrita next week.

It goes without saying that if I were there, I would not have permitted the separation. I would of course have supported the organisation of a separate department but not an entirely new institution with a completely different name. Anyway there is no other way now. We have to plunge into work in the belief that what has happened has been for the good. You have done the right thing by drawing up a Constitution.

I hope you will not have any conflict with the Balak Samity over the collection of rice and subscriptions. If a number of societies start collecting subscriptions and rice in the same locality, the householders tend to get fed up. You should therefore be careful about this.

I think if you can get one or two of your teachers trained at the Cossimbazar Polytechnic, it will be very useful for teaching technical subjects. I had once been to the Cossimbazar School. I liked it a lot. They teach some such new subjetcs which are not taught in an ordinary school, viz, clay-modelling, doll-making, smithy, tailoring, electroplating, etc. When I visited them, electro-plating machinery was just arriving. I have received copies of the Constitution of the School and the Samity sent by you.

It is a pity that the work of the Health Department has not been satisfactory. This is because the public were not approached in the right way. They are bound to respond if the call goes out to them in the right spirit. Our principal aim is to rouse intuition ad the will to work in them. The purpose of the Health Department is entirely different from that of the Charitable Dispensary. If you want to create the will to work in them, you have to win them over to your cause by love.

You may perhaps not be aware that I am primarily responsible for the shortcomings of the Dakshin Kalikata Sevasram. I failed to organise it properly while I was free. Then came my sudden arrest. When the Sevasram was located at Kalighat, I used to be personally responsible for house rent and the salary of the Assistant Secretary. Only the maintenance of the boys had to be met from public subscriptions. I have a clear conscience so far as the Sevasram is concerned, because I have not misused even a single pice out of public donations. Since my arrest my elder brother (Sarat Babu) has been paying my share of the expense. Recently, expenditure has gone down while the income has gone up ; so he has not to pay as much as before. When I used to spend Rs. 200/- per month on the Sevasram, my friends would say that I was unnecessarily spending so much money on six or seven boys, and that the money could be better utilised otherwise. But they did not know that I had not taken up Sevasram work as a whim. I took up this work to relieve myself of a deep-seated pain that has been smouldering within me for well-nigh twelve to fourteen years. I can give up Congress work but it is impossible for me to give up Sevasram work. Where else shall I get such a wonderful opportunity of serving "Daridra Narayana".[1] Some day I shall tell you the long history behind the Sevasram, when and why the idea got hold of me and how I gave up the world of contemplation to enter the field of action. To try to say all that in a letter will make a volume.

I have written enough, let me stop now. You have asked about myself, what can I say ? One of Rabindranath's poems I like very much. Will it sound impertinent if I replied to you in the poet's words. Poets are held in high esteem because they can express our innermost thoughts more eloquently and clearly than we can do ourselves. So I say :

"এখনো বিহার কল্পজগতে
জেলখানা (অরণ্য) রাজধানী,
এখনো কেবল নীরব ভাবনা
কর্মবিহীন বিজন সাধনা
দিবানিশি শুধু বসে বসে শোনা
আপন মর্মবাণী।

* * *

[1] The Needy in whom God dwells.

মানুষ হতেছি পাষাণের কোলে
* * *
গড়িতেছি মন আপনার মনে
যোগ্য হতেছি কাজে।
* * *
কবে প্রাণ খুলি বলিতে পারিব
পেয়েছি আমার শেষ।
তোমরা সকলে এস মোর পিছে
গুরু তোমাদের সবারে ডাকিছে,
আমার জীবনে লভিয়া জীবন
জাগরে সকল দেশ।"[1]

I am not physically so well, but I do not worry about that. I send you my love and greetings. How are Amrita and other comrades ? I shall be happy to have news of your well-being. But, it is not necessary for you to take time off your work to write to me. Please accept my affectionate regards. So long.

Yours
SUBHAS

[1] I still reside in the world of imagination,
The forest (the prison) is the seat of my kingdom,
Only silent contemplation is still my refuge
And lonesome meditation devoid of all action,
Only to listen to the musings of my soul day and night.
* * *
I am growing up to be a Man nursed by the rocks.
* * *
I am building my mind all by myself
and growing worthier for the tasks ahead.

Who knows when shall I be able to declare with all my heart:
I have reached my Realisation,
Come all, follow me,
The Master is calling you all,
May my life bring forth new life in you all
And thus may my country awake.

59. *To Haricharan Bagchi* *

Mandalay Jail
1926 ?

What you have said is true—there is a real dearth of honest workers; but we have to function with what material is available. Just as one cannot have the right to live without being prepared to die—just as one cannot expect to be loved without loving others, so also one cannot produce men without being a man himself.

Politics is continuously getting so polluted that at least for some time it will not be possible to do much good to the country through politics. The more the twin ideals of truth and sacrifice become less and less operative in the political field, the utility of political activity diminishes. Like the currents of a river, a political movement is sometimes clean and sometimes dirty; this happens in every country. Whatever may be the state of politics in Bengal today, you should take no notice of it but go on with your mission of service.

* * *

I do not know if you have been able to determine the cause of the mental turmoil that you are having at present; but I know the reason. One cannot attain self-fulfilment through work alone. Together with external work there must be study and contemplation. Just as work helps to overcome external indiscipline and to make man disciplined, study and meditation establish internal discipline. Without internal discipline, external discipline does not last long. One word more, just as regular exercise improves the physique, similarly regular meditation cultivates the good faculties and destroys the evil ones. Meditation has two aims:—(1) Destruction of the evil faculties, principally to overcome lust, fear and selfishness, and (2) Manifestation of love, devotion, sacrifice, intellect and such other noble attributes.

The best means of conquering lust are to visualise the

* Translated from the original Bengali.

mother-image in all women, to invest women with that halo and to worship God in the mother-form, such as Durga and Kali. When man contemplates God or Guru in the form of the mother, he learns to see divinity in all women ; when he reaches this state he has overcome lust. That is why our forefathers, in order to create an image of Divine Power, thought in terms of the form of woman. In practical life, man becomes pure and clean through the process of contemplating "mother" in all women.

Devotion and love render a man selfless. As man develops devotion and love for a person or an ideal, he correspondingly becomes less and less selfish. It is possible for one, through his own efforts, to develop love and devotion and thus reduces selfishness. By gradually enlarging love, man can leave all narrowness behind and eventually lose himself in the Infinite. So, one should think of and meditate on objects of love, devotion and reverence. Man becomes exactly the image of what he contemplates. He who considers himself a "weak sinner" becomes weaker every day ; he who considers himself to be strong and pure all the time becomes strong and pure. "Yadrishi bhavana jasya siddhirbhabati tadrishi".[1]

The way to conquer fear is to worship Power. The images of Durga, Kali etc. are the expressions of Power. Man can attain power by invoking any of its forms in his mind, praying to Her for strength and offering all his weaknesses and faults at Her feet. Infinite strength lies dormant inside us, we must bring it to life. The purpose of worship is to develop strength within one's self. You must contemplate some form of Power every day, seek strength from Her, offering all the five senses and all evil at Her feet. The five-pointed lamp symbolises the five senses. Worship of the Mother is performed with the five senses. We have eyes to see ; so we worship with sweet-smelling things like incense, etc. By sacrifice is meant sacrifice of evil—because the goat is the physical form of lust.

The purpose of spiritual exercise is, on the one hand,

[1] As one feels and thinks, so does one become.

to destroy evil and on the other, to cultivate the noble propensities. As evil is destroyed the heart fills up with divine bliss. And once divine power has entered the soul, all weaknesses will disappear.

Your should meditate on the above lines every day, twice if possible. You will feel stronger after meditating for some time and you will experience inner peace also.

For the time being you may read the following books by Swami Vivekananda. Of his books, the letters and the speeches are the most instructive. You will probably find all of them in "Bharate Vivekananda". Separate editions are probably available also. One should not try other books before reading his letters and speeches. Please do not take up books like "Philosophy of Religion", "Jnanayoga", etc. in the first instance. You may of course read "Shri Shri Ramakrishna Kathamrita" simultaneously. Some of Rabi Babu's poems are very inspiring. There are many books of D. L. Roy, such as "Mebar Patan", "Durgadas", etc., which bring a lot of strength. The historical novels by Bankim Babu and Romesh Dutt are quite instructive ; you may also read Nabin Sen's "Battle of Plassey'. "Sikher Balidan", probably by Shrimati Kumudini Basu, is a good book ; please read Victor Hugo's "Les Miserables" (you will, probably, find it in the library) and you will profit from it. I have not been able to mention many titles in haste. I shall draw up a list at leisure and send it on to you.

*60. To Haricharan Bagchi**

Mandalay Jail
(1926 ?)

It will be beneficial if you take daily physical exercise for improving your health. You will find it profitable to secure a copy of Muller's "My System" and take physical exercise according to it. I take Muller's exercises from time to time and with good results. The special features of

* Translated from the original Bengali.

Muller's exercises are :—(1) No expense is involved and very little space is required for them ; (2) The exercise do not result in too much fatigue and there is no risk due to such fatigue ; (3) All the muscles of the system and not merely certain parts of the body are worked ; (4) Digestive power improves.

I think that adoption of Muller's system in our country, particularly amongst the student community, will do a lot of good.

Man must not feel satisfied just by fulfilling his daily routine. One must never forget the ultimate aim and purpose of all activity, viz., achievement of self-fulfilment. Work is not the end in itself ; through work one must build up character and achieve an all-round development of one's life. Man must of course attain specialisation in a certain direction in accordance with his personality and tendencies : nevertheless, there must be an all-round development as the basis of such specialisation. He who has failed to achieve this all-round improvement can never be inwardly happy ; a sense of vacancy and want persists in his mind till the end. What you require for this all-round improvement are :—(1) Physical exercise ; (2) Regular study ; (3) Daily meditation or contemplation. Sometimes, owing to pressure of work all these things are overlooked ; or even if they are not overlooked, there is no time for them. But, as soon as pressure of work lightens, one should attend to them. One must not be content with merely doing the daily chores ; one must arrange to allot time for physical exercise, studies and meditation. If one can devote one and a half to two hours daily to these three very essential items, one will be greatly benefited. Muller is of the opinion that if a person takes physical exercise for at least fifteen minutes daily according to his instructions, it should be enough. And then, if one spends fifteen minutes daily on thinking or meditating in seclusion, the total time taken will be half an hour. And if you set apart another hour for studies (not reading newspapers—the time taken for that is to be counted separately) the total time spent daily will be an hour and a half. At least an hour and a half must be made available. Of course "Adhikontu na doshaya"[1]—the more time you can devote the better. Each person should arrange for this time according to his convenience. I probably wrote something about meditation in my previous letter—so I shall not say more about that now. I am giving the titles of the books in this letter. First, I shall mention those which you will find in the library and then the others :

(A) On religion

(1) 'Shri Shri Ramakrishna Kathamrita'; (2) 'Brahamacharya'—Surendra Bhattacharya; Ditto by Ramesh Chakraborty; Ditto by Fakir Dey; (3) 'Swami-Shishya Sanbad' by Sarat Chakraborty; (4) 'Patraboli' by Vivekananda; (5) 'Prachya O Paschatya' by Vivekananda; (6) 'Baktritaboli' by Vivekananda; (7) 'Bhabbar Katha' by Vivekananda; (8) 'Bharater Sadhana' by Swami Prajnanananda; (9) 'Chicago Baktrita'—by Swami Vivekananda.

(B) Literature, Poetry, History etc :—

(1) 'Deshbandhu Granthaboli' (Basumati edition); (2) 'Banglar Roop'—Girija Sankar Roy Chowdhury; (3) 'Bankim Granthaboli'; (4) Nabin Sen's 'Kurukshetra', 'Prabhas', 'Raibatak' and 'Palaseer Yuddha'; (5) 'Jogendra Granthaboli' (Basumati edition); (6) Rabindra Nath Tagore's 'Katha O Kahini', 'Chayanika', 'Gitanjali', 'Ghare Baire'. 'Gora'; (7) Bhudeb Babu's 'Samajik Prabandha' and 'Paribarik Prabandha'; (8) D. L. Roy's 'Durgadas', 'Mebar Patan', 'Rana Pratap'; (9) 'Chhatrapati Sivaji'—Satyacharan Shastri; (10) 'Sikher Balidan'—Kumudini Basu; (11) Rajnarayan Bose's 'Sekal O Ekal'; (12) Satyen Dutt's 'Kuhoo O Keka' (Poetical works); (13) Maharshi Debendra Nath's 'Atmajibancharit'; (14) 'Rajasthan' (Basumati edition); (15) 'Nabya Japan'—Manmatha Ghosh; (16) 'Sipahi Yuddher Itihas'—Rajanikanta Gupta; (17) Upen Babu's 'Nirbashiter Atmakatha' and other works; (18) 'Col. Suresh Biswas'—Upendra Krishna Bandopadhyaya. Three anna editions of short biographies of many great men of India suitable for children's reading are available.

This list of book is adequate. You will find enough

[1] Something extra does no harm.

material in it for a whole year. Now let me say something about primary education.

One big difference between primary education and higher education is that in the former what is more important is to teach new facts. In higher education cultivation of the reasoning faculty must go hand in hand with the teaching of new facts. In primary education one has to depend to a great extent on the senses, because imagination and memory have not yet developed properly. So, if you wish to teach certain objects, viz., cow, horse, fruit, flower, etc. you have to arrange for direct visualization to teach without difficulty. In higher education such subjects are taught that the student has never seen, but the student can grasp them without having seen them by his power of imagination. Moreover, the more the senses are utilised for teaching purposes, the easier is the teaching. If you wish to explain something about the flute or some such musical instrument, the student will learn about it quickly if you let him see it, touch it, and listen to its sound by playing it himself. Because he has thus utilised the sense of vision, touch and hearing simultaneously. An infant wishes to touch and mouth any object that he sees, because infants want to learn about external objects through all the senses. So, if we follow the laws of Nature and try to acquire knowledge by the use of all the senses, the results will be very quick. While teaching arithmetic, if we do not depend only on cramming but demonstrate addition, subtraction, multiplication and division with such objects as 'Kori', marbles, pieces of stone etc., children will pick up these subjects very speedily.

One more important matter. Instead of confining ourselves merely to intellectual training, we must arrange for training in handicrafts simultaneously. One must arrange for training in doll-making, making relief maps of clay, drawing, use of colour, popular music, etc. This will not only make education all-embracing but also contribute to better intellectual training. If you can teach your boys a variety of things, they will become alert, more intelligent and more attentive to and less fearful of, studies. Instead of learning a variety of things, if the student devotes himself only to cramming, he does not feel a lively interest in studies, learns to fear them and his intellect fails to develop. If a child's eyes, ears, hand, tongue and nose find objects of enjoyment and interest, then the senses also sharpen ; as a result his intellect is roused and the knowledge he acquires makes his studies enjoyable. Without manual training education is rendered basically defective. The pleasure that one gets by making something with his own hands is a rare pleasure in this world. There is genuine happiness in creative activity. This joy of creation is felt even by children of tender age when they make things with their own hands. Whether by planting seedling and growing trees or making dolls with their own hands—anything new that comes out of their own efforts gives them unbounded joy. You must make such arrangements that students, even while they are very young, are able to taste this happiness. Such activity will promote originality and the development of their personality and they will learn to enjoy studies rather than fear them. In England, in most of the primary schools students learn gardening, do physical exercise, take part in drill, participate in sports between study hours, are taught music, undertake route marches and go round in organised groups, learn clay-modelling and are taught about various subjects and countries through stories. It is most essential that teaching is done in the form of story-telling. Let not the students think that they are having formal teaching ; let them rather feel that they are listening to stories or having a game. In the initial stage, text-books are quite necessary. When you teach about trees, flowers, etc., you must see that you have trees and flowers in front of you. When you want to talk about the sky, stars, etc., you should take them out into the open and teach them there. Whatever may be the object of teaching—it should be available to all the senses. When you teach geography, maps and globes should be on hand ; when you teach history, you should take them to museums and similar places conveniently. You must arrange for instruction in music, painting, drawing, gardening, etc. even if it has to be on a very modest scale. Otherwise, primary education will be utterly useless. Practical sense is what is most necessary. Cramming of lessons is not so essential.

I have said something of the principles of primary education. I intentionally did not mention text-books. There is very little need of text-books and the importance of what books you have to keep is also small ; only good teachers can make a success of primary education. The teacher must first grasp the fundamental principles of primary education. He may then introduce new methods of teaching. The teacher must view things with affection and sympathy, from the point of view of the student. How else can he appreciate the difficulties and mistakes of the student ? Thus, the personality of the teacher is of prime importance. The corner-stones of education are three : (1) Personality of the teacher, (2) Teaching methods, (3) Subject and text-books. No education can achieve its purpose unless the teacher has the requisite personality. Once a teacher of character is available, we may proceed to determine our educational methods and then it becomes easy to teach books on any subject.

. . . .

I hope you are well. So long.

Yours v. affly
SUBHAS

S. C. Bose Esq.
38/1, Elgin Road
Calcutta

61. From Sarat Chandra Bose

Censored and Passed
Illegible
6/1/27
for D.I.G., I.B., C.I.D.
Bengal

38/1, Elgin Road
6.1.27

My dear Subhas,

I received your letter of the 24th Dec, day before yesterday.

I received the telegram from the I.G. of Prisons Rangoon on the afternoon of Thursday, the 23rd Dec. In the morning papers, I read an Associated Press message saying that you had left Rangoon. I was rather taken aback and wondered what might have been the cause of your sudden return to Mandalay. The same afternoon I received your telegram from Mandalay and then I understood what the position was.

I was rather disappointed at the result of the medical examination. I was expecting that it would reveal what the real trouble with you was. I asked the I.G. of Prisons by telegram to send me a copy of the report of your medical examination and he has referred me to the Bengal Govt. I have asked the Deupty Secy., Political Department for a copy and he has sent me a reply that the "matter is receiving consideration." Yesterday I have written another letter to the Deputy Secy., Political Department, copy of which I enclose herewith.

I am sending your temperature chart (Rangoon) to Kaviraj Mahasay. Your Mandalay chart was handed over to Kaviraj Mahasay last week by Dada. Kaviraj Mahasay told Dada that he had received all your letters but he was not quite sure if you were receiving his, as there was no reference in any of your letters to his. Subsequent to that Kaviraj Bimalananda called and he promised to write to you in detail about medicines and diet.

Your election expenses return was filed yesterday. Today is the last date for filing them.

I received yesterday from the Secy., Bengal Legislative Council a notice of motion (Govt. motion) for demand for grant for salaries of two Ministers. The motion will come up on the 17th instant. Has the Secy. to the Council been sending you Council notices ?

I am anxiously awaiting your next letter in which you have promised to write more about your health.

Father has gone down to Cuttack. Mother is still here. This leaves us fairly well.

Yours very affly

SARAT

Subhas C. Bose Esq.

62. To Sarat Chandra Bose

Censored and Passed
Illegible
21/1/27
for D.I.G., I.B., C.I.D.
Bengal

Mandalay Jail
12.1.27

My dear brother,

Your letter of the 6th January along with the enclosure was to hand yesterday. I have written to the I.G. of Prisons to send you a copy of the report of my medical examination and a copy of the X-ray photograph.

Kaviraj Mahasay has informed me that he is sending me 10 days' medicine for the present and that he will prescribe again after he gets details about my present condition. A copy of my temperature chart from the 23rd December up to date is being sent to him by the Supdt. by today's mail. If necessary Kaviraj Mahasay can consult Dr. Bidhan Roy about the chart. I have already written other details about my health to him in my last letter.

I think I have received all the letters of Shyamadas Kaviraj. In my next letter to him I shall mention the dates of the letters I have already received.

I have been receiving the notices etc. from the Secretary, Bengal Legislative Council. I am glad to learn that my election expenses have been duly filed.

In one of my previous letters I mentioned certain books about parliamentary procedure which would be useful to you in your future work in the Council. I would also like to read the article on "Parliamentary Privilege" by Mr. T. Chakravarti M.A. which appeared in the *Calcutta Review* for February, 1925. The article is interesting and important and it will not take you more than half-an-hour to go through it.

Please keep the Baidyasastrapith matter in view at the Corporation Finance Committee. I am told that the Ashtanga are again coming up for an additional capital grant.

My condition continues unchanged—Yesterday afternoon the temperature rose to 99.4°. Please do not feel alarmed—especially when there is hardly any remedy. Hope this will find you quite well.

Yours v. affly
SUBHAS

S. C. Bose Esq.
38/1, Elgin Road
Calcutta

63. *From Sarat Chandra Bose*
Censored and Passed
Illegible
22.1.27
for D.I.G., I.B., C.I.D.
Bengal

38/1, Elgin Road
22.1.27

My dear Subhas,

Your letter of the 12th came in just now. Along with my last letter, I sent you a copy of the report of Lt.-Col. Kelsall which I received from the Deputy Secretary, Political Department, Government of Bengal.

On the 18th instant, the Deputy Secretary, wrote to me that the Government of Bengal had no objection to Sunil *seeing you and medically examining* you if the Government of Burma had no objection. On the 20th I sent a telegram to the Inspector General of Prisons Rangoon asking for the necessary permission and he wired back to say that his Governmnt had no objection provided the permission of the Bengal Government was first obtained. I forwarded the telegram of the Inspector General of Prisons, Burma to the Deputy Secretary yesterday and asked for the Bengal Government's permission but have not received any reply yet.

I have been reading up the books on Parliamentary Practice and have collected the available materials on the subject of members' privileges. Yesterday there was a discussion on that subject in the Assembly and I believe you will find a report of the debate in the Burma papers. I am sending you the article on "Parliamentary Privilege" by Mr. T. Chakravarti and shall see what new materials I can get there.

At the last meeting of the E.G.P. Committee we have recommended that the *Dhobikhana* land on Upper Circular Road (total area 3 bighas 6 cottahs) should be divided between the Baidyasastrapith and the Bani Bhawan (of Lady Bose)—2 bighas to the former and 1 bigha 6 cottahs to the latter. The matter will come up before the Corporation at an early date. Nripen Babu (who is one of the redoubtable champions of Ashtanga) and Ram Taran Babu opposed us in the E.G.P. Committee.

Since your return to Mandalay, has the temperature risen *every day* or has there been any break ? Father is naturally feeling alarmed but I don't see what can be done in the circumstances. I am now waiting for *permission* for Sunil to go and examine you there.

This leaves us well.

Yours very affly
SARAT

Subhas C. Bose Esq.

64. *From Sarat Chandra Bose*
Censored and Passed
Illegible
13/1/27
for D.I.G., I.B., C.I.D.
Bengal

38/1, Elgin Road
13th Jany, 1927

My dear Subhas,

Your letter of the 31st Dec, from Mandalay reached my hands on the 8th instant. I shall let you know later which of the letters mentioned in your letter under reply I received. I received all the telegrams mentioned by you.

I have received a reply from the Additional Dy. Secy.,

Govt, of Bengal to my letters of the 20th Dec, and the 5th January. It is apparent that Govt. take delight in half-truths which are really more dangerous than falsehoods. I have drafted my reply to Mr. Martin's letter and shall send you a copy of the same along with my next letter.

Mrs. Das told me that she wrote you a letter some time ago. Haven't you received it?

This leaves us fairly well, except that Baby is not doing well. We are taking steps to cure her but I cannot tell you when I can give you the information that Baby is doing well.

I have asked for permission to send Sunil to see and examine you at Mandalay. Are you any better?

Yours very affly

SARAT

Subhas C. Bose Esq.

65. To Sarat Chandra Bose

Censored and Passed
Illegible
28/1/27
for D.I.G., I.B., C.I.D.
Bengal

Mandalay Jail
21.1.27

My dear brother,

Your letter of the 13th January along with the enclosure reached me yesterday. I have received Mrs. Das's letter and have already replied to it. You do not say how she is keeping now. Is she going to remain in Calcutta for treatment? I find from the notices that Bhaskar has joined his post. How is he working?

The Superintendent told me this morning that you had wired to the I.G. of Prisons for sending Chotodada to Mandalay to interview and examine me. If Chotodada comes, let him bring a blood-pressure apparatus with him.

I am anxious to know that Baby is not doing well. I hope you are taking steps to treat her properly.

Yesterday my temperature rose to 99° and the day

before to 99.4°. Other symptoms continue unchanged. I have had to give up strenuous exercise owing to the strain and do not play any games now. I am now under the treatment of the local Superintendent.

I have had a letter from father in which he asks for details regarding my health and this has put me in a fix. I cannot help writing now—but I know that the effect of my doing so would be to make him worried, if not alarmed.

Hope this will find you all quite well.

Yours v. affly
SUBHAS

S. C. Bose Esq.
38/1, Elgin Road
Calcutta

66. *To Sarat Chandra Bose*
Censored and Passed
Illegible
27/1/27
for D.I.G., I.B., C.I.D.
Bengal

Mandalay Jail
19.1.27

My dear brother,

Since the 11th instant I have not received any letter from you. Father's letter was to hand yesterday.

Ever since my illness took a serious turn I had been thinking deeply whether I should continue Kaviraji treatment, being far away from my physician. My hesitation was great because of my faith in Ayurveda and if I had no faith I would not have the slightest hesitation in discarding Ayurveda. But I felt that it was not fair to my Kaviraj to ask him to treat me from a distance and it was not desirable from my point of view to entrust myself to an absentee physician. I therefore came to the conclusion that I should stop Kaviraji treatment for the present and place myself under the treatment of the local medical officer. As a result of this decision I wired to Kaviraj Mahasay yesterday asking him to discontinue sending any fresh medicine. I would like to have your opinion on this point, as also the opinion of other relatives and friends. In the meantime please explain the position to Kaviraj Mahasay so that he may not feel offended. I am also writing to him by this mail.

About a month ago I sent a representation to the Governor-General regarding my family and establishment allowance. I have not had any reply yet.

I am getting the Council notices and papers regularly. I have not so far sent any questions or resolutions but I am sending by this mail a representation to the Governor asking for permission to attend the Council.

My temperature chart up to the 13th January has been sent to Kaviraj Mahasay in two lots. Please get the chart from him and consult Dr. Bidhan Roy about it. You will get some idea of the daily rise of temperature from the following figures :—6th Jan.—99.6° ; 7th Jan.—99.4° ; 8th Jan.—99.4° ; 9th Jan.—99° ; 10th Jan.—99° ; 11th Jan.—99.4° ; 12th Jan.—99.4° ; 13th Jan.—99.4° ; 14th Jan.—99.2° ; 15th Jan.—98.6° ; 16th Jan.—99.4° ; 17th Jan.—99.4° ; 18th Jan.—99.4°.

My condition continues unchanged and the old symptoms are persisting. I am anxious to have a correct diagnosis of my ailments. The I.G. of Prisons told me that the Rangoon medical authorities would be able to give their final opinion when they got a further report on my health a fortnight after my return from Rangoon. That report has been sent and I have asked the Superintendent to remind him about it. I hope to get the final opinion of the Rangoon medical authorities shortly.

After my return from Rangoon I had taken up tennis hoping that it might do me good. But I began to feel too much strain and I have had to give it up.

Father seems to be alarmed over my illness. Please try your best and see that he does not worry too much over the matter.

How are you all doing ? How are the children and how

is Baby? I believe mother is now in Calcutta. I shall be writing to her shortly.

Yours v. affly
SUBHAS

S. C. Bose Esq.
38/1, Elgin Road
Calcutta

P.S.
Before you give your opinion about continuing Ayurvedic treatment, please consult Kaviraj Mahasay.

SUBHAS

67. *From Sarat Chandra Bose*

Censored and Passed
Illegible
29/1/27
for D.I.G., I.B., C.I.D.
Bengal

38/1, Elgin Road
Calcutta
29.1.27

My dear Subhas,

I received your letter of the 19th yesterday evening and your letter of the 21st this morning.

I am sending copies from your letter of the 19th to Kaviraj Mahasay and shall also confer with him on the subject and let you know his opinion regarding your treatment. I shall anxiously await the report of the Medical Officer at Rangoon. Please send it on to me as soon as you get it.

No, you cannot help writing to father now, specially when the facts regarding your health are public property now. You should however, write in such a way that he might not feel much too worried.

I am enclosing herewith the correspondence between me and the authorities from the 18th to the 28th. I have every hope now that Burma will not object to Sunil examining you medically. Sunil will leave for Mandalay as soon as the necessary permission is received from Burma. I shall ask him to take a blood-pressure apparatus.

When did you write to the Governor-General for family and establishment allowance ?

I think you have acted rightly in asking for permission to attend the Council.

This leaves us well, except Baby who I am sorry to say, is still not doing well. I am trying to make the necessary arrangements for proper treatment but haven't succeeded so far.

Father is expected here during the Saraswati Puja holidays.

Mrs. Das is better now, after a course of radium treatment at the Seva Sadan. She has taken on lease Jiten Sarker's new house on Priyanath Mullick Street (which is very near Sudhir's house) and intends to shift there shortly.

So long today.

Yours very affly

SARAT

Subhas C. Bose Esq.

Enclos :

Five letters and copies of two telegrams.

68. To Sarat Chandra Bose

Censored and Passed
Illegible
13/1/27
for D.I.G., I.B., C.I.D.
Bengal

Mandalay
5.1.27

My dear brother,

I have already replied, partly at least, to your letter of the 11th December.

I am sorry you could not take any rest during the X-mas Vacation.

I am eager to know if you consider it desirable to

appeal against the judgement in *The Statesman* libel suit. You need not make any further reference to me on the subject before steps are taken, as I have left the matter entirely in the hands of my legal advisers. I have cursorily glanced through the proceedings of the case and it struck me that it would not have been superfluous to lay more emphasis on two facts :—(1) I was not present at the Sirajgang Conference and was totally ignorant of the proceedings of the Conference till they appeared in the papers and I had no more connection with the Conference than the man in the moon. I took charge of the C.E.O.-ship on 16.5.24 and the Conference was held after that date—probably during the first week of June 1924. (2) I had given up all connection with *Forward* before I became the C.E.O. and even before 16.5.24, I had no connection with the Editorial Department of that paper. Sir B. C. Mitter did refer to these two points but if I am to believe the newspaper reports, the defence seemed to make so much of these 2 points that it would have been worthwhile laying more emphasis.

We are all anxious for Mrs. Das's health. I have written to her day before yesterday.

Your letters of 24.12.26 and 30.12.26 were to hand yesterday. You know by now the reasons which induced me to leave Rangoon. I arrived here on the 23rd in the morning and immediately after, I sent a wire through Intelligence informing you that I had arrived. I am in a way glad that I left Rangoon, otherwise all of you, including father, would have been put to the trouble of coming to Burma.

I think I have written the details of the medical examination but I have not got a copy of the written report of Col. Kelsall with me. I wanted to have the spine and the lungs X-rayed in Rangoon and I suggested that to the I.G. of Prisons but Col. Kelsall did not consider that necessary. I wanted particularly to have the spine X-rayed as the pain is located there. I am writing to the I.G. of Prisons to send you a copy of the report together with X-ray photograph of the viscera as you want to consult Sir Nilratan, Dr. Bidhan, Shyamadas Kaviraj and other eminent physicians. You may also write to him.

The temperature is still persisting. Yesterday it rose to 99.6° and the day before to 99.4°.

I have received the summons to attend the Council on the 10th January and I am writing to H.E. the Governor of Bengal in Council to allow me to attend.

The Burma Government has issued a communique about my health which has also been published in the Calcutta papers. I believe you have seen it by now.

Along with my letter of 13.11.26 to you I forwarded a letter from Sj. Sabitri Chatterji regarding some of his dues from *Forward.* I hope you received it duly.

Have you been able to find the testimonials of Mr. S. K. Sen (Bhombal's father-in-law) which were with me? If so, please return them to him.

Please see that parents do not get too alarmed. I am afraid it is not possible to prevent them from feeling anxious.

How are you all doing? How is the cold this year?

Yours v. affly

SUBHAS

69. From Sarat Chandra Bose

Phone Cal. 4434
Censored and Passed
Illegible
21/1/27
for D.I.G., I.B., C.I.D.
Bengal

38/1, Elgin Road
Calcutta
20th January, 1927

My dear Subhas,

Your letter of the 5th came in on the 14th.

I believe I have already told you that we have decided to appeal against the judgement in *The Statesman* case. B. C. pressed his points hard but failed, not because he did not do justice to the case but because of the Judge's mentality. The judgment is very unsatisfactory specially at the place the Judge deals with the offending article.

Mrs. Das is, I think, decidedly better. Radium treatment has done her good. She told me night before last that she had received your letter.

The Additional Deupty Secretary, Political Department, Government of Bengal has sent me a copy of Col. Kelsall's report. I enclose herewith a copy of that report as also copies of my letter to Mr. Martin dated 13.1.27, Mr. Martin's letter to me dated 18.1.27 and my reply of the same date. I am not at all satisfied that you are having proper medical treatment but I don't know what to do. All that I can say now is that you must be *extremely careful* about your health.

Goswami left for Delhi on Sunday last. He has been told how you have been keeping.

Yes, I received Sabitri Babu's letter which you sent me some time ago. I am very doubtful if Sabitri has really any claim against *Forward* now. He has drawn quite a big sum on account of commission.

I can't find the testimonials of Mr. S. K. Sen.

I have hardly anything more to write today except to ask you once again to take as much care of yourself as is possible under the circumstances.

Yours evry affly

SARAT

Subhas C. Bose Esq.

70. *To Sarat Chandra Bose*

Censored and Passed
Illegible
5/2/27
for D.I.G., I.B., C.I.D.
Bengal

Mandalay Jail
28.1.27

My dear brother,

Your letters of the 20th January (together with all the enclosures) and 22nd January were to hand yesterday.

I am in agreement with your decision to appeal against

Justice Buckland's judgment. I only hope that better luck will be in store for us this time.

I am glad to learn that Mrs. Das is better now.

It is clear from Col. Kelsall's report that he has not given his final opinion yet and has recommended careful watching. As you already know, I am at present under the treatment of the Superintendent who is watching me carefully. He has told me more than once that he feels concerned about my health.

The daily rise of temperature has been continuous since the last attack of influenza in November and there has been practically no break in spite of the Rangoon trip. The temperature chart from the 23rd December 1926 to the 6th January 1927 was sent to Kaviraj Mahasay on the 12th January and the temperature chart from the 7th January to the 13th January was sent to him on the 14th instant. Since then the daily afternoon rise has been as follows :—

14th January—99.2° ; 15th January—98.6° ; 16th January —99..4° ; 17th January—99.4° ; 18th January—99.4° ; 19th January—99.4° ; 20th January—99° ; 21st January—99.6° ; 22nd January—99.4° ; 23rd January—99.6° ; 24th January—99° ; 25th January—99.4° ; 26th January—99.4°.

On two days an hourly afternoon chart was recorded and the following results were obtained :—

25th January, 1927

1 p.m.—98.8° ; 2 p.m.—99.4° ; 3 p.m.—99.2° ; 4 p.m.—94.4° 5 p.m.—99.2° ; 6 p.m.—99° ; 7 p.m.—99° ; 8 p.m.—98.4°.

26th January, 1927

1 p.m.—98.8° ; 2 p.m.—99.4° ; 3 p.m.—99° ; 4 p.m.—99.2° ; 5 p.m.—99.4° ; 6 p.m.—99.2° ; 7 p.m.—98.4°.

At noon the temperature is usually normal i.e. 98.4°.

Have you received a copy of the X-ray photograph ?

The other complaints continue as usual.

I am anxious to know how Baby is doing. I hope she is quite well by now.

I wrote to father day before yesterday. Hope this will find you all quite well.

Yours v. affly
SUBHAS

S. C. Bose Esq.
38/1, Elgin Road
Calcutta

71. *To Sarat Chandra Bose*

Censored and Passed
Illlegible
5/2
for D.I.G., I.B., C.I.D.
Bengal

Mandalay Jail
2.2.27

My dear brother,

I have already replied in part to your letters of the 20th and 22nd January.

I do not think that the Bengal Govt. will have any objection to my being treated by a doctor of my own choice—if I am to judge by their past attitude. When I was in the Presidency Jail in 1921 with Maulana Azad, the latter used to be treated by his own doctor, Dr. K. Ahmed. Col. Hamilton was then the Superintendent. When Deshbandhu was in the Presidency Jail and the Alipore Central Jail, he used to be treated by his own doctor, Dr. D. N. Roy. Major Salisbury was then the Superintendent of the Alipore Central Jail. When Sj. Satyendra Mitra was in the Alipore Central Jail and Dr. Young and Major Salisbury were successively the Superintendents—he used to be treated by his own Kaviraj. Govt. as far as I am aware, have always been accommodating in this matter.

I am sorry and anxious to learn that Natunmamababu is now bebridden. What is the latest news about him ? Is he improving ?

I do not know why Mr. S. K. Sen's testimonials could

not be found. They must be mixed up with my papers. Did they search for the testimonials all over ? Namamababu or Sailesh might be able to find them. I am sorry for Mr. Sen—he must have missed them badly for the last 2 years or more.

If Chotodada comes, you may consider the desirability and necessity of sending an independent doctor along with him.

The debate on parliamentary privileges was not in my opinion up to the mark and it should have been richer. The points were mostly there, facts would have been welcome.

I am glad that the E.G.P. Committee have recommended a plot of land for the Baidyasastrapith. But I am afraid the plot will not be big enough for the College—at least if one considers future requirements. Was it necessary to give the Bani Bhawan a share of that plot ? The Bani Bhawan could be given a plot elsewhere. The Bani Bhawan is, I think, a Widow's home. The proximity of such an institution to a college like the Baidyasastrapith, will not be conducive to the latter's welfare.

I think I have told you that I have addressed H.E. the Governor of Bengal and the Hon'ble the President over the question of privilege in my case. I have received the summons of H.E. the Governor to attend the meeting of the Bengal Legislative Council fixed for the 21st February.

Dr. T. N. Mazumder, Acting Health Officer, wrote to me for my opinion regarding his work. His request somewhat embarrassed me but I ultimately decided to send him my opinion. I felt that he would be entitled to a testimonial if I had been in office and I would not be right in refusing the request. I however suggested that it would be better if my opinion were asked for officially and I requested him not to make use of my remarks officially if he could help doing so. I may say that I have a good impression of him and of his work.

My health continues the same as before and all the

symptoms are persisting. Hope this will find you all quite well.

Yours v. affly
SUBHAS

S. C. Bose Esq.
38/1, Elgin Road
Calcutta

72. *To Sarat Chandra Bose*
Censored and Passed
Illlegible
12/2
for D.I.G., I.B., C.I.D.
Bengal

Mandalay Jail
4.2.27

My dear brother,

Your letter of 29/1/27 together with the enclosures was to hand on the 2nd inst. I have duly received your letters of 11/12/26, 24/12/26, 30/12/26, 6/1/27, 13/1/27, 20/1/27 and 22/1/27 during the last 2 months.

We are glad to learn that Mrs. Das is better now.

I have already asked you for your opinion about my treatment and I hope I shall get it shortly. You will—I take it—consult parents and Kaviraj Mahasay about the matter. I don't remember if I told you that I tried Kaviraji medicine for 3 months or a little over. Though I did not improve much, I might have been worse without it. I started the treatment in September (with the knowledge and consent of the Medical Officer and the Local Government of course) and carried on till the early part of January—the expenses of my treatment being borne by the Government. It is possible that I would have been benefited if influenza had not made its appearance in November last.

Since I wrote to you last, the temperature has risen as follows :—29th January—99.2° ; 30th January—99.4° ; 31st January—99.4° ; 1st February—100° ; 2nd February—99.8° ;

3rd February—100.8°.

It appears that the temperature is tending to go higher up than before. The symptoms are otherwise unchanged.

The Superintendent informed me that Chotodada would be coming on Wednesday or Thursday next.

Hope this will find you all quite well.

Yours v. affly
SUBHAS

To
S. C. Bose Esq.
38/1, Elgin Road
Calcutta

*73. To Bivabati Bose**

Mother Durga be with us.

Mandalay Jail
7.2.27

My dear Mejobowdidi,

Your letter of the 16th January reached my hands on the 22nd together with Asoke's letter. I was happy to hear from you after a long time. It is still cool here but I expect the cold season will end at the end of this month. We shall have the Spring breeze in March and then in April the hot weather will be in full swing. Last year, April was the hottest month.

Our garden looks quite pretty with flowers of many colours in bloom. But most of these are season flowers. They will therefore disappear at the end of the cold weather and when the Summer's assault begins. For the time being a look at the garden makes one happy.

Yesterday we performed the Saraswati Puja. The image was made locally and it was fairly good. Those who perform the Saraswati Puja in these parts do not have the immersion in the Ganges (that is, the Irrawady).

You are no doubt getting news of my health from my

* Translated from the original Bengali.

letters to Mejdada. I am feeling no better, rather worse. The weight has gone down further—to 138 lbs. Chotodada will be arriving here probably on Wednesday or Thursday next.

I was very happy to learn that Natunmamababu was somewhat better than before. Where is he now ? Please let me have his address.

I presume father came down to Calcutta during the Saraswati Puja holidays.

Our pigeon population is growing fast. We have simultaneously to add to the number of pigeon boxes. There has been a marked increase also in the number of cocks and hens (Hinduism will not be in peril, I hope, as a result). We have had a practical demonstration of how two or three pairs of cocks and hens of good foreign breed could produce a large good breed within a relatively short time. The same applies to the pigeons. But we were not able to save those with wings like the peacock's—they tend to die out fast. The parrot lives—happily or not, I cannot say. It whistles in a variety of tunes. It has not learnt parrotry yet but may learn eventually.

I was very sorry to learn that the Abhoy Ashram lost your hand-spun yarn. I hope you will not feel discouraged on account of that. Asoke's long vacation will start in a few days—he will also be able then to spin at leisure. I shall reply to Asoke later.

The Government have informed us that even after the lapse of two years since January 1925, the order of detention under the ordinance will continue. We had a feast on a small scale to celebrate our continuance in our jobs !

I hope all of you are keeping well. Please accept our *pronams* and convey same to superiors.

Yours

SUBHAS

P.S.

It has not yet been decided if the interview with Chotodada and the medical examination will be held here or at Rangoon. Probably I shall have to go down to Rangoon.

SUBHAS

74. To Sarat Chandra Bose.
Censored and Passed
Illegible
16/2
for D.I.G., I.B., C.I.D.
Bengal

Mandalay Jail
8.2.27

My dear brother,

I am leaving for Rangoon this afternoon and shall reach there tomorrow morning. I shall have the interview and medical examination there and Chotodada will be—or has been—asked to await my arrival at Rangoon. I am told that I shall be back here within a week or so.

The municipal elections will be on very soon and no one knows how the votes will be cast. I only hope that the results will show that a well-defined disciplined group—whatever their party complexion may be—with a definite programme, will come into power and take charge of the civic administration of the city. My past experience tells me that the success of municipal administration depends mainly on two factors : Firstly there must be a cordial relation between the Councillors and the Executive and the latter should be so chosen as to command the confidence of the former. Secondly there must be a well-defined majority group with a definite democratic programme. What concerns me more is not so much the complexion of the group as the existence of the group itself with a particular programme. From the point of view of the Executive such a majority group is thrice welcome because in that case the Executive know where they stand and how they should act. In the absence of such a group, it is difficult for the Executive to decide in the face of a heterogeneous body how they should act and what policy they should pursue. It is for the electors to decide what party complexion they prefer—but if the cause of civic welfare is to be furthered they should in any case see to it that such a majority group is returned with a mandate to carry on the work of civic advancement for the next three years.

Are you standing for election as a Councillor ? I suppose most of the Councillors would like to be returned again.

My health continues unchanged. The temperature rose to 99.4° yesterday.

Hope this will find you all quite well.

Yours v. affly
SUBHAS

75. To Sarat Chandra Bose

Censored and Passed
Illegible
for D.I.G., I.B., C.I.D.
Bengal

Rangoon Central Jail
14.2.27
Monday

My dear brother,

I arrived here on Wednesday last (i.e. the 9th inst.). It was decided at the eleventh hour that the interview should take place in Rangoon so that Col. Kelsall (who examined me last time) could be present. I left Mandalay accordingly on Tuesday the 8th inst.

Chotodada is seeing me every day. The medical examination took place on Saturday last. Chotodada is having a consultation with Col. Kelsall this morning. He is leaving by tomorrow's boat—so that he will have seen you before this reaches you and you will get a firsthand report from him.

Father will be anxious—so please send him a report soon after Chotodada reaches there. Kaviraj Mahasay will also be anxious—so I am asking Chotodada to call on him when he arrives there. Please see that Chotodada does not forget to pay him a visit.

I have no definite information about my future movements. I am not comfortable here and I would like to go back to Mandalay. I don't mind going to Insein if there is probability of an early transfer. I am going to have a talk with the I.G.P. about this when I meet him next.

The Rangoon papers of yesterday's date say that Messrs. Bannerji, Sasmal and others have resigned their offices.

My last letter to you was on 7.2.27

Hope this will find you quite well.

Yours v. affly
SUBHAS

Sarat Chandra Bose Esq.
Bar-at-law
38/1, Elgin Road
Calcutta

*76. To Sarat Chandra Bose**

Rangoon Central Jail
18.2.27
Friday

My dear brother,

I am still here. No letter came to me since I reached here—probably the letters are lying there at Mandalay. They did not care to send the letters to me under the impression that I would be back to Mandalay soon. So I have written to Major Tarapore to arrange for sending all my letters from Mandalay to Rangoon.

I am now in a state from which the mythical Trisanku suffered, that is I am neither in heaven nor on earth hovering in mid-air. The authorities are waiting for official verdict about me coming from Calcutta. After waiting for a few days I shall try to go back either to Mandalay or to Insein. It is highly inconvenient here to live with restrictions on movements. I have informed Major Tarapore all these and he has asked me to wait for a few days—no better arrange-

* Translated from the original Bengali.

ments can be made at present. Most probably *Chotodada* reached Calcutta last night. Probably, you will get all the news orally from him. *Chotodada* was here till last Sunday and after that my temperature has been shooting up to 100° every day. Otherwise I am as I was before. When I shall be transferred from here, I shall inform you by sending a telegram.

This morning I got a telegram from Kaviraj Shyamadas Vachaspati and he wanted to know my state of health. I told *Chotodada* that as soon as he would reach Calcutta he should meet Kaviraj Mahasaya and tell him everything. If by any chance *Chotodada* has forgotten to do so then you must send him to Kaviraj Mahasaya once. A few days back I wrote a letter to Kaviraj Mahasaya. Please inform him about my state of health.

I hope all of you are keeping well. What's the news about municipal election ?

I told *Chotodada* that as soon as he would be back in Calcutta he must inform father—I hope that he had done so.

How are father and mother. Accept my *pronam* and give my *pronams* to elders.

Yours affectionately
SUBHAS

77. *To Sarat Chandra Bose**
Censored and Passed

Rangoon Central Jail
25/2/27
Friday

My dear brother,

I sent you a letter last Saturday and I think it reached you in time. I did not receive any letter from you for a long time and the last letter which I got from you was probably of 29th January—and I sent a reply on 4th February. I hope that by now *Chotodada* has informed Father and Kaviraj Mahasaya about the state of my health. I got a telegram

* Translated from the original Bengali.

from Kaviraj Mahasaya about a week ago and in that telegram he wanted to know the present state of my health. I am going to send a reply to him on coming Monday, the 28th February. For the last few days I am taking a motor-ride every afternoon—and always accompanied by a C.I.D. Officer and allowed to take this motor-ride for an hour and a half. My health is not at all better than before, on the contrary it is worse than before. I have informed the Inspector General of Police that if I have to stay here for a long time my health will most probably deteriorate. *Chotodada* himself saw the condition of the prison where I am now, its advantages and disadvantages and you will come to learn everything from him. The temperature of my body is still going up—as for example, 18th Feb.—99.8°, 19th Feb.—100°, 20th Feb.—99°8, 21st Feb.—100.1°, 22nd Feb.—100°, 23rd Feb.—99°, 24th Feb.—100.4°. I do not know what kind of medical treatment will be or should be arranged for me. No medical treatment has yet been arranged for me. I hope that a decision whether I shall be kept here or not will be taken soon. How are the children? I hope that Khuki (Baby) has by now recovered. How has Asoke fared in examination? How are the parents? I hope that all of you are keeping well.

I was happy to learn from *Chotodada* that the Saraswati Puja was celebrated by the children.

Yours affectionately
SUBHAS

P.S. Has anything been settled regarding Gora's marriage? How is *Natunmamababu*? Send Rs. 50 in my account in Mandalay Jail.

SUBHAS

78. To Sarat Chandra Bose

Censored and Passed

Rangoon Central Jail
2.3.27
Wednesday

My dear brother,

After coming here I sent three letters to you—on 14th, on 18th and on 25th Feb. I hope that you received all those letters in time. Two or three days before Colonel Tarapore conveyed to me the news that you had sent him a wire informing him that as there was no certainty of my staying here you did not send to me any letter after 29th of January. I do not know how long I am going to stay here. I do not feel like staying here even for a moment because of so many inconveniences but I am helpless.

Summer is already here and it is quite hot specially during the day though mornings and nights are comparatively cold. My health is no better than before and there is no indication of any change. On the contrary, my temperature is shooting up more than before and here is the chart—

25th	February	—	99.2°
26th	"	—	100.4°
27th	"	—	100.2°
28th	"	—	100.4°
1st	March	—	99.4°

Other symptoms are as they were before. Nowadays, I go out for an hour for the motor-ride. I hope that all of you are well. I have come to learn from newspapers that a lot of noise is being made regarding the coming municipal election. How is *Natunmamababu* ?

Yours affectionately
SUBHAS

79. *From Sarat Chandra Bose*
Censored and Passed
Illegible
3/3/27
for D.I.G., I.B., C.I.D.
Bengal

38/1, Elgin Road
Calcutta
3.3.27

My dear Subhas,

Since I wrote to you on the 29th last, I have received the following letters from you—28th Jany., 2nd Feby., 4th Feby., 7th Feby., 8th Feby., 14th Feby., and 18th Feby., (the last two from Rangoon). I didn't write to you all this time because of the uncertainty of your movements.

I sent a telegram to the Inspector General of Prisons Rangoon a few days (ago) asking him how you were keeping. He sent a reply to the Bengal Govt. saying that your condition was the same and that reply was forwarded to me by the Deputy Secy., Political Dept., Govt. of Bengal.

Are you being taken out on a motor drive every evening? Are you feeling better as a result of that?

Sunil has told us in detail about your physical condition. I really cannot understand how the Mandalay authorities could keep a person who was suffering from tuberculosis with you all for 18 long months.

I think you should stay on at Rangoon for some time more and not go back to Mandalay or to Insein, unless of course, living at Rangoon is particularly uncomfortable.

So long today.

Yours very affly
SARAT

Subhas C. Bose Esq.

80. *To Sarat Chandra Bose**

Censored and passed

Rangoon Central Jail
11th March, 1927
Friday

My dear brother,

I received your letter after a long time. The letter written by you on 3rd March reached me yesterday. Last morning I sent a letter to the I.G. of Police requesting him to send a telegram to you, as I got no news from home for about three weeks. Probably the telegram was sent in time and then I received the letter from you yesterday noon. I am free from anxiety now on learning that all are well at home.

Yes, every afternoon I am taking a motor-ride, but what is the good of going out by a motor-car for 1 or 1½ hour when a day consists of 24 hours. Yet I enjoy the time while I travel by the car and then after the ride back to the cell again. Meanwhile I have lost my weight more and now it comes to 135 pound. I am also running temperature more than before and here is the chart—7th March—99.8° ; 8th March—100.4° ; 9th March 100.4°; 10th March 100.8°. I do not at all want to stay here any longer and after waiting here till 17th inst. I would like to leave this place. I apprehend that my health will be worse if I stay here any longer.

For the first ten or twelve days Mr. Rafi a barrister who practises here sent his own car for my use—so that I can go out and have a motor-ride and this arrangement was made by the I.G. of Police himself. After that Mr. Chandu is sending his car. In between Justice Das too sent his car for my use, but as Mr. Das himself is not keeping well I do not like the idea of putting him in trouble. I am indebted to Mr. Rafi and Mr. Chandoo and I think if they are thanked by you on my behalf, that will be very nice. If I go on writing letters now I think half of my letters (if I write four letters a week, at least

* Translated from the original Bengali.

two) will be tampered and damaged. Moreover my letters will take a lot of time to reach you after making their detour via the C.I.D. office. Most probably *Chotodada* knows the address of Mr. Chandu. Probably Mr. Chandu is an officer of Scindia Steam Navigation Company. Here is Mr. Rafi's address—

M.M. Rafi Esq. M.L.C.
Bar-at-Law
Rangoon.

Mr. Bose was ready to spare his car twice a week, but I do not feel like disturbing him.

Last Monday I sent to Kaviraj Mahasaya the chart of my temperature—from 14th Feb. to 6th March.

I hope all of you are well there.

Yours affectionately
SUBHAS

*81. To Bivabati Bose**

Censored and passed.

Mother Durga be with us.

Rangoon Central Jail
Wednesday, 16.3.27

Dear Mejobowdidi,

A few days ago I got your letter written on 24th Feb. I am still now in Rangoon and do not know how long I shall have to stay here. I think you know all about my state of health which is gradually deteriorating. Anyway I am not going to be worried about it. Rangoon is getting hotter and hotter, but I hope Rangoon will not be as bad as Mandalay which is hotter than Rangoon.

This year the image of goddess Saraswati was quite nice. The man who makes the image, usually takes the

* Translated from the original Bengali.

image away after the Puja is performed and most probably he either immerses the image in the river or keeps it at his home. I am happy to learn that *Natunmamababu* is better than before.

I am also happy to learn that Gora's marriage was solemnised properly.

A few days ago I wrote to *Mejdada* to send Rs. 50/- in my account through the Superintendent of Mandalaya Jail. If the money has not yet been sent tell *Mejdada* to send it by telegraph money-order to Mandalay Jail. When this letter will reach you, if at that time by any chance I shall have to stay on here in Rangoon, ask *Mejdada* to send fifty rupees more directly here to Rangoon Jail to me. The money which I get as yearly allowance from the Government, has been exhausted by now.

(incomplete)

82. *To H. E. the Governor of Burma*
Through the Superintendent, Rangoon Jail and the I.G. of Prisons.

May it please Your Excellency,

I have the honour to bring to your Excellency's notice an incident which happened only this morning which has given me considerable pain. I sent the following note to the Chief Jailor, Mr. Solomon this morning :—

"*Mr. Solomon*

Please send for the *Englishman* of the 14th and 15th March and please see that I get them before you leave the office for breakfast.

S. C. Bose 19/3/27"

About an hour and a half later the same note was returned to me with the following footnote in the Superintendent's handwriting and with his signature :—

"Mr. Bose is requested not to give orders to my Chief Jailor.

Sd/- R. E. Flowerdew 19/3/27"

(The initials are not quite legible but I think I have deciphered them correctly.)

I do not think that the note I sent to the Chief Jailor, Mr. Solomon, can be regarded as disrespectful or discourteous on any construction. I have been in confinement under the Bengal Ordinance for nearly 2½ years and have visited quite a number of jails in Bengal and Burma. I have always sent my requisitions to the Jail authorities in the same form in which I wrote to Mr. Solomon this morning. Even in Rangoon Jail where I have been living for over a month and a half I have written in the same form almost daily. But I have never heard or seen anyone remarking that I have been discourteous or have "given orders" to use Major Flowerdew's expression.

I respectfully submit that my knowledge of the English language is not altogether meagre—otherwise I would not have stood first in English composition at the I.C.S. open competitive examination in the year 1920. I would even be so bold as to claim that though Major Flowerdew is a Britisher my knowledge of the English language and literature is more profound than his.

I am painfully conscious of the fact that whatever my status in society and my position in the public life of India may be—within the four walls of the Rangoon Jail I am to a great extent at the mercy of the Jail officers from the Superintendent downwards. Though I possess the legal right to have my legitimate requirements (including newspapers) supplied by the Jail officers in accordance with the orders of Government and though I am aware that the work for which Jail officers here are paid by Government includes that of looking after my comforts, I am not so presumptuous as to think that I can "give orders" to Jail officers. I am making this statement from my experience in dealing with subordinates as the Chief Executive Officer of the Calcutta Corporation. Your Excellency may be aware that as an officer I have European subordinates of high education and international reputation some of whom at least draw salaries almost double that drawn by Major Flowerdew. I therefore claim to know in what form and style orders to subordinates are issued and in the light of that experience I can say without hesitation that no fair-minded man will hold that by writing the note referred to above, I "gave orders' to Mr. Solomon the Chief Jailor.

Before I close I would like to say a few words by way of personal explanation. I am entitled according to Government rules to get the *Englishman* a Calcutta paper and it is the duty of Jail officers to supply me with this paper. When I was in Mandalay I used to get the paper regularly without having to ask for it every time. In Rangoon Jail owing to the negligence of the Jail officers I have had to remind them about getting the paper for me every time the Calcutta mail is delivered here and I have found from experience that whenever I have not reminded them the paper has not been supplied. I have had to complain to the Jailors several times about irregularity in the matter of supplying newspapers and on at least one occasion I told Major Flowerdew myself about the matter. Owing to these troubles I had made it a part of my habit to send a memo. to the Chief Jailor every time the Calcutta mail was delivered here and uptill this morning this practice was working very well.

It is known to the Superintendent, Deputy Superintendent, Chief Jailor and other officers that I am quite alone in this Jail and have no company whatsoever and that I have to kill time somehow with the help of newspapers. It is also known to them that my stock of books and periodicals is exceedingly scanty as I had been advised by the Superintendent, Mandalay Jail not to take more than what was required for a short stay of 2 or 3 days. I have therefore to while away my time with the help of such papers as I can procure through the mercy of Jail officers. At the time I wrote the memo to Mr. Solomon the Chief Jailor, I was feeling very lonely and so I asked him to send me the papers in the morning before he left for breakfast (i.e. before 11-30 a.m.).

What little commonsense I possess tells me that if I had meant to give an order to the Chief Jailor I would not have taken the trouble to write the word "please" twice in the same sentence. Moreover, if I had intended to "give orders" I would have written Chief Jailor—which is the official designation—and not Mr. Solomon.

Under the law of the land I as a detenu am entitled to treatment in keeping with my rank and station in life. I therefore feel that the Superintendent of the Rangoon Jail Major Flowerdew has in an unwarranted manner hurt my feelings as a gentleman and humiliated me in the eyes of his staff by writing a note which to all fair-minded and reasonable men will appear as discourteous and insulting. At present I am at a loss to decide how I should communicate with the Jail staff and I am afraid I should forego my necessities rather than court fresh insult by writing to the Jail staff.

That I am not unduly sensitive will be apparent to Your Excellency from the fact that during the last 2½ years this is only the second occasion on which I have had to complain of discourtesy at the hands of an IMS officer. I conclude by appealing to Your Excellency to do justice to me by calling upon Maj. Flowerdew to withdraw his remarks and express regret.

I have the honour to be
Your Excellency's
most obedient servant
S. C. Bose, B. A. (Cantab),
Chief Executive Officer, Calcutta
Corporation and member, Bengal
Legislative Council.

Rangoon Jail
Dated the 19th March
1927

83. *To H.E. the Governor of Burma Through the Superintendent Rangoon Jail and the Inspector General of Prisons.*

Dated Rangoon the 21st March 1927.

May it please Your Excellency,

In my representation to Your Excellency dated the 19th March 1927 I brought to Your Excellency's notice one specific complaint which I had against the Superintendent, Major Flowerdew. I purposely refrained from mentioning other grievances therein as I did not want to complicate the issue. I would now with Your Excellency's kind permission submit other facts which would go to illustrate the manner in which I have been treated during my short stay in Rangoon Jail.

2. When I came to this Jail in Decembr last, during the first conversation I had with Major Flowerdew I was told or rather warned by him that I must not communicate with anyone outside. The nature of the warning, the language in which it was couched and the way it was uttered in their cumulative effect were as a detenu not only not complimentary to me but were somewhat insulting. I have met several I.M.S. officers and have lived in several jails in Bengal and in Burma but nowhere has it been my misfortune to be greeted with a warning of the kind uttered by Major Flowerdew. Of course I am not aware if Major Flowerdew did not possess sufficient keenness of perception to realise that such a warning was not due to me in view of my rank and station in life. However I was too conciliatory to be provoked at the time and I made the best of a bad situation by replying with a smile—I have been long enough in jail to know that.

3. During my visit to Rangoon Jail in December last I did not receive any attention from Major Flowerdew in the matter of diagnosis and treatment. On the other hand he seemed to be extremely anxious to belittle my aliments. When I told him that I had been running a temperature and showed him the temperature chart—his remark was—"But where is the temperature ?"—probably meaning there-

by that unless the daily temperature went up to 101° or 102° it did not deserve notice. However I was fortunate enough to get better attention from Col. Kelsall the senior physician of the Rangoon General Hospital and I dismissed the incident from my mind for the time being.

4. When I came to the Rangoon Jail a second time in February last I reported myself to the Superintendent in his office. No chair was offered to me while I was exchanging a few words with him and in order to avoid an awkward situation I had to avail myself of the earliest opportunity of slipping out of the room with a good grace. During the last 2½ years of jail life this was the first time when the Superintendent did not have the courtesy to offer me a chair. I feel emboldened to make this complaint because I know that Government do not approve of discourtesy on the part of their officers and because I am aware that these acts of discourtesy are the exception rather than the rule.

5. The attention that I have received from Major Flowerdew this time and the interest that he has taken in my treatment during my illness will be at once apparent if it is only asked how often he has visited me during the last 40 days. It is his usual practice to look in once a week on Mondays but even this practice is not sometimes kept up and a whole fortnight elapses before I have a chance of seeing him. During his inspection on Monday the 14th inst. he peeped in from the cell-door and put in the remark —are you quite well ? In view of the present state of my health the question was so palpably absurd that I could only reply with a smile—"Yes, thank you." Such a question could be justified either on the assumption that he was deliberately belittling my ailments or on the assumption that he was not aware that I was having fever daily, that my weight was going down, that I was suffering from dyspepsia and loss of appetite and from physical pain. The latter assumption if true would be damaging to him in view of the fact that my weight is being carefully recorded, a four-hourly temperature is being charted and other notes about my health are being recorded by the subordinate medical officers from time to time. I fail to see how with a medical

officer evidently so callous one can receive any attention or sympathetic treatment and it is no wonder that during my stay in Rangoon Jail for the last 40 days I have had no treatment at all till this morning.

6. The degree of isolation to which I have been subjected in this ward will be apparent from the fact that the prisoners have been prohibited on pain of punishment to converse with me. On one occasion a prisoner who happened to be a new arrival unacquainted with the rules was reported by the Deputy Superintendent Mr. Sutherland for asking my convict-attendant whether a particular bathroom was meant for general use or not.

7. I am fully conscious of the contrast between this sort of treatment and what I have received at the hands of other I.M.S. officers. Even Major Cormack of the Rangoon General Hospital who X-rayed me has taken more interest in me than the Superintendent of the Jail and whenever he has met me he has gone out of his way to make detailed enquiries about my health.

8. I had no desire to bring these trivial matters to the notice of Your Excellency but in view of recent developments I feel that I shall not be doing my duty to myself if I do not rake up the past. It is necessary for me to inform Your Excellency as the head of the Government that during my stay in the Rangoon Jail I have been anything but comfortable.

I have the honour to be,
Your Excellency's most obedient servant
S. C. BOSE
(Chief Executive Officer, Calcutta Corporation and member, Bengal Legislative Council)

84. To The Inspector General of Prisons
Rangoon

Rangoon
21st March, 1927

Dear Sir,

I am sorry that when I asked you yesterday morning

to transfer me to Insein or Mandalay, I did not state clearly what induced me to make the request. The real and only reason for which I made the request was to protest against the discourteous treatment I had received at the hands of the superintendent of this jail, Major Flowerdew. I have no desire to remain one moment longer in a jail where the superintendent does not treat me as I would expect a gentleman to treat me. I have already submitted a petition to his Excellency The Governor of Burma in this connection which will pass through your office and it is not necessary for me to enter into details here. I am anxious that the local government should not have a wrong impression as to why I want to be transferred from this jail.

In his last letter my brother had advised me to stay on in Rangoon unless I felt particularly uncomfortable. I would have accepted his advice but for the development referred to above. My knowledge of English have failed me and if I want anything I do not know how and what to write to a member of the jail-staff, for it is possible that whatever I write may be construed as an order given by me. Incidentally, this is a most unnatural state of affairs and it is telling on my health and sooner I get out of this place, better.

I am yours faithfully,
SUBHAS C. BOSE

85. To The Inspector General of Prisons
Rangoon

Rangoon
21st March, 1927

Dear Sir,

I desire to send the following two telegrams due to Pandit Motilal Nehru, Delhi and the other to Mr. J. N. Sengupta, Calcutta. I shall be obliged if you pass them and in case you cannot send them direct, I hope you will be good enough to send by wire to Calcutta CID who will forward them to the addressees. If necessary I shall pay the telegram charges out of my own pocket.

Telegram

Pandit Motilal Nehru, Delhi.

Please move home member for early transfer from Rangoon Jail owing superintendent's discourteous treatment.

Telegram

Sengupta, Mayor Calcutta.

Please move Bengal government for early transfer from Rangoon Jail owing Superintendent's discourteous treatment. If necessary wire Delhi also.

Bose Chief Executive Officer.

I am yours, faithfully

S. C. Bose

86. *To The Hon'ble Mr. Justice J. R. Das*
Barrister-at-law
High Court of Judicature
Through the Superintendent,
Rangoon Jail

Rangoon Jail
Dated, the 21st March, 1927
7-15 A.M.

My Lord,

I am an inmate of the Rangoon Jail having been detained under the Bengal Ordinance. I have certain complaints against the jail authorities which I desire to bring to the notice of the local Government.

One of the surest means whereby I can catch the ears of the local Govt. is to seek the help of the official visitors to the jail. Your Lordship as an honourable judge of the High Court of Judicature at Rangoon is, I understand, an ex-officio visitor to this jail. If your Lordship can conveniently spare a few minutes for a visit to this jail, I shall be enabled to place my grievances before your lordship for transmission to the local Government.

I have the honour to be
Your lordship's most obedient servant
S. C. Bose

87. *To The Deputy Inspector General of Police, Rangoon*

Rangoon
21st March, 1927

Subject : Manner of Bhowmick's removal from the Rangoon Jail

Dear Sir,

I have been asked by my friend Detenu Mr. M. M. Bhowmick who has been transferred from Mandalaya Jail to Alipore Jail (Calcutta) via Rangoon Jail to bring to your notice the circumstance of his removal from Rangoon Jail. As your department is in charge of the transfer of detenus from our jail to another it is desirable that all the facts should be brought to your notice so that similar unpleasant incidents may be avoided in future. It would have been better if Mr. Bhowmick had related the whole story himself, but unfortunately he had no time to do so.

Mr. Bhowmick arrived at the Rangoon jail at about 10 o'clock on Saturday the 19th instant. I met him soon after and asked him whether he would be leaving in the same afternoon by the 1-30 P.M. steamer. He said that he could get no information on the point from Chief Jailor who rather gave him the impression that he would have to travel by the next boat. He also said that he had just shaken off a really severe attack of Malaria which had left him very weak. Exposure at night had given him bad headache, which was persisting and he would rather have some rest for a day or two before risking a fresh exposure. Thereupon we explained the circumstances to the jailor in charge of our ward Mr. Conway and asked him to go over to the jail office at once and inform the C.I.D. office over the phone that Mr. Bhowmick was not feeling fit to travel and that it would be advisable to put off his departure till the next available opportunity. To avoid any risk or mistake the message that was to be conveyed to the C.I.D. office was written out and handed over to the Jailor. It was explained to him that the message was to be communicated to the

C.I.D. soon, so that they could go ahead with the arrangements for Mr. Bhowmick's departure by the afternoon steamer.

The Jailor went to the office and saw the Chief Jailor and Deputy Superintendent. What transpired there I do not know but the Jailor came back and said that Mr. Sutherland the Deputy Superintendent told him that no message could be sent directly to the C.I.D. office in the absence of the Superintendent. They would have to wait till the Superintendent came—which by the way would be either on Monday morning or on Saturday afternoon after the steamer left. We told the jailor that we had done our duty in the matter of informing the jail office and if the message was held up there that was not our fault. No one could blame us if the C.I.D. officer pushed on the arrangements for sending Mr. Bhowmick the same day and if the escort arrived Mr. Bhowmick would not be in position to travel. The jailor thereupon remarked that he did not see how Mr. Bhowmick could travel in the same afternoon in the existing circumstances.

All this took place at about 10-30 A.M. that is some time later and about 10-45 A.M. a lot of furniture had arrived for Mr. Bhowmick including a bedstead, table, chairs, tripod etc. and there was an enquiry from the chief Jailor as to whether anything else was required. Three cells next to mine were vacated and placed at the disposal of Mr. Bhowmick. This left no doubt in the mind that the jail authorities were making arrangements for Mr. Bhowmick to stay on for a few days. The warder who does my shopping was also sent by the chief jailor to enquire if any more shopping was required for my friend.

As Mr. Bhowmick was not well, he had breakfast and lay down to rest. At about 12-30 P.M., a written message came to him from jail office to say that he should be in readiness, also the escort were expected shortly. Mr. Bhowmick replied in writing saying that in view of the state of his health, he was not feeling fit to travel and he had asked the jail officer at about 10-30 A.M. to inform the CID about that. Reply was sent from the jail office purporting to be a communication from the CID office to the effect that CID had completed the arrangements for sending Mr. Bhowmick the same afternoon and that he *must* go. A reply to this was sent by Mr. Bhowmick saying that as it was a medical question, it was not possible for the CID to say without reference to the state of his health that he must go. Soon after at about 1 o'clock Mr. Bhattacharya Deputy S.I. appeared on the scene. The circumstances were explained to him. He said that he had not received any message from the jail office that Mr. Bhowmick was unable or unwilling to go by Saturday's boat. Only a few minutes ago, he had been told by his superior officer that Mr. Bhowmick was unwilling to embark the same afternoon, and he had been commissioned to see into the matter. Mr. Bhattacharya said that after 11 A.M. and possibly at about 11-30 A.M. Mr. Sutherland telephoned to him to say that it was not possible to accommodate Mr. Bhowmick in Rangoon jail and arrangements should be made to send him the same day. He had to work against time in order to make the necessary arrangements at the eleventh hour and he would have been only too glad to put off Mr. Bhowmick's departure if he had been informed an hour ago. We told him that we were quite convinced that the CID were not to blame over this affair but that was no reason why Mr. Bhowmick should be put to needless trouble and inconvenience owing to the lapses of some jail officers. Mr. Bhattacharya then requested Mr. Bhowmick to avoid an unpleasant situation by not deciding to go and the latter ultimately agreed to travel but under protest.

I would like to point out that—why Mr. Sutherland told Mr. Conway between 10-35 and 11 A.M. that he was unable to send any message direct to the C.I.D. office in the absence of the superintendent regarding Mr. Bhowmick's inability to travel and why after 11 a.m. or rather at about 11-30 a.m. he telephoned to Mr. Bhattacharya in the absence of the Superintendent asking him to arrange the departure of Mr. Bhowmick the same afternoon as there would be difficulty about accommodating him ? The talk about difficulty in accommodating him was a pure myth as the necessary accommodation had already been provided for him.

It is also clear beyond a shadow of doubt that before the telephone call was conveyed to Mr. Bhattacharya by Mr. Sutherland table, chairs, bedstead and other furniture were sent for Mr. Bhowmick, thereby giving us the reasonable impression that Mr. Bhowmick was going to stay for a few days. We are of the opinion that it was wrong to compel Mr. Bhowmick to embark when he was a convalscent and in a very weak state of health and he was laid up with a severe headache which is usually the symptom of a relapse of Malaria. In view of Mr. Bhowmick's past medical history was it not a sort of gross negligence and callousness on the part of some jail officers to arrange for his transfer without handing any notice and employing means which any gentleman would hesitate to use? Even if Mr. Bhowmick had not been unfit to travel he could still claim that reasonable notice be given him in order to give him necessary time to pack up. On this occasion the packing had to be done at breakneck speed and when Mr. Bhowmick had got into the taxi at about 1-15 p.m. he was panting for breath.

It is not for me to pronounce him responsible for this unpleasant episode, but as I can judge Mr. Sutherland the Deputy Suprintendent should come in for a major share of the blame.

I am bringing these facts to your notice as your department is responsible for the transfer of detenus. Further when this matter was brought to the notice of the I.G. Prisons on Saturday last I understand that he expressed his inability to interfere as the affair rested entirely in the hands of the C.I.D. I am anxious, as no doubt you are, that similar incidents should not be repeated in future. Whatever our political views may be we have had so far no quarrel with or complaints against the Burma C.I.D. and I see no reason why our cordial relations should be disturbed owing to the interference or mismanagement by some member of another department via the jail department. I hope that if necessary you will be so good as to bring this matter to the notice of the local government.

I am, yours faithfully,
SUBHAS C. BOSE

88. To Sarat Chandra Bose

Rangoon Central Jail
22.3.27

My dear brother,

My condition has been growing worse—the loss of weight has been persistent and since my arrival here I have lost 7 pounds in all. It is getting hot here—specially in the day time and for some time past the drop in weight has been at the rate of 2 pounds a week. The temperature usually goes up higher than 100° and yesterday it rose to 100.1°. Indigestion and loss of appetite have been my friends for some time past and the pain in the spine is persisting. I am afraid summer will aggravate my trouble.

I have read Mr. Moberly's speech at yesterday's meeting of the Bengal Council in today's Rangoon papers.

How are you all doing? I have had no news of you all for a long time.

Yours very affectionately
SUBHAS

To Mr. S. C. Bose
38/2, Elgin Rd. Calcutta.

89. To Sarat Chandra Bose

Censored and passed
Illegible
31/3
for D.I.G., I.B., C.I.D.
Bengal

Rangoon Central Jail
22.3.27
10 a.m.

My dear brother,

I am not pulling on well with the Superintendent of this Jail Major Flowerdew—whose treatment has been discourteous. I have therefore requested the Inspector General of Prisons to transfer me to Insein or Mandalay pending final orders. Yesterday I forwarded to the Insp.-General the following wire which I wanted to be despatched to you—either direct or through the Calcutta C.I.D.

Escibos Calcutta

Anxious no news since telegram tenth March stop despite your advice have requested Inspector General transfer me Insein or Mandalay pending final orders owing Rangoon Superintendent's discourteous treatment stop my health worse wire health all—Bose.

I have read in today's Rangoon papers a fairly full report of Mr. Moberly's speech at yesterday's meeting of the Bengal Council regarding the conditions of my release (?)

I have had no official communication yet—nor have I received any telegram from you.

Hope this will find you all quite well. How are mother and father?

I have written to Chotodada under a separate cover about my health at present.

I am

Yours v. affly
SUBHAS

To
Sarat C. Bose Esq.
38/1, Elgin Road
Calcutta

90. To Motilal Nehru

Rangoon Central Jail
23.3.27
(Address : C/o D.I.G.,I.B.,C.I.D.
13 Elysium Row, Calcutta)

Dear Panditji,

I am writing this only to inform you that on the 21st March I sent the following telegram addressed to you to the I.G. of Prisons Rangoon to be despatched either direct to you or through the Calcutta C.I.D. I hope you have got the telegram by now.

Telegram

Pandit Motilal Nehru, Delhi

Please move Home member for early transfer from Rangoon Jail owing Superintendent's discourteous treatment

SUBHAS

The trouble had been brewing for some time past but the climax was reached on Saturday the 19th inst. I am purposely refraining from mentioning details as this letter may be withheld on that ground.

I have already addressed two representations to H.E. the Governor of Burma regarding the treatment I have received in this Jail. My object in writing to you was that in case this Government felt that they could not move in the matter without a direction from Delhi—you could help by bringing this to the notice of Sir Alexander Muddiman. I would prefer staying in any other jail—say Insein or Mandalay—rather than here.

Hope this will find you in good health and spirits in spite of a very busy session. With my "pronams" and deepest regards to you.

I am

Yours affly

SUBHAS C. BOSE

Pandit Motilal Nehru

Delhi

P.S. Sir Alexander's statement before the Assembly and Mr. Moberly's statement before the Bengal Council on the 21st March regarding the detenus have appeared in the Rangoon papers and I have seen them.

S.C.B.

91. *To J. M. Sengupta Esq.,*
B.A., L.L.B., (Cantab) M.L.C.
Mayor, Calcutta Corporation,
10/4 Elgin Road, Calcutta.

Rangoon Central Jail
23.3.27
(Address: C/o D.I.G., I.B., C.I.D.
13 Elysium Row, Calcutta)

Sir,

I am writing this only to inform you that on Monday the 21st March I sent the following telegram addressed to you to the I.G. of Prisons, Rangoon, to be despatched either direct or through the Calcutta C.I.D. I hope you have received the telegram by now.

Telegram

Sengupta, Mayor, Calcutta
Please move Bengal Govt. for early transfer from Rangoon Jail owing Superintendent's discourteous treatment stop if necessary wire Delhi also

Bose, Chief Executive Officer

I have already addressed two representations on the subject to H.E. the Governor of Burma regarding the treatment that has been meted out to me in this Jail but my object in writing to you was that in case this Government felt unable to move without instructions from Bengal, you could help by speaking to or communicating with Mr. Moberly. I would prefer to go to any other Jail—say Insein or Mandalay—rather than stop here for one moment longer.

Mr. Moberly's statement at the meeting of the Bengal Council on the 21st March regarding the conditions of my release have appeared in the Rangoon papers and I have seen it.

The friction with the Jail authorities here have been

going on for some time past but matters came to a head on Saturday the 19th inst.

I have the honour to be Sir,
Your most obedient servant
S. C. Bose
(Chief Executive Officer)

92. From Sarat Chandra Bose

38/1, Elgin Road
Calcutta.
24.3.27

My dear Subhas,

I wrote to you last on the 14th. I have received your letters dated 25th February, 2nd March, and 11th March and am very disturbed to learn that you have gone down in weight further. I sent yesterday a telegram to Inspector General of Prisons, Rangoon asking him to place you under proper treatment immediately and send you back to Mandalay, if you are particularly uncomfortable at Rangoon. Sunil told me that the room allowed to you at Rangoon was unsuitable. I did not say anything all this time about your bringing back to Mandalay, as I was fondly hoping all this time that motor-drive would do you some good. But as it has not had the desired effect I think you should consult at your convenience regarding the place where you should stay.

Mr Moberly made a statement on the Bengal Council on the 21st about you. I enclose a copy of the statement for your use. Please go through it and let me have your opinion as early as possible. Apparently Sunil's suggestion regarding stay in Switzerland has elicited the response that externment is due remedy.

I have written to father also for his opinion. And I expect he will write you back to say that I should ask you to express you so.

I shall not write anymore today except to ask you to take as much care of yourself as possible in the circumstances.

Yours affectionately
Sarat

93. To Sarat Chandra Bose

Censored and Passed
Illegible
2/4/27
for D.I.G., I.B., C.I.D.
Bengal

Insein Jail
28/3/27
Monday

My dear brother,

I hope you have got my letters of the 7th, 11th, 14th and 22nd March by now.

I came over here on Friday the 25th inst.

I received your letter of the 14th March a few days ago at Rangoon. On the 21st inst. I sent a wire to you to the office of the I.G. of Prisons to be despatched from there. I hope you received it in due course.

I am sorry to learn that Baby is not well yet. I hope you will not neglect her treatment. How is Natunmamababu now ? I was informed some time ago there was a slight improvement.

At the last weighment my weight was 131 lbs—which implied a drop of 7 lbs (seven pounds) during my stay in Rangoon Jail. The temperature rose as follows :—11th March 100.6° ; 12th March—100° ; 13th—99.6° ; 14th—99.8° ; 15th—100°; 16th—100.2°; 17th—99.6°; 18th—100.4°; 19th—100.4°; 20th—100.2° ; 21st—101° ; 22nd—100.4° ; 23rd—100° ; 24th —100.4° ; 25th not recorded ; 26th—100.6° ; 27th—99.6°.

I am a little better off here than at Rangoon—as there is some company here—otherwise things are much the same. It is dry here at present but I am told that the rains will commence in May and then there will be practically one long continuous downpour till November. I do not know how long I shall be here.

Have you written to Messrs. Rafi and Chandoo thanking them for lending me their cars ?

How are you all doing ?

Yours v. affl·
SUBHAS

S. C. Bose Esq.
38/1, Elgin Road
Calcutta

94. *From Sarat Chandra Bose*

38/1, Elgin Road
Calcutta
31st March, 1927.

My dear Subhas,

I received on the 22nd instant through Elysium Row, a copy of the telegram from the Superintendent, Insein Jail, informing me that you have arrived there. I sent a telegram to the Superintendent, Insein Jail, asking him how you are keeping there. He wrote back to say that you were no worse and that you had gained somewhat in weight. I was surprised to hear that two day's stay in Insein had made any change in your weight.

Did you prefer Insein to Mandalay or had you no choice in the matter? What sort of a place is Insein? Is it as hot as Mandalay? Is the climate in Insein any better than Mandalay? I hope you have asked the Superintendent to put you under proper treatment. Have not the medical authorities at Rangoon made any suggestion regarding treatment?

Please let me know how you are keeping at Insein and the nature of the accommodation you have been given there.

Yours affectionately
SARAT

Subhas Chandra Bose Esq.

95. *To Jatindra Nath Chakrabarty**

Insein Jail
Rangoon
2 April, 1927

My dear Mr. Chakrabarty,

I was happy to receive your letter of 5th Chaitra. You have asked so many questions—I hardly know what to say in reply. I feel like writing about so many things—but can

*Translated from the original Bengali.

one write all that?

I have nothing new to say about my health—I am in the same state. I do not know what will eventually happen—I no longer worry about my health. During the past few months my thoughts have been speeding along in certain directions. I have become convinced that it is not possible to keep your head high unless you are prepared to devote hundred per cent of your life to the cause. In the morning of my life, I embarked on my career with this prayer: "Give unto your chosen one the strength to bear the cross" ("Tomar pataka jare dao, tare bahibare dao sakati"). I do not know about the future but so far God has fulfilled my prayer. So, I feel extremely contented today—sometimes I wonder how many are there in this world as happy as I? As the prospect of going out of the high encircling wall grows dimmer and dimmer, my mind is getting more and more peaceful and free of worry. To live from within and to lose your life in inner self-fulfilment bring absolute peace —inner peace is the only sustenance in prolonged incarceration—thus the prospect of long imprisonment is bringing me limitless peace. Emerson used to say—"We must live wholly from within". These words are wholly true and my faith in this truth is getting stronger day by day. If those who are in the same position as I am assess success or failure in life in terms of external events, then death is inevitable (Mrityurena na sansaya'). The yardstick that has to be used to evaluate our life (that is, of prisoners) relates to the inner self, because according to the external yardstick our lives are probably utterly valueless. If all ends here, no enduring impress of our existence will be left in the material world. But even if I cannot achieve anything else in life and do not have the chance to translate my ideals into reality, my life will not have been in vain. If I have accepted a great ideal deep inside my life—if I have been able to bring my body and mind in tune with that great ideal—if my existence has merged with that ideal, I am satisfied,— even if my life is valueless to the world at large, it is not so to myself (and perhaps to the arbiter of my destiny). Everything in this world perishes—only one thing never perishes or dies and that is an idea or an ideal. Our ideals, our aims and aspirations and our thoughts are immortal. Can one imprison ideas by a wall ?

If one has to receive hundred per cent, one must give up hundred per cent at the other end. In other words, if an ideal is to be attained in its entirety, one must be prepared to dedicate his whole being. 'Tyaga' and 'Amrita', renunciation and realisation, are two faces of the same medal. To attain hundred per cent and to sacrifice hundred per cent have now become the passion of my life. Will He who has led me through all my weaknesses to the height of power not be kind to me ? The Upanishads say 'His chosen one alone can attain to it'—now let us see what happens. I have been compelled to give up systematic study since long. I had started studies and research on the solution of certain fundamental problems providing the basis of nationalism—the work remains suspended for the present. I do not know when I can resume it. Once I go out, such work will be drowned by others—that is why I wanted to complete it while I was here. The assignment that I had in prison has probably not been completed—that may be the reason why my return is being delayed. I have a desire to write about some of the problems of our collective life. I shall try to write something if I receive a reply to this letter.

May God keep you all well and may He shower his blessings always on all your work—this is my earnest prayer.

Yours sincerely,
SUBHAS C. BOSE

96. To Sarat Chandra Bose

Censored and Passed
Illegible
13/4/27
for D.I.G., I.B., C.I.D.,
Bengal

Insein Central Jail
4.4.27

My dear brother,

You must be anxious to know what I think of the offer that has been made by the Hon'ble Mr. Moberly and it is time to unburden myself on the subject. I don't know if I shall see eye to eye with you but I am giving my opinion for what it is worth.

I have read and re-read very carefully the statement of the Hon'ble Member. I have pondered over every sentence and every word in his statement—which by the way, I must say is a carefully drafted one. I have taken time to weigh the pros and cons of his proposal and have not been in haste to come to a definite decision. What I am going to write to you represents my opinion at his moment, formed after prolonged deliberation but I am open to correction and if there are any facts or arguments which I have overlooked or which have not been brought to my notice I am prepared to reconsider my decision.

Let me say at the outset that I appreciate the frankness of the Hon'ble Member's statement and I shall be failing in my duty if I do not reciprocate it. I have always believed in frankness and I think that frankness pays in the long run. There are certain points in the Hon'ble Member's statement for which I cannot but feel thankful to him. When he said that he did not want any admission regarding the past or promise about the future—when he stated that he was prepared to release me if I gave my "word of honour" etc.—when he remarked towards the end that he did not make the offer to me first because he did not want me to feel that the offer was being forced on me—he showed commendable consideration for my feelings as a gentleman and as a man of honour. And though I feel unable to accept the offer owing to reasons into which I shall presently enter—I none the less appreciate the honourable elements in the offer. Further, as a member of the Bengal Legislative Council I cannot fail to welcome the Hon'ble Member's action in taking the house into his confidence in at least one case. But when I have said this I am afraid I have said about all that could be urged in favour of the proposal.

There is one preliminary point on which I should like to disabuse your mind viz. that Chotodada's report and recommendation were made without any reference to or prior consultation with me. If he had consulted me I would have objected to a recommendation of that kind and when after submitting it, he acquainted me with the nature of his recommendation, I expressed misgivings as to its expediency—which I now find have been amply justified. Of course Chotodada was here to examine me as a patient and to give his opinion as a medical man and I think he performed his duty with scientific impartiality and professional dispassionateness. He was not concerned with the political implications of his recommendation nor with the question as to whether Government would make political capital out of it—and no one, not even I, can blame him for ruling out all extra-medical questions and for ignoring the political consequences of his recommendation. He advised in my case as he would in the case of any other patient of his and he told me that as several of his patients had been cured by treatment in a swiss Sanatorium—he strongly advised all tubercular patients who had means, to undergo a course of treatment in Switzerland. In these circumstances it is clear that I have not in any way committed myself in advance as to what offer I would welcome.

It appears that Govt. do not accept Chotodada's diagnosis (though they are prepared to make use of his recommendation) for the Hon'ble Member said, "It will be seen that at the moment Mr. Subhas Chandra Bose is not seriously ill and certainly not incapacitated." It would be interesting to know at what stage Govt. would regard me as either incapacitated or seriously ill. Is it when doctors will declare me as past cure and my death as a question of a few months or days ? Further, if Govt. do not accept Chotodada's diagnosis—why are they so anxious to accept what on the surface—and only on the surface—appears to be his recommendation ? Chotodada's recommendation does not say that I should not be allowed to go home and meet my people before I sail abroad. Nor does it say that the ship by which I must travel should not touch at any port in India. Nor again does it say that even if I am restored to proper health, I should not return home before the expiry of the Bengal Criminal Law Amendment Act. All this leads me to doubt if the real object of the Govt. is to give me an opportunity to recoup my health.

The Hon'ble Member said in effect that the only 2 alternatives which were open in my case were (1) confinement in Jail and (2) treatment in a foreign country for an undefined period. But is there really no via media between the two ? I am not sure that there is not.

The Bengal Govt. want me to stay abroad till the expiry of the Bengal Criminal Law Amendment Act i.e. ostensibly till January 1930. But who can be sure that the Act will run out in 1930 and that it will not be given another lease of life ? The last conversation I had with Mr. Lowman, D.I.G., I.B., C.I.D. in October, 1926, was anything but reassuring on this point and I shall not be surprised if in 1929, serious attempts are made to put the Bengal Criminal Law Amendment Act of 1925 permanently on the Statute Book. In that case my absence from home will be made permanent and I shall have to thank myself alone for exiling myself from India by a twentieth century "self-denying Ordinance". If the intentions of Government had been quite clear on this point they would have mentioned a definite date till when I would have to stay abroad.

Again, I have not been given any assurance as to the extent of freedom I shall be allowed in Europe. Will the Govt. save me from the kind attentions of the numerous spies that swarm in Switzerland ? There is no gainsaying the fact that I am a political suspect and shall continue to be one, as long as I do not turn a somersault and become a police informer and it is possible that my life abroad may be made miserable by spies shadowing me at every step. I understand that in Switzerland there are not only British spies but Swiss, Italian, French, German and Indian spies in the employ of the British Govt. and what is there to prevent some of these overzealous agents from sending false reports regarding myself with the object of further blackening me in the eyes of the Govt. ? I honestly think—and told Mr. Lowman about it last year—that it is possible for the Intelligence Department if they feel so inclined to concoct a plausible case against any citizen concerned with politics which will suffice for the purpose of securing orders for his detention under the Ordinance. This is more true of those political suspects who live in Europe for a time. No one can forget the difficulty that some of these political suspects had to encounter in order to obtain permission to return home with impunity. Even a leader of the position and eminence of Lala Lajpat Rai could return home only with the help of influential M.P. friends, some of whom are ex-Ministers of the Cabinet. Unfortunately I am now "bete noire" to the Govt. and the difficulty that I shall have to encounter can be easily imagined.

Moreover, I feel so helpless in the face of overzealous police agents that I am almost sure that however cautious, and even timid, I may be during my stay in Europe—I shall never be able to prevent unfavourable reports regarding myself from reaching the Govt. of India. All my caution and even timidity will be put down as shrewdness and cunning and all sorts of sinister activities, of which I shall be the author, will be imagined where there are none. And the tragedy of the whole situation will be that I shall have no means of knowing what reports are being sent about me and I shall not be given any opportunity of explaining things and incidents which are really harmless. It is thus possible that by the time 1929 draws near, I shall have been painted as a Bolshevik agent (for in Europe there is only one nightmare today viz. the Bolshevik nightmare) of the darkest dye before the India Govt. and the inevitable consequence will be that I shall either be prevented from returning to India or shall be arrested again on my arrival. I have no desire to become a voluntary exile from the land of my birth and I would therefore like Govt. to look at this matter for a minute from my point of view.

If I had the remotest intention of becoming a Bolshevik agent, I would have jumped at the offer made and taken the first available boat to Europe. If I succeeded in recouping my health, I could then have joined the gay band who trot about from Paris to Leningrad talking of world revolution and emitting blood and thunder in their utterances. But I have no such ambition or desire.

When I read that I was required to undertake not to return to India, Burma and Ceylon I rubbed and rubbed my eyes and asked myself—"Am I so dangerous to the existence of British rule in India that a deportation from Bengal is not regarded as an adequate safeguard or is all this but a hoax?" If the former, then from one point of view it is somewhat flattering to a nationalist to be told that he is so much of a nuisance to the bureaucracy. But when I come to look at facts and analyse my life and activities before I was arrested, I cannot help feeling that my political complexion is not so red as some interested and malicious people have led Government to think. I have not done any political work outside Bengal and I have hardly any desire to do so, at least for some years to come—for Bengal is big enough for me and for my ambitions. I do not think that any other Govt. (whether the Govt. of India or any other provincial Govt.) besides Bengal has anything to say against me and so far as I remember, I do not think I left Bengal during the last 6 years except to visit members of our family or to attend meetings of the A.I.C.C. or the Congress. Why then this attempt to prejudice me in the eyes of other Govt.s by holding me up as a dangerous person and prohibiting me from entering India, Burma and Ceylon? Ceylon being a Crown Colony, I doubt if it is within the jurisdiction of the Govt. of Bengal or even of the Govt. of India to lay down such a condition.

The Bengal Government want to have control over my

movements now—but I moved but little when I was free. Between October 1923 and October 1924 I do not think I left Calcutta on more than two occasions—on the first occasion to attend the Khulna District Conference and on the second occasion to address some election meetings in Nadia District for a prospective M.L.C. And between February 1924 and October 1924, I do not think I stirred out of Calcutta at all. All attempts made to connect me with the Sirajganj Conference are futile and malicious for when the Conference met, I had just taken over charge of the C.E.O.-ship and was too busy with municipal work and in warding off a threatened sweepers' strike, to be able to leave Calcutta for a minute. Between May and October 1924 my activities and movements need no enumeration for they are a matter of common knowledge. The Government were perfectly aware of my movements before my arrest and if the object of my imprisonment was to control my movements, there was no necessity at all for arresting me.

There is one aspect of the Hon'ble Member's proposal which struck me as particularly callous. Government know that I have been away from home for nearly 2½ years and I have not met most of my relations—including parents—during this period. They nevertheless propose that I should go abroad for a period which will be at least 2½ or 3 years without having an opportunity of meeting them. This is hard for me—but much more so for those who love me—whose number is I think very large. It is not easy for a Westerner to appreciate the deep attachment which Oriental people have for their kith and kin and I hope that it is this ignorance—rather than wilfulness—which is responsible for what I cannot but regard as a heartless feature of the Government offer. It would be typical only of a Western mind to presume that because I have not married—therefore I have no family (taking the word in its large sense) and no attachment for anyone.

Government seem to have clean forgotten the suffering to which they have subjected me for the last 2½ years. I am the aggrieved party and not they. They have locked me in for such a long period without any justification. I was only told that I was guilty of being a member of a conspiracy for importing arms, manufacturing explosives and murdering police officers and was asked if I had anything to say. I wonder if the Late Sir Edward Marshall Hall or Sir John Simon could have put up any other defence beyond saying "not guilty"—and this is exactly what I did. When the "allegations" were presented to me a second time, I raised the question myself as to why I of all persons happened to be victimized by the Police—and I think I was able to give a satisfactory explanation. Since my arrest the Bengal Govt. have not granted me any allowance for the maintenance of my dependents or the upkeep of my establishment and when, as a last resort, I appealed to H.E. the Viceroy, my representation was withheld by the Bengal Government. On the top of this they want me to exile myself for nearly 3 years and to find the money for maintaining myself during my exile in Europe. Is this a fair and reasonable proposition ? If Government do not recognise any other moral obligation they should at least feel obliged to set me at liberty in the same state of health in which they found me in 1924—and if my health is impaired owing to my incarceration, they should compensate me. Even if they do not recognise the obligation to compensate me—they should at least meet all the expenditure that has to be incurred till I recoup my former health. How long will Government go on ignoring all moral obligations ? If Government had allowed me to go home once before I sailed abroad, had agreed to meet all my expense in Europe and had permitted me to return without let or hindrance on my recovery, there would have been something human about the offer.

Lastly the Hon'ble Member has shown me the mailed fist appearing in a velvet glove. He said—"Both Government and Mr. Bose realise that they can detain him until the expiration of the Criminal Law Amendment Act." I perfectly agree with him and I would go further and say that I realise that Government can detain me as long as they like—for when the Amendment Act expires—they can either prolong its life or serve a fresh order on me under Regulation III of 1818. As a matter of fact I have told many Government officers, including Mr. Lowman, that I feel to my utter despair that there is absolutely nothing to prevent Government from detaining us all our life—though M.L.A.s and M.L.C.s may fret and fume and throw out Executive Councillors' touring expenses. And I have yet to learn that Government do not really intend to keep us here all our life.

I am reminded of what the late Deshbandhu of hallowed memory used to call me (viz. a "young old man") because of what he regarded as my pessimism. I am pessimistic from one point of view for I always try to picture the worst that may happen. I have on this occasion tried to anticipate the worst that may befall me, if I do not accept the offer of Govt. but I have not been able to persuade myself that a permanent exile from the land of my birth would be better than life in a Jail leading to the sepulchre. I do not quail before this cheerless prospect for I believe as the poet does, that "the paths of glory lead but to the grave."

I believe I have said about all that could be said both for and against the Government offer. Let no one grieve that the chances of my release are few and far between. Above all please console our dear parents, for theirs is the hardest lot, and all those who love me. We have yet to suffer a lot, both individually and collectively, before the priceless treasure of freedom can be secured. Thank God I am at peace with myself and I can face with perfect equanimity any ordeal that He in His wisdom may choose to visit me with. I regard myself as doing penance in my own humble way for the past sins of our nation and I am—and shall be—happy in my atonement. Our thoughts will not die—our ideals will not fade from the nation's memory and posterity will be the heirs of our fondest dreams—this is the faith which shall sustain me in my tribulation forever and forever.

Please let me have an early reply.

Yours v. affly
SUBHAS

S. C. Bose Esq.
38/1, Elgin Road Calcutta

97. *To Gopal Lal Sanyal**

Insein Jail
5th April, 1927

My dear friend,

I was delighted to receive your letter of the 5th Chaitra. You have asked me so many questions—I hardly know what to reply. I feel like writing so much but how can I ?

There is nothing new to report about my health—it is the same old story. I do not know how it will end—I do not worry about my health any more. During the last few months my thinking has been developing fast on certain lines. I am getting more and more convinced that unless one is prepared to sacrifice a hundred per cent of his life, it becomes impossible to remain firm and unshakable. I had started my life with this prayer—

"তোমার পতাকা যারে দাও,
তারে বহিবারে দাও শকতি।"[1]

I do not know what the future holds for me. But, uptill now God has fulfilled my prayer. I therefore feel completely happy—I often wonder if there is anybody else in this world happier than myself. The more the chances of my going out of these tall circular walls are receding, the more calm and free my mind is becoming. There is infinite bliss in living wholly from within and entirely devoted to the development of one's inner self. And, in order to put up with long incarceration a mind at peace provides the only sustenance. Thus, the prospect of a long imprisonment fills my mind with a rare composure. Emerson has said : "We must live wholly from within." This is completely true and my belief in it is getting stronger every day.

If those who are in the same position as myself judge success or failure in life by external events, then things would appear to be beyond redemption. The yardstick with which we prisoners must be judged relate to inner and not external achievements. Because in terms of external things,

*Translated from the original Bengali.
[1] "O Lord, give unto your chosen one the strength to bear the Cross".

our lives are probably futile. If all ends here, our lives may not leave any lasting impression on the material world outside. Nevertheless, even if I am not able to achieve anything else—if I do not get the opportunity to translate my ideals into reality—my life will not have been in vain. If I have accepted a great ideal with all my heart and soul—if I have been able to identify my body and spirit entirely with that great ideal—if my earthly existence and the ideal have become inseparable—then I am content; even if the world looks upon my life to be useless, it is not so to me and probably to my God as well. Everything in this world is ephemeral but ideals and ideas are imperishable and indestructible. Our hopes and aspirations and our dreams of an ideal social order are immortal. Who can keep ideas confined within stone-walls ?

To be able to give away completely, one must accept one's ideal in its entirety. On the other hand, in order to achieve one's ideal, one must be prepared to give up one's all. Renunciation and realisation are like the two sides of the same medal. My mind and spirit now yearn for absolute achievement and absolute sacrifice.

He who has led me to the pinnacle of spiritual power in spite of all my weaknesses—will He not bless me now ? The Upanishads say: "Yamebaisha brinute tena labbya"[1]—now let us see what happens.

I was compelled to give up systematic study a long time ago. I had started studies and research on certain fundamental problems of nationalism. For the time being all work is in abeyance. I do not know when I shall be able to resume it. Once I go out, such work will be shelved; I therefore wanted to complete it here. The purpose of my imprisonment is probably yet to be fulfilled—there will therefore probably be yet some time before I go out.

May God keep you all well and may He bless your work always—this is my fervent prayer.

Yours

SUBHAS

[1] It can be attained only by one who has His grace.

98. *To Sunil Chandra Bose*

Censored and Passed
Illegible
15/4/27
for D.I.G., I.B., C.I.D.
Bengal

Insein Central Jail
8.4.27
Friday

My dear Chotodada,

As you know I arrived here on the 25th March from Rangoon Jail. Insein is dry and breezy now but it will be very wet from the end of May onwards. It is not so hot as Mandalay. I have been informed officially that if I do not accept the Govt. offer, I shall be transferred to Almora Jail or Bangalore Jail or Ootacamund Jail in the near future—so my stay here is in any case a temporary one.

The temperature has been rising here as before e.g. 26th March—100.6°; 27th—99.2°; 28th—100.4°; 29th—100°; 30th—100.4°; 31st—100.4°.

Major Findlay examined me carefully the other day and found some suspicious signs—crepitations—on the right side below the scapula. Prior to this, the senior sub-assistant surgeon had examined me and he had made a note of the same signs.

A few days before I left Rangoon, I was given some mixture which was meant to be an appetizer. It did not however do any good.

I don't know if it is necessary to take anything by way of medicine. I am not taking anything now. I am having motor drives here since the 29th March.

The accommodation here is not as suitable as at Mandalay—but I have told Major Findlay that if I am going to be here for a short while, I am not going to bother. At present the bathroom, kitchen etc. are in another ward at some distance from where we are living. We are occupying the upper floor of the under-trial ward which is airy and roomy though rather hot during the day. I am getting some company here which I so badly needed in Rangoon Jail.

I have informed Mejdada already about my opinion on Mr. Moberly's offer.

I hope you have received my letter of the 22nd March. Please write to me when you have time. Hope this will find you all quite well. How is Natunmamababu?

Yours v. affly
SUBHAS

Dr. S. C. Bose., M.B., M.R.C.P., D.T.M.
38/2, Elgin Road
Calcutta

99. *To Sarat Chandra Bose*
Censored and Passed
Illegible
13/4/27
for D.I.G., I.B., C.I.D.
Bengal

Insein Central Jail
8.4.27
Friday

My dear brother,

Your letters of the 24th and 31st March were to hand on the 5th and 7th March respectively. I hope you have duly received my letters of the 14th March, 22nd March, 28th March and 4th April. The last two I have written from Insein.

I have written in great detail in my last letter re: the Hon. Mr. Moberly's offer. It is not necessary to repeat what I have said there. Apart from the difficulty of accepting an offer of conditional release, certain conditions are unsatisfactory, and the offer as it stands is therefore unacceptable. I take it that Govt. have said the last word on the subject.

I have not had any reply from the President, Bengal Legislative Council yet.

By the time this reaches you, the election of Aldermen,

Mayor and Deputy Mayor will have been over. If you can spare the time, why should you shirk the offer of election as Alderman ?

I sent a wire to you on Saturday the 2nd April saying that I had not received your letter of the 24th March.

The Govt. offer was communicated to me on Tuesday the 5th inst. by the I.G. of Prisons. It was precisely the same offer as was made before the Bengal Council. The same day I sent you two telegrams in succession. I am giving you the contents of the telegrams *from memory* :—

(1) "Your letter twenty-fourth March not received yet but Govt. offer being precisely what was stated in Bengal Council formally presented this morning stop certain points in Govt. offer appear vague and unsatisfactory stop desire interview for discussing details."

(2) "Received letter twenty-fourth March containing no further information stop Govt. offer unless modified in certain respects appears unacceptable consequently desire replying Govt. accordingly stop interview with you may be unnecessary wire reply."

I am having motor drives here since the 29th ultimo.

Insein is more or less like Rangoon—perhaps not so hot in summer—as far as I can gather. It is a rainy place. The rains commence towards the end of May and continue till October. I don't think it will be as hot as Mandalay but much wetter. I don't know if the climate would be better than Mandalay on the whole—I don't expect it will, at least for me.

The I.G. of Prisons told me before I left Rangoon that the question of sending me back to Mandalay was out of the question as *in any case* I would be leaving Burma. He offered me a choice between Rangoon and Insein—and after that incident in Rangoon Jail I had no option but to accept the latter.

The remittance you sent to Rangoon has been forwarded here.

I shall be writing to you on Monday again. I am writing to Chotodada today under a separate cover. I am anxiously awaiting a reply from you to my telegrams of the 5th inst.

referred to above.

Has Chotodada got my letter of the 22nd March ? The temperature is rising as before and is usually on the wrong side of 100°. Hope this will find you all quite well.

Yours v.affly
SUBHAS

S. C. Bose Esq. M.L.C.
38/1, Elgin Road.

100. From Sarat Chandra Bose

38/1, Elgin Road,
16th April 1927

My dear Subhas,

Your letters of the 4th and 8th April were delivered to me on the evening of the 13th instant. On receipt of those letters, I sent a telegram to the Superintendent, Insein Jail to the following effect :—

"Please inform Subhas received today letters 4th and 8th April stop shall wire tomorrow whether coming Insein."

I could not avail myself of the mail on Friday last nor could I send you a telegram as to whether I was coming to Insein as I was waiting to know what modifications (if any) in their original offer of last month Government were agreeable to. I had of course received on the 12th the Superintendent's telegram of the 11th informing me that you did not want me to come to Insein for the purpose of discussing the Government offer with you. But I thought that if any modifications were suggested which might be acceptable, I would come over and discuss the same with you. Moreover, I wanted to avail myself of the holidays to come and see you, not having seen you for well nigh two years.

Now about your letter of the 14th. I could well anticipate that the two main points for discussion were (I) about taking a boat direct from Rangoon to Europe and (2) about giving your word of honour that you would not attempt to come back home until the expiry of the Cr. Law Amendment

Act of 1925 (which has about three years to run, unless of course, it is further extended). I had a long discussion with Mr. Moberly on Sunday last on these points the idea being that after learning each other's views, I might place them before you during Easter. As regards (1) I suggested that you should be sent to Almora or any other dry hill station and released there, so that you may live there with some members of the family for at least three months. The objection raised was that it might become a place of pilgrimage and Government might want some sort of understanding that persons other than members of the family should not flock there; otherwise once Government released you in Almora they would have no further control in the matter of visitors. I said there might be some sort of understanding that visitors other than members of the family will apply for the Bengal Government's permission to see you in Almora. All this, of course, would be subject to your confirmation.

As regards (2) I found that Mr. Moberly was very stiff. I said that I did not understand why a word of honour was necessary or should be asked for. Once you went to England en route to Switzerland or any other Sanatorium you would need a passport to come back home and the India Office would consequently have control over your movements and therefore the question of giving your word of honour not to come back for three years could easily be dropped. Mr. Moberly did not agree. He said in fact that the Home Government could not appreciate their difficulties and a passport was treated in England more or less as a certificate of identity. After further discussion, I gathered that the only formula the Bengal Government might agree to was that if you desired to come back home, you would have to apply to the Government of Bengal for permission to do so and that they would lay down the conditions under which you could return to India. The matter rested there on Sunday last and I told Mr. Moberly that after I heard from him as to how far the Government were prepared to go, I would go to Insein and discuss the matter with you. Not having heard from him till the 14th I wrote to him on the morning of the 15th asking him to let me know Government's views. I got his reply yesterday evening in which he said that Government were prepared to agree to the following modifications, viz., that you will stay at Almora (en route to Europe) for three months with your relatives but that you should give your word of honour not to receive or communicate with any one there except relatives save with the permission of the Government of Bengal and (2) that you would undertake not to return to India, Burma or Ceylon except with the permission of the Government of Bengal and to abide by any conditions attached to such permission if accorded.

I wrote two letters to Mr. Moberly yesterday before I received his letter last evening, and in both of them I suggested certain modifications of the original offer made last month. Shortly speaking, my suggestions were that you should be taken to Almora or Bangalore or Ootacamund and released there, that you will be allowed to stay there for six months or such other time as may be necessary for your recovery and that the question as to whether you were to go to Europe or to live outside Bengal or to live in Calcutta or to be again detained under the Cr. Law Amendment Act should be left open for decision in future. I said in those letters that having had the advantage of knowing your views now, I thought that was the most satisfactory solution. Those suggestions have not found favour with Mr. Moberly and he has made the offer mentioned above. He has also said in his letter of yesterday's date that he has seen your letter to me of the 4th April. I wrote to him at Darjeeling this morning that I did not think that the modified offer of Government would be acceptable to you and consequently it was no use my going to Insein now.

I have really nothing to say regarding your letter of the 4th. I do think that no one—not even Government—can take exception to anything you have said. The sentiments you have given expression to are worthy of you and I hope the Lord will grant you strength—both physical and spiritual—to bear all the wrongs that may be inflicted on you.

I cannot conceal, however, our anxious concern for your health. I hope you will not attempt to take any physical exercise because that will do you harm. Absolute rest and evening drives are expected to do you good. What is most necessary is change to a climate like Almora and now that you have declined the Government offer, there is no reason why you should not be sent there at once.

Any one of us can come and see you at Insein any time you want us, whether there are holidays or not. So please don't hesitate to write or wire as the occasion requires.

Father was to have gone to Puri yesterday. He is fairly well but you can well imagine that his mind is not at peace on account of your illness. I have forwarded a copy of your letter of the 4th April to him.

I shall send you by next mail copies of my letters to Mr. Moberly. I am sorry I haven't the copies with me just now; otherwise I would send them on today.

This leaves us fairly well. Please let me know all about yourself and about the treatment the authorities place you or propose to place you under. I hope you have not lost any further in weight.

Yours very affly
SARAT

101. From Sarat Chandra Bose

38/1, Elgin Road
Calcutta
9th April, 1927.

My dear Subhas,

Your letter of 22nd March from Rangoon was to hand on the 1st of April and your letter of 28th March from Insein was to hand on the 2nd of April. The telegram which you say, you forwarded to the Inspector General of Prisons on the 21st March was not forwarded to me.

In your letter of 28th March last, you say that rains will commence at Insein in May and there will be continuous downpour till November next. I mentioned that fact casually to Dr. Bidhan Ray and he thereupon said that in his opinion Insein would be a bad place for you from May to November. Dampness will aggravate your illness—that was his impression.

I find from your second telegram of the 5th that you have received my letter of the 24th March and from your first telegram that Governmental offer was formally made to you. I have had correspondence with Government on the subject and enclose copies of same herewith (5 letters).

Are you feeling any better at Insein ? I hope you have not lost further in weight there. This leaves us fairly well.

Yours affectionately,
SARAT

102. To The Superintendent
Insein Jail

Insein Jail,
11.4.27

Dear Sir,

I desire to have the following telegram sent to my brother today and I shall be obliged if you be too good as to pass it.

Yours faithfully
S. C. BOSE

Telegram
Intelligence Calcutta
Please convey following message to Sarat Bose 38/1, Elgin Road from his brother.

Your telegram eigth replied Govt. today offer unacceptable. Interview for this purpose unnecessary

103. To The Inspector General of Prisons, Burma, Rangoon
Dated Insien the 11th April 1927
Subject—The offer of the Govt. of Bengal

Sir,

I am thankful to Govt. for the offer that they have been pleased to make and particularly so, for having taken the Bengal Legislative Council into their confidence over my case and for the consideration they have shown for my feelings in dropping all reference to my past or future conduct. But I regret that certain conditions introduced therein prevent me from accepting it.

2. The position that I have taken up from the very beginning is that I have ben imprisoned illegally without trial and without any justification. The people of India have all along looked upon the Bengal Ordinance of 1924 and its sequel the Bengal Criminal Law Amendment Act of 1925 as lawless laws promulgated and enacted for the purpose of suppressing their fundamental rights and liberties. In a civilized state no such law would be tolerated for twentyfour hours. The injustice which my incarceration exemplifies has been heightened since my election as a member of the Bengal Legislative Council for the parliamentary privileges—"the ancient and undoubted rights"—to which members of legislatures all over the world are entitled, have been denied to me. By committing people to custody for an indefinite period without trial or justification the Government have set at nought the fundamental principles of Criminal Law. By bringing the B.C. Law A. Act into force by certification after its rejection by the Bengal Legislative Council, the Government have exposed the sham which the legislatures in India represent. And by sanctioning an encroachment on parliamentary privileges (viz., immunity from arrest, detention and molestation) the Government have subordinated the legislature to the executive thus reversing the normal relation which should subsist between these two divisions of the body-politic. In these circumstances my release is demanded for undoing an act of injustice already committed and allowed to stand unredeemed.

3. I have always maintained that I am entitled to reparation for the physical and mental suffering I have been subjected to and for the pecuniary loss I have had to undergo. No one can repudiate this claim without giving the go by to all ethical principles, canons of equity and rules of fair play. From this point of view, the utter inadequacy of the offer will be quite apparent.

4. The Government are not so unsophisticated—and neither am I—as to think that the real and only purpose

of the offer is to give effect to the recommendation of Dr. Sunil Chandra Bose regarding treatment in a Swiss Sanatorium. The recommendation is undoubtedly a very sound one from the medical point of view but I can act up to it only when I am a free agent and my choice is unfettered.

5. My conception of honour, my duty as a political sufferer and my position in public life preclude me from accepting the conditions with which Government have been pleased to qualify their proposal. It is too late in the day to talk of conditions, when I have already been in jail for nearly 2½ years. To accept the conditions imposed by Government would be tantamount to admitting the validity of the act and it is impossible for me to surrender the position I have taken up. While the fight for constitutional liberty is going on—the honour of our nation is in our keeping and we cannot betray that trust. Much as I value my life—I love honour more and I cannot for the life of me barter away those sacred and inviolable rights which will form the basis of the future body-politic of India. I foresee the additional suffering which this attitude of mine will entail but I take it that it is a part of the legacy I inherited when I was born a member of a subject race.

6. I regret that I cannot see eye to eye with those members of the Government who may feel that they have been generously inclined in making the offer. But I have faith in human nature and I have no doubt that the decision I have arrived at is one which even members of Government will in their private moments not only endorse but appreciate.

7. In conclusion I repeat that I am thankful to Government for the offer of release but I would request Government to make it acceptable by dropping the conditions.

I have the honour to be Sir
Your most obedient servant
S. C. Bose

104. To The I. G. of Prisons, Burma, Rangoon.

Insein Jail
12. 4. 27

Dear Sir,

In view of the reply to the Govt. that I sent in Yesterday an interview with my brother will not be necessary. In connection with this matter I have conveyed to my brother through the CID to that effect after I sent in the reply. In these circumstances I would request you not to inconvenience yourself any further by holding up your latest programme.

Yours faithfully,
S. C. Bose

105. To Janakinath Bose

Jnsein Central Jail
13.4.27
Wednesday

My dear father,

My last letter to you was on 21/2/27 from the Rangoon Jail. I came here from Rangoon on the 25th March. Insein is a small but rapidly growing town at a distance of about 10 miles from Rangoon. There is a fine road from Rangoon to Insein as well as a frequent railway service. Insein is dry and breezy now and not very hot—certainly not as hot as Mandalay but it will begin to rain in May and the rains will continue till October.

You are aware by now of the reasons which induced me to leave the Rangoon Jail.

The Govt. offer was formally presented to me on the 6th inst. I took some time to think over the matter. On the 11th I sent a reply to say that the offer was unacceptable and I requested Govt. to make it acceptable by dropping the conditions.

I wrote to Mejdada on the 4th in great detail giving him

my reasons for not accepting the offer.

The offer which was formally presented was precisely the same as that which was stated before the Bengal Council on the 21st March.

I have been officially informed that if the offer is not accepted, I shall be transferred to Almora Jail or Ooty Jail or Bangalore Jail.

My health is much the same as before. I have some company here which I did not have in Rangoon.

I feel confident that you will approve of my decision which will also find general support among the public.

How are you keeping now? Hope this will find you all well at Cuttack and Calcutta. I believe mother is now at Elgin Road.

With my *pronams,*

I am
Yours v. affly
SUBHAS

J. N. Bose Esq.
Cuttack

106. To Sarat Chandra Bose

Insein Jail
13.4.27
Wednesday

My dear brother,

I am enclosing herewith a copy of the reply to the Govt. offer which I sent in on Monday, 17th April. I sent the following wire to you on Monday afternoon through Intelligence Calcutta.

Telegram

Your telegram Eighth replied Govt. today offer unacceptable stop interview for this purpose unnecessary and in a hurry to be in time for todays mail and shall not write more. Hope this will find you all quite well.

Yours v. affectionately
SUBHAS

107. *To Sunil Chandra Bose*

Jnsein Jail
13.4.27
Wednesday

My dear Chotodada,

I hope you have duly received my letter of the 22nd March and 8th April. Please keep Kaviraj Mahasaya informed about my health as I am not able to write to him as frequently as I would like to. Sometimes I do not write to Mejda when I happen to write to you.

On Monday I felt a pain on the right chest and told Major Findlay about it. The pain came down and was not acute. It was not extensive. Major Findlay examined me carefully, and noted some sounds. He ordered me to bed for a few days and I have had to drop the motor drive since then. Yesterday I felt a pain on the left shoulder—but the pain on the right side was less than on Monday. Today I am feeling somewhat better.

The temperature has been rising during the last few days as follows—

1st April—99.8°; 2nd April—100.4°; 3rd April—100.4°; 4th April—100°; 5th April—100.4°; 6th April—100.2°; 7th April—100.4°; 8th April—100.2°; 9th April—100.4°; 10th April—100.2°; 11th April—100.6°; 12th April—99.4°.

Major prescribed Codliver Malt which I shall be taking from tomorrow. He has also prescribed another medicine for cough.

Hope this will find you all quite well.

Yours affectionately
SUBHAS

*108. To Prabhabati Devi**

Mother Durga be with us.

Insein Jail
13.4.27

Revered Mother,

A long time ago I received your letter written on 25th February. Due to laziness I failed to answer your letter.

On 25th of Magha I was transferred from Rangoon Jail to this jail. This place is ten miles off from Rangoon.

My health is now in the same state as it was before and my health has not undergone any definite change after my transfer from Rangoon.

Knowing about the health of Polly I am worried and how is Polly now ?

How is Namamababu now ? Has he regained his health ? Does he come to Bhowanipur ? I am greatly worried to hear about the state of health of Natunmamababu. Who is now treating him ?

I am happy to learn that Gorarani's marriage has been performed nicely.

It is good that Sarada has gone to Gorakhpur. There she will be able to forget things. The chance of my getting released is almost nil. Everything depends on the will of God and I firmly believe that wherever I may be, I will always be protected by His blessings.

Where are Sejo-Jyathamoshai and others now ?

I have written to the Govt. that I cannot simply accept the conditions under which they are ready to set me free. I presume that you have heard about those conditions from my elder brother and I am not going to write about them in this letter.

Bestow on me the blessing always that I may never deviate from the path of duty. Ask others not to be worried about me. I am passing my days quite happily.

*Translated from the original Bengali.

Please accept my respectful *pronams*.
How are you all? How is father doing?

Devotedly yours,
SUBHAS

109. To Sarat Chandra Bose
Censored and Passed
Illegible
20/4/27
for D.I.G., I.B., C.I.D.
Bengal

Insein Jail
14.4.27
Thursday

My dear brother,

I had no time to write to you at length in my last letter. Your letter of the 9th April is to hand. I hope you have received duly—or will receive—my letters of the 14th March, 4th April, 8th April and 13th April. In my last letter (13th April), I enclosed a copy of the reply I sent to the Govt. offer. In my letter of the 4th inst, I stated all the pros and cons of Government offer (the letter is a long one) and have shown that it is unacceptable as it stands.

Have you written to Messrs Rafi and Chandoo thanking them for lending me their cars while I was in Rangoon Jail?

I had a pain in the right chest (or lungs—I don't know which) on Monday last, followed by a pain on the left side on Tuesday. Major Findlay examined me carefully on Monday and notice(d) sounds. He advised me to keep to bed all the time and give up the evening drives and I have been acting accordingly since Monday. The pain has subsided now, I hope it won't recur. I have written other details about my health to Chotodada on the 22nd March, 8th April and 13th April. I am feeling too lazy to repeat what I have written him. Please ask Chotodada to keep Kaviraj Mahasaya informed—as I don't feel up to writing many letters as I used to write before.

I have seen the result of the election of Aldermen on Monday last in the Rangoon papers of yestedray's date.

I know that during the rains Insein will be a bad place for me and the local authorities are desirous of seeing me off before the Monsoon breaks. I have been officially informed that I shall be transferred in the near future to Almora Jail, or Bangalore Jail or Ootacamund Jail.

No, I did not write to the Inspector General of Prisons for permission to interview you. The I.G. of Prisons took the initiative in obtaining the local Government's permission so that the interview, if it came off, would be expected. In the telegram I sent you on the 5th inst.—which the I.G. of Prisons happened to see as he was here then—there was a probability of the interview taking place.

After replying to the Government offer on the 11th inst. I wrote to the I.G. of Prisons on the 12th asking him not to inconvenience himself further by holding up his tour, as the interview was unnecessary.

Physically I am not better here than at Rangoon but I have some company here and am not troubled by hosts of prisoners living in adjoining cells. We are occupying the upper floor of the under-trial ward which is airy.

I shall shortly be sending you a list of books I want. Please ask the Book Company to supply them. Do you want Ronaldshay's *Heart of Aryavarta*? I have done with it. Please let me know if you want any other books I have with me at present.

Hope this will find you all quite well.

Yours v. affly
SUBHAS

S. C. Bose Esq.
38/1, Elgin Road.

110. To Sarat Chandra Bose
Censored and Passed
Illegible
25/4
for D.I.G., I.B., C.I.D.
Bengal

Insein Jail
20.4.27
Wednesday

My dear brother,

On the 11th inst. I sent you the following telegram through Intelligence :—"Your telegram eighth replied Government today offer unacceptable stop interview for this purpose unnecessary".

Since then i.e. on the 14th and 16th inst. two telegrams have come in and in the 2nd you say that you will come to Insein if a fresh offer from Government is received.

I have written to you on the 13th and 14h inst. Along with the former letter I have sent you a copy of my reply to the Government offer.

I think Lt. Col. Kelsall made it clear in the presence of Chotodada and Lt. Col. Tarapore that he had come to examine my present condition and give his opinion on it and that he was not concerned with the problem of my treatment.

I gave up Kaviraji medicine about the middle of January. In Rangoon an appetizing tonic was given me on the 20th March and the following days.

I have been keeping to bed under medical advice since Monday before last. The trouble started with pain in the chest which has now subsided, but complete lack of exercise makes me feel weak and affects my appetite further. Major Findlay wants to see if complete rest has any appreciable effect on the temperature—so I shall keep to bed for some time longer. The temperature has been slightly lower than before though the difference has been hardly appreciable as the following figures show :—13th April. 100° ; 14th—100.2° ; 15th—99.8° ; 16th—100° ; 18th—100.6° ; 19th—100.2°.

My weight is now 130 lbs.

Col. Tarapore came here yesterday and told me that he had received a wire from you enquiring if the pain in the chest was due to pleurisy. The Superintendent received a similar wire too.

Mr. Justice J. R. Das came to see me on Saturday the 9th April.

Please ask somebody to send me my copy of Bergson's *Creative Evolution.*

How is Mrs. Das keeping ?

Hope this will find you all quite well.

Yours v. affly
SUBHAS

S. C. Bose Esq.
38/1, Elgin Road
Calcutta

111. Sarat Chandra Bose

Insein Jail
29.4.27

My dear brother,

Bardada has come and gone. You will hear my views from him. I shall however try to recapitulate the conclusions if I feel like writing a long letter during the course of next week. At present I am not feeling up to it.

During the last few days the temperature has been rising .... ; My weight has dropped further to 128 lbs. I am still keeping to bed. It is rather tiresome at times but I have to be patient.

I doubt if these palliative measures will do me any good—while the general conditions and environment remain unchanged. As a matter of fact my condition has been going from bad to worse. I am thinking seriously of taking to Yoga as a curative. Yoga has its dangers as well and that is why I am hesitating. But I have no alternative and Yoga is the only means whereby it is possible that I may be able to save my life. It is no use shutting one's eyes to the fact that tuberculosis is an incurable and fatal disease and once the disease has set in, one can only seek to put off the evil day.

Hope this will find you all quite well.

Yours v. affly
SUBHAS

P.S. Do not be anxious on any account for my sake—for I am always prepared for the worst.

S.C.B.

S. C. Bose Esq.
38/1, Elgin Road.

112. To Sarat Chandra Bose
Censored and Passed
Illegible
13/3/27
for D.I.G., I.B., C.I.D.
Bengal

Insein Jail
The 6th May, 1927

My dear brother,

I do not feel up to writing a long letter and I must wait till I can summon sufficient energy for the purpose. I had a long heart-to-heart talk with Bardada about the Govt. offer and he must have acquainted you all with my views. I appreciated the opportunity given me of having a private interview and the Hon'ble Home Member has my profound thanks for the courtesy shown. It is a welcome departure from the sort of treatment hitherto meted out to me.

The reply from the Bengal Govt. which Bardada communicated to me on the 27th April (the day before he left) has made the issue clearer for both parties. Taking stock of the present position I have to say that I reaffirm the attitude I took up in my reply of the 11th April to the Govt. offer.

My decision follows directly from my general outlook on life and closer thinking only serves to confirm it. The longer I live in gaol, the stronger does the conviction grow within me that the struggles in this world are at bottom conflicts of ideas—conflicts between false ideas and true—or as some would like to say, between different degrees of reality or different degrees of truth. Ideas are the stuff of which human movements are made and they are not static but dynamic and militant. They are as dynamic as the Absolute Idea of Hegel, the Blind Will of Hartmann and Schopenhaur, the *elan vital* of Henri Bergson. Ideas will work out their own destiny and we who are but clods of clay encasing sparks of the Divine Fire have only got to consecrate ourselves to these ideas. A life so consecrated is bound to fulfil itself regardless of the vicissitudes of our material and bodily existence. My faith in the ultimate triumph of the ideas for which I stand is unflinching and I am not therefore troubled by thoughts about my health and future prospect.

I have stated my point of view clearly and unambiguously in my letter to Govt. and no sophistry is possible thereafter. I am sorry that some critics should be so unkind as to say that I am bargaining for better terms. I am not a shopkeeper and I do not bargain. The slippery paths of diplomacy I abhor as unsuited to my constitution. I have taken my stand on a principle and there the matter rests. I do not attach so much importance to my bodily life that I should strive to save it by a process of higgling. My conception of values is somewhat different from that of the market place and I do not think that success or failure in life should be determined by physical or material criteria. Our fight is not a physical one and it is not for a material object either. As St. Paul said, "We wrestle not against flesh and blood but against principalities, against powers, against the rulers of the darkness of this world, against spiritual wickedness in high places." Our cause is the cause of freedom and truth and as sure as day follows night, that cause will ultimately prevail. Our bodies may fall and perish but with faith undiminished and will unconquerable, triumph will be ours. It is, however, for Providence to ordain who of us should live to witness the consummation of all our efforts and labours and as for myself, I am content to live my life and leave the rest to destiny.

One word more before I close. It is not possible for me at this stage to decide whether I should go to Switzerland. I am at present physically incapable of undertaking a journey to Switzerland and I need preliminary treatment at some health-resort in India. How long it will be before I am declared as fit to travel abroad following a course of preliminary treatment—I do not know. One thing is certain—until I am very much better, a journey to Switzerland is from the medical point of view, out of the question. Further, if I improve remarkably well while I am at a health-resort in India, it may not be necessary at all to go abroad, except for the purpose of voluntary externment. Then there is the financial question—I shall have to consult my purse which is none too full. I shall also have to consult members of our family, particularly our parents, before I can decide to leave home and country for an indefinite period. The political situation in India may change during the next few months and the Bengal Govt. may of their own accord feel inclined to alter their angle of vision. All these factors have to be weighed carefully before I can finally make up my mind. Above all I would like to feel myself a free agent before I make my choice and I would prefer not to be stampeded into signing my warrant of exile. If the question of my compulsory residence in Switzerland is regarded by Govt. as a sine qua non—you need have no hesitation in breaking off all negotiations. God is great and certainly greater than his own handiwork—man—and while we trust in Him, we shall not come to grief.

I am pained to realise what anxiety and worry I have been causing in so many loving and sympathetic hearts. But I console myself by thinking that those who believe in a common motherland (I shall not say fatherland)—have a common heritage—and have to share their joys and sorrows.

Hope this will find you all quite well.

S. C. Bose Esq.
38/1, Elgin Road
Calcutta

Yours v. affly
SUBHAS

*113. To Sarat Chandra Bose**

Insein Jail
9.5.27

My dear brother,

My last letter to you was dated the 6th May. The same day I wrote to Chotodada as well.

As at present arranged I leave for Calcutta tomorrow or on Thursday next en route to Almora. I have already received orders for transfer and shall leave tomorrow unless the weather is too bad.

On the 6th Major Findlay communicated your wire to me asking me not to start Yoga pratice yet. The next day i.e. the 7th May I sent the following wire through Intelligence.

"Your telegram 6th shall await Mrs. Das's letter stop leaving Tuesday next for transfer Almora".

Yesterday I had a peculiar experience. I had pain in both chests which lasted about an hour. The sensation was exactly like that of cramps and as long as the pain lasted I felt awfully uneasy. The pain I formerly had was a dull one and in no way like this.

May be, I shall meet you before this letter reaches you. In the absence of any information to the contrary I take it that I am going to Almora Jail.

Hope this will find you all quite well.

Yours v. affly
SUBHAS

S. C. Bose Esq.
38/1, Elgin Road
Calcutta

[1] Translated from the original Bengali.

*114. To the Superintendent**
Insein Jail.

Insein Jail
10.5.27

Dear Sir,

As my people may feel anxious at my departure being postponed and may be alarmed by imagining that my condition has suddenly taken a serious turn I shall be obliged if you kindly pass the following telegram which I desire to send today.

Yours faithfully
SUBHAS C. BOSE

Telegram
Intelligence Calcutta

Please convey following message to Sarat Bose 38/1, Elgin Road from his brother. Begins, departure postponed owing cyclonic weather. Leaving Thursday unless I inform contrary.

*115. To Basanti Devi***

Kelsall Lodge
Shillong
14.6.27

Revered mother,

I arrived here day before yesterday—there was no particular inconvenience or discomfort on the way. I am feeling about the same since coming here—only one does not feel so tired in the absence of heat. It rains from time to time—it is depressing when it does. It would be nice if it did not rain. The scenery here is quite pretty although there is not the grandeur of the snowy ranges of Darjeeling. There will of course be some improvement due to the cool weather, but I do not know if my digestion will get better.

* With this letter ends the correspondence from Burma—Ed.
** Translated from the original Bengali.

Bhaskar Babu came to the station and travelled in the same train up to Barrackpore. How is Justice Das ? I should like to have detailed news of his health. Please let me know how you and all the rest are doing. All is well here. So long.

Devotedly yours
SUBHAS

116. To Satyendra Chandra Mitra

Censored and Passed
Illegible
28/6/27
for D.I.G., I.B., C.I.D.
Bengal

Kelsall Lodge,
Shillong,
The 25th June, 1927

My dear Satyen Babu,

I arrived here on the 12th. Shillong seems to be a cool and healthy place—except for the rains. The cold is bracing but uptill now I have not noticed any improvement in digestion. The temperature is still persisting—but the daily rise is much lower. The acute symptoms, viz., pain in the chest, troublesome cough etc. have abated and on the whole I am better than what I was a month ago. The weather is unfortunately against me—as also my chronic dyspepsia—otherwise I would have picked up much more quickly. However, let me hope for the best.

Anil Babu wrote to me from Pondicherry when I was at Insein asking me to accept the Government offer of the 21st March and conveying your opinion which agreed with his. Lt. Col. Tarapore also after he returned from Mandalay saw me at Insein and told me what your views were. However, I hope we are now all agreed that "All's well that ends well".

Life has been a romantic drama to me of late. From C.E.O.'s chair to the Alipore Central Jail was as sudden a transition as a transfer from the Insein Jail to His Excellency's launch on the Hooghly. I wanted to write about the details of my journey from Insein to 38/1 Elgin Road as they would interest you all, but I found that the newspapers gave practically everything. Only one point need be cleared up. You know that convict-warder Gafur, my attendant, was accompanying me. He was dressed in Khadi and on arrival at Outram Ghat was taken for a state prisoner by the *Englishman's* reporter.

The letter you wrote to your brother regarding parliamentary privileges and Mr. Patel's reply to you—has appeared in the papers. My letter to the President, Bengal Council, appeared in the press a few days before. I sent it to the press before I left Calcutta.

It is distressing to be released all alone, while all of you are still rotting in Jail. It is so difficult for me to feel at ease under the present circumstances—I feel as if a burden is pressing on my mind all the time.

I should be the last man to hold out any hopes to any friend in jail because I know from experience that no one can be sure of being released until he is actually set free. With this qualification I can say in a general way that the future is hopeful.

If I can be of any service to any of you while you are in jail and I am out—please do not hesitate to write to me. You can easily judge what is possible for me.

If there are any books I have left behind and you have done with them, please send them on to me at your convenience. My parents are here as also some other members of our family. They are doing well except my youngest niece who is almost a baby. She has been somewhat neglected owing to my illness which has drawn all the attention. However, we are now trying to have her treated properly.

Please show this letter to all my friends as I am not writing to any one else today. I am anxious to learn from the papers that Suren Babu is down with his old friends dysentery and dyspepsia. How is he doing now ?

With love to all,

I am,

Yours affectionaely

SUBHAS C. BOSE

Satyendra Chandra Mitra, Esq., M.L.A.
C/o. D.I.G., I.B., C.I.D., Bengal.
13, Elysium Row,
Calcutta

*117. To Basanti Devi**

Kelsall Lodge
Shillong
17.7.27

Revered mother,

I received your letter of the 10th July on the 13th inst. I did not write to you as I had promised—the fault is therefore mine and I hope to be forgiven. If a man accepts certain relationships, certain responsibilities also come upon him automatically and it is wrong for him not to fulfil those responsibilities. So there is no doubt that I am at fault.

You often say and sometimes even write: "my company cannot bring joy any more to anyone in this world". This is not at all true. Don't you know with what reverence the youth of Bengal (not mentioning others for the sake of argument) look up to you even today ? Is it not an injustice to them for you to consider them "outsiders" ? Have they not offered at your feet the best in themselves ? How they had hoped that when Deshbandhu left this world, you would come forward and take up their leadership ! When their hope was not fulfilled, where could they contain their immeasurable sorrow and disappointment ? In his time Deshbandhu used to say that you might not openly participate in public work so long as he was alive, but in his absence you would fill the void left by him.

Perhaps you will say that a Hindu woman's duty lay

* Translated from the original Bengali.

within the limits of her family—behind the scenes and not on the public platform. I do not have the impudence to offer advice as to the duties of my mother. But I think this is not a normal phase in the life of our country and society. Mother, today our house is on fire. When the house is on fire, even a woman observing *purdah* has to take courage in both hands and come out on the street. She has to work as hard as a man to save her child, to protect valuable property from fire. Does that detract from her prestige or grace ?

The spiritual quest of Bengal has always been voiced through the cult of the Mother. Be it God or be it motherland—whatever we have worshipped we have done so in the image of the Mother. But alas ! Today the menfolk of Bengal have become so impotent and cowardly that they are incapable of preventing the molestation of women that is going on in the districts of Bengal. The other day (several months ago) *Sanjeebani* wrote—"O Mother, you must take up arms yourself to protect your honour". I was touched by these words. Indeed, the condition of our country today is very much so ; what is more, most probably the mother will have to come forward to protect the honour of her children as well—the nation has become so degenerate and cowardly.

Sometimes I have the feeling that if you could occupy yourself with various public welfare activities, that would perhaps at least partially lessen the agony of your mind. Is it proper that our life should be entirely controlled by domestic weal and woe ? You were an Empress once ; today you are a pauper in the material sense. Whoever thinks about it cannot but feel a pang in his heart. But we have this consolation that from time immemorial the people of India have considered the glory of renunciation to be greater and more covetable than the fortunes of a king. Perhaps you are not even aware how high you have risen in the estimation of your countrymen because of your background of glorious renunciation.

I do not know whether it is childish on my part to say all this to you ; my only justification is that the deep sorrow that afflicts you also haunts me now and then,—may be to a lesser degree; and it will be no exaggeration to say that so does it affect countless youngmen of Bengal.

You wrote in your previous letter—"everything in my cursed life has come to an end. Now there is nothing else for me but to wait patiently for the final end. I do not know how many ages must pass before I reach my fulfilment".

I am afraid due to excessive brooding you sometimes forget where your place is in the hearts of your countrymen and in our hearts. Had you not forgotten this, you could never have described your life as "cursed" despite these terrible domestic disasters? Those whom the God loves are victims again and again of sorrow and disaster. Is this absolutely untrue? And the bigger a man's heart the more he gets his share of sorrow—is this also entirely untrue? Please fulfil our hopes and desires—your place shall always remain secure in the hearts of your countrymen. The devotion, the respect, the affection that the people of your country have offered at your feet—and are still offering and will continue to offer—could any so-called fortunate man expect even a tenth of it. Deshbandhu has left us with many of his hopes and dreams unfulfilled. Those dreams of his are his best legacy. You have also inherited that legacy along with us. So, can you honestly declare that your work is done and the time has come for you to quit? It would be impudent of me to say so but still I wish to say that your God will never support your stand but rather support me.

You have written "it is here that my soul has a perfect union with mute nature. I like this dense, impenetrable darkness". Perhaps, nowadays you like darkness all the time—well, everyone likes darkness at least now and then. If you love darkness can't you also love the light that lies hidden in darkness? What is wrong with that? The light is meant to make everybody happy, by bringing the glow of happiness.

Perhaps you do not wish to have any bonds—be they of work or of human relationship. But we have no other way. The day we called you 'mother' we accepted the relationship. This bond is not to be severed—at least not in our lifetime. In this material world there are narrowness, obstacles, social obligations—but in spite of all this, kinship of the spirit can never be false.

Man hankers for a corner in his life where there will be no arguments, no critical judgment, no intelligent appraisal but only "Blind Worship". That explains the creation of "mother". I pray to God I may go on worshipping 'mother' in this spirit.

My health is better than it used to be. I feel stronger. I am sleeping well (may be a little too much) and indigestion is a little better. I may have gained in weight but I cannot be sure because I have not checked it. I shall recover quickly if my digestion improves further. It is raining a lot—I do not like this incessant rain. Incessant lamentation is a fact of this world but laughter is perhaps equally true. So, it is not that we are not happy when the moon shines.

I have given expression to a lot of silly ideas—in the hope that I shall be forgiven. Please let me know if all is well with you. Please accept my respectful *pronams*.

Devotedly yours
SUBHAS

P.S. The list of donors of the Seva Sadan has come with me. I am sending it back by registered post within a couple of days.

118. To Santosh Kumar Basu

Kelsall Lodge
Shillong
18.7.27

My dear Santosh Babu,

Kindly go through the enclosed letter and other papers in connection therewith. Sj. Anil Chandra Biswas is the Asst. Secy. of the South Calcutta Sevak Samity and is our best worker. You probably remember that he got into trouble as he was *alleged* to have confined and assaulted an agent provocateur of the name of Divakar Mukherjee. Though Anil Babu managed to escape the hospitality of

His Majesty's Guest House at Alipore—he lost his job (a seven year old one) as a sequel to this incident. He is a political sufferer in every sense.

I am interested in Anil Babu for more reasons than one. He has been my right hand man in the field of social service for the last 5 or 6 years. Without him, the Sevak Samity would not have been what it is. Secondly he is in great pecuniary trouble as a result of several bereavements and mishaps in his family. Thirdly he has lost his job for having the courage to stand up against the police at very great risk and sacrifice. I therefore feel it to be my duty to help him in every possible way.

I do not desire to approach Mr. Sengupta myself, being doubtful how far that would help. I am therefore writing to you as a last resort.

I confess I am greatly disappointed at the attitude Kshitish has taken up. But I still hope that if strong support is forthcoming from some quarter, we shall be able to get Anil Babu in, in spite of Kshitish's opposition. I hope that once you are interested in Anil Babu's case—you will, with your characteristic vigour and driving power, be able to see matters through.

It is not necessary for me to write more. I shall feel content that you at any rate will do your very best in the matter.

I am progressing though not very fast. Hope this will find you quite well.

With kindest regards,

Yours v. sincerely
SUBHAS C. BOSE

P.S. If there is any attempt to reopen the question of the grant of a plot of land to the Baidyasastrapith—for the purpose of withdrawing the gift already made by the Corporation—I hope you will be there with all your energy for frustrating that attempt.

SUBHAS

119. To Satyendra Chandra Mitra

Censored and Passed
Illegible
28/7/27
for D.I.G., I.B., C.I.D.
Bengal

Kelsall Lodge,
Shillong,
25.7.27

My dear Satyen Babu,

Your letter of the 5th inst. reached me on the 17th inst. The lower half of the second page and the upper half of the third were however missing.

We selected Shillong after a good deal of cogitation owing to several reasons. In spite of its proximity to Cherrapunji, it is not so rainy as Kurseong or Darjeeling at this time of the year. This was the verdict of all those who have been to both places and I find that they are right. Moreover, unlike Kurseong and Darjeeling, if it rains in the morning here, it is usually bright in the evening and vice versa. Simla and its vicinity are no doubt drier but my doctors advised me not to undertake a long journey in my present state of health. There were other minor advantages e.g. accessibility to my relations and my doctors etc. which had to be considered. I was at first doubtful whether Shillong would be a right choice but I am now satisfied that we were not wrong. It is possible as you suggest, that Col. Kelsall's name had some mysterious influence in the matter.

Both my Doctor brother and Dr. Bidhan Roy were here—Dr. Roy left only the other day. I have decided not to take up any work until I am quite fit—at least that is what I feel now—though, as you can easily understand, this period of inactivity is in some respects exceedingly painful.

I am very much concerned to learn about the ill-health of Messrs. Chakravarti, Ghosh and Ganguli though I feel so helpless in the matter.

I received my silk loongyi from Mandalay when I was

in Calcutta, though I did not expect it, as I had left it for the prisoner Maung Tin, who used to massage me. I had spoken to the Superintendent about this and had promised to leave the loongyi for him which he would get on his release. I am afraid the poor man must have been awfully disappointed. Did I forget to tell you when I left Mandalay that I was leaving the loongyi behind purposely for Maung Tin ? I am ready to send the loongyi back to Mandalay for Maung Tin in order to redeem my promise. I have a faint recollection that I received a book along with that, though I forget which. If you can send me the name of the book, I shall verify my stock and see if that book is with me now. By the way, have I left behind my Michael Madhu Sudan Dutt's works and some books of Bhudev Mukherji including 2 vols. of *Bibidha Prabandha* ? The books may be with Suren Babu if they are there at all. Please ask him and let me know.

The D.I.G., C.I.D. having kindly agreed to pass it, I sent you on the 22nd inst. a copy of this year's Deshbandhu Number of *Forward*. Elysium Row will send it on to you in due course. I have enquired of the D.I.G. if he would pass *Bichitra* a monthly magazine in Bengali recently started in Calcutta by some of Dr. Tagore's following. I have the first issue with me and shall send it on to you as soon as I get the necessary permission.

I have nothing more to write for the present. My second brother (M.L.C.) was here on a visit for about a week. He has gone down with his family as my little niece was ailing. She is better now and is on the safe road to recovery.

I shall be glad to hear from the others and promise to reply to them if they write. For the present I am not writing to them separately but I hope they will not mind it.

I find that Bipin Babu's letter to his people regarding the Govt. offer has appeared in the papers.

I am improving steadily and intend to be here for some time longer. With fraternal greetings to all,

I am,

Yours affly

S. C. Mitra Esq. M.L.A. SUBHAS CHANDRA BOSE

P.S. I sent you a copy of the *Illustrated Weekly, Times of India* and the *Indian Pictorial Magazine* some time ago when I was in Calcutta. Did you get them ? They were sent to the Jail Superintendent.

S.C.B.

*120. To Basanti Devi**

Kelsall Lodge
Shillong
30.7.27

Revered mother,

In my previous letter out of impudence I had tried to enlighten you about your duties. You have affectionately forgiven my childishness. I have more than my share of impudence, otherwise how could I aspire to achieve the impossible ? After all, we are a pack of vagabonds.

It is not because of our lack of self-confidence that we are still looking up to our mother. We have enough self-confidence, perhaps a little too much. Still why do we want our mother ? The reason is that no worship is complete if we leave the mother out. In our social history, whenever we have faced danger and misfortune we have invoked the Mother. We have created the image of the Mother with all that was best in our being. Our national struggle began with the song "*Bande Mataram*" (salutations to the Mother). That is why we are calling upon our mother in this manner. But will not the heartless image respond ?

As I am proclaiming to myself that I am a son of the mother—bless me so that I may not do anything that will sully the name of my mother. I do not have the impertinence to declare that I shall be a worthy son of the mother. My path is full of thorns—bless me so that I may march on in the same way till the last. May my life not wither away in the desolation of *Sannyasa* ; may my life blossom forth in beneficent fulfilment with the touch of the inspiration that

* Translated from the original Bengali.

is behind this desolation—I crave for this blessing. Need I say how I value your blessings ?

Looked at from one point of view there is no limit to my impudence ; on the other hand I am always troubled by the thought of my unworthiness. It is not an imaginary conflict—it is very real. I always pray to God—"Grant your chosen one the strength to carry your banner". Still, sometimes I get apprehensive that I may not be able to give to the country what she expects of me. I am afraid that my boat may not sink in midstream—that my attempt may not turn out to be like that of a dwarf trying to reach up to the moon ! Would you not give me a word of assurance ?

There is something else I wish to say—I have been trying to say this for some time but I could not. Your son has a duty and a right. Shall I always be deprived of my right to serve you ? Shall I forever remain an 'outsider' to you ? In this vast world, is the narrow family circle created by man the greatest truth ? You have much to give—your country is still waiting for that. It is not an idea manufactured in my brain—it is the voice of your country. But whether you'll give your due or not depends on you. If the country does not get what it expects to get, the country is unfortunate, what more can I say ?

You have written—"The trends of thought and the line of action cannot be the same for the old and the young". True, but many old people can be found among the so-called young and among the so-called old, a number of youthful people. If the youth consider you to be one of them, if they wish to bestow their leadership on you—what objection can you have to that ?

The question I put to you in Calcutta has been solved. The answer is that if you do not accept our leadership there is no one else in Bengal whom we can accept from our heart as the leader. If someone is invited to be the chairman of a meeting he does not necessarily become the leader. There are many such leaders in Bengal. But a real leader—to whom one's heart bows down with reverence is rare in Bengal today. If we do not get you, then this pack of vagabonds will have to fend for themselves. Your blessings will undoubtedly be a priceless thing for us but we want a little more than that.

We are fairly well. My sister's health is better. Mother is also well. I am also gradually getting better but my weight is not increasing so well. Of course, I do not want to gain in weight—but the doctors are keen about it. Every day we go out and have a good walk.

I had found Shreemati Aparna Devi's health in a very bad state. How is she ? I hope Minu and others are well. Let me have news of all. How is Justice Das ?

Please accept my respectful *pronams*.

Devotedly yours
SUBHAS

P.S. The other day I heard from mother that you had a suggestion about a medicine for my illness in a dream. But neither did you give me the medicine nor mention anything about it. I am very upset to hear this. Would you treat me as an outsider forever ? You know very well that I would have gladly and respectfully accepted any medicine that you gave me.

*121. To Bivabati Bose**

Kelsall Lodge
Shillong
7/27

My dear Mejobowdidi,

I got your letter dated 13th July in due time. Here it sometimes rains heavily and then for two or three days its intensity diminishes and we get light rains. After you left we had three or four bright sunny days. We take walks in the afternoon (provided that the weather is fine) and all join in it. If it does not rain we walk a mile.

After medically checking up Polly's chest Bidhan Babu said that the trouble on the right side of the chest which he

* Translated from the original Bengali.

diagnosed earlier was no longer there. Meanwhile as Polly was suffering from stomach upsets Bidhan Babu prescribed a medicine for her. Anyway Polly is certainly a little bit better than before. Yet it so happens that she has aged untimely and lost the zest of life which pains me very much. Polly is taking regularly twice a day Bengers food for her stomach trouble and as a result suffers less from it. Biswa is quite well—he does not behave like a cry-baby, though he is rather lonely and does not get much scope for play. I myself do not indulge in sports much nowadays and I think, I have grown oldish. It seems mother is now comparatively well. Bidhan Babu checked her blood-pressure and said it was within 140-145—but her right-hand thumb has not yet cured. I do not know what form it will take (the state of her right-hand thumb).

By reducing the number of domestic staff no inconvenience has been created—though it means more work for Kalu Singh. Though the burden of work on Biru Buro has been lessened, yet he has started playing truant, but it seems he is feeling less restless. Yesterday I told him (Biru Buro) "If you don't feel like working take the railway fare from me and go back to Calcutta. Don't you think that we are being inconvenienced by your absence?" Today, it appears he is in a better mood.

The fruits reached us undamaged, though just one promegranate went rotten. No *Makarajdhaja* from Kavirajmahasaya came to me yet. Kavirajmahasaya is not ready to allow me to pay the price of the medicine, but I feel so ashamed of taking the medicine free of cost. This is the reason why I have refrained from writing him asking him to send *Makarajdhaja*. I think I can do without *Makarjdhaja* now—I took it for five weeks. But, I think, Polly needs that medicine.

We are happy to have news about *Natunmamababu*. Meanwhile I wrote a letter to *Nutanmamima* and got a reply.

We got the coat sent for Polly by parcel. I hope that Chhabi is by now well, cured of the fever. I am sorry to learn about Chhabi's marriage being arranged. Though they

(Chhabi's guardians) are not prepared to listen to our advices, yet on our part, it is our duty to ask Swaraj Babu ardently not to arrange her marriage—and then leave the rest to Chhabi's fate.

How are Chhaya and Radhu? Has X-Ray treatment done any good to Chhaya?

Have you been to Belta? How is mother?

I am so so. My digestion is not very satisfactory. I have not taken my body-weight all these days. Anyway I have gained some weight after coming here—though I am not quite sure about it. The weighing machine is lying in a dilapidated state. There is no scope for getting it repaired here. I wanted to send the broken part to Calcutta with Bidhan Babu for repair but I just forgot to do so. Bidhan Babu carried with him a pair of socks and two pencils for Ami, two scarves and also a letter written to you by mother and I hope you have got all those things.

(Unfinished)

*122. To Bivabati Bose**

Mother Durga be with us.

Kelsall Lodge
Shillong
3.8.27

My dear Mejobowdidi,

I duly received your letter of the 28th July. It has been raining here day and night for the last few days—it cleared up somewhat today and we all went out for a walk. How are you feeling nowadays? How is Mejdada? Please request him on my behalf that he should stop dining so late. During the few days I was in Calcuta I noticed irregularity about his meals. Probably even I have never been so irregular myself. Please also request him on my behalf to rest for the month of September. Health is more valuable than money—although money is badly needed now. His position is such

* Translated from the original Bengali.

as they would say in English—that he cannot afford to be ill. He is not a vagabond like myself, so that it hardly matters whether I live or die.

Polly is improving steadily—but the progress is very slow. Miss Harmen saw her today after a long time and commented that she had improved considerably. Whenever it is possible to go out, she walks about a mile. She is also not so depressed mentally nowadays—she keeps herself fully occupied teaching the child. Your sympathetic attitude to Polly has made me very happy.

Mother is nursing a bad finger—fomentation has not done much good. It looks as if the trouble will continue till the end of our stay.

Bir has not been particularly troublesome these days. The chauffeur has been working well all along. Minor repairs had to be carried out on the car. The bill for June and July has come to Rs. 30/-. The car is behaving well now.

We received the fruit parcel yesterday—the fruits were in reasonably good condition. Lalit (Nani's husband) has also sent a fruit parcel through a friend—we got it yesterday.

I felt happy that you went down to Calcutta as a matter of duty. I could appreciate from the very beginning that it was not right for you to stay on here. I therefore told you repeatedly and wrote to Mejdada that you should not feel embarrassed in any way. I would feel extremely sorry if you had continued to stay here for my sake neglecting your duties and at personal inconvenience. Considering the path that I have chosen for myself, putting other people to inconvenience and trouble for my own comfort would be a great sin. I know the ideal is very difficult to live up to and I cannot always prevent trouble and inconvenience to others on my account; even so, I must function with this ideal in front of me as far as possible.

What you have written about money is true, but what I wrote in this regard is also correct. For one who is earning it is desirable to have the feeling that money is a worthless commodity. He will then not have selfish or miserly tendencies. But this cannot apply to me. To me every rupee is extremely valuable. Whenever I spend a rupee on myself I have the feeling that I would be happier if I could spend it on somebody else. I cannot get rid of this feeling and perhaps I should not (speaking from my point of view, not yours). Once having accepted the ideal that I must give away my personal fortune to the last pie for public welfare, I must not allow even a trace of selfishness to enter my mind ; if I do, I am doomed. In spite of all that I have said, the fact remains that I am quite selfish and I do so many things in my own interest. Because, one cannot attain one's ideal so quickly and prolonged effort is necessary to conquer selfishness completely.

I would not feel happy at all if *Nabowdidi* came here at her own or *Nadada's* inconvenience. I would be happy of course if she came here for giving Chhaya and Radhu a change of climate. I must always keep myself prepared for all kinds of situations and the necessary preparation has to be over a long period of time. Otherwise, if I am faced with an adverse situation all of a sudden, I shall not be able to keep my mental equilibrium. I used to be an utterly inferior being and extremely weak-minded ; whatever strength I have been able to muster has been the result of continuous internal struggle during the last sixteen or seventeen years. There is no end to this struggle because there is no limit to one's mental elevation ; the more you rise, the more is the desire to rise further. The result is that the struggle goes on and on.

Well, I have written so much rubbish—I hope you will not mind, I am not mad, but if you take me to be one I will not mind. Eccentricity to a limited degree is useful, is it not ? Is it desirable to be absolutely level-headed ?

I am not worried about myself—I am quite well. Polly is probably feeling somewhat lonely. There is nobody here of the same age.

Please let me know when something is decided about Rangamamababu's coming here. Please ask Asoke to send me the books.

The weighing machine has come back after necessary repairs. But it does not record correctly. There is variation of two to four pounds. Please tell Mejdada that my weight now is 144-146 pounds. On my arrival from Calcutta it was

134 pounds.

I wish to read "Mother" once again. If possible, please send the book through somebody. I have a mind to write a review of the book.

I have found a solution of the question that was exercising my mind so much.

Did Mr. Saha bring milk for father at Santahar station during your journey back to Calcuta ? None of you have mentioned about this in your letters. It is necessary to send him a letter of thanks.

My views about my stay here are as follows :

(1) If necessary, I shall go down to Calcutta about the 20th or 22nd of this month—to attend the Council. After the Council session is over, I shall leave Calcutta and go somewhere.

(2) If all of you come up to Shillong in September, I shall return to Shillong. Then towards the end of September (or, if possible, about the middle of October), we shall go down to Calcutta all together.

(3) If you and the children do not accompany him, Mejdada will not probably agree to come here alone. He will say that he does not need a change, that he is keeping quite fit and that he should rather earn some money in Calcutta. But if you tell him that children need a change, he will not be able to refuse. If it is so badly necessary to earn during the vacation, he might as well spend the month of September here and October in Calcutta. But it is absolutely essential for him to take rest for a month at the least.

(4) If you come, Bardada, Bowdidi and others may come also. Your room is lying vacant—you have only to come and occupy it. Bardada and Bowdidi will take my room. I can stay in the cottage with the older children (viz., Asoke, Ami) ; that will give me a chance to occupy the cottage.

(5) If nobody comes here from Calcutta in September, I do not wish to return here at the end of the Council session. In that case, I would rather go to Cuttack or Puri.

(6) If my attending the Council does not materialise and nobody comes here in September, all of us who are here

now may go down towards the end of this month.

I have written so much. My health is steadily getting better. My digestion has also improved. I am taking very light dinner nowadays, viz., Bengers food, toast, etc.

I hope all is well at home. Please accept my *pronams*.

Yours affectionately
SUBHAS

123. To Santosh Kumar Bose

Kelsall Lodge,
Shillong
6.8.27

My dear Santosh Babu,

Your kind note of the 2nd inst. was to hand this morning.

I am so glad that you have taken up both the cases in right earnest. With regard to the second case you will have to be vigilant and insistent in your demand. You know what Mr. J. C. Mukherji is like. You will have to get the signature of appointment made in your presence before you can be sure that your candidate will be accepted. Of course, he has difficulties—so many masters to serve. Unless you can force things, you won't get what you want.

The second applicant writes to me to say that here are two vacancies going—stock verification officer (pay 150-200) and Market Superintendent of Entally. He cannot, of course, get the latter job straight away. He will have to get in as Market Inspector—which is not a bad job I think. If you want to get anything done—please go into Mr. J. C.'s room and sit tight till you get what you want. If you leave it to him you can rest assured that nothing will be done.

Regarding the first case, please have the clause regarding teachers' training certificate deleted when the matter comes before the E.G.P. Committee.

I shall eagerly await your next letter. I have already told you (when I met you in Calcutta) what I expect of you in the present ramshackle Corporation. I have said that, because I believe that you will fully rise up to popular expectation. What is more, I expect you to enter on a wider field of activity in the days to come.

I am improving steadily though not very rapidly. I have an evening drive and a little walk as well. I have gained in weight and strength, only my indigestion is still giving trouble. I hope to get rid of it gradually.

Trust this will find you quite well.

With kindest regards,

Yours very sincerely
SUBHAS CHANDRA BOSE

124. To Satyendra Chandra Mitra

Confidential

Kelsall Lodge
Shillong
The 7th Aug. 1927

My dear Satyen Babu,

So glad to receive your letter of the 2nd August from S. S. Ellenga this morning. I am eager to know the details of your journey from Mandalay and how our friends there are doing. I find a brief note regarding the Bengal detenus in Burma in *Forward* of the 6th inst. (Dak Edition).

Did you get my letter of the 25th (twentyfifth) July before you left Mandalay ? Your letter to me from Mandalay Jail reached me in a mangled form—the lower half of the 1st page and the upper half of the 2nd. page were missing.

It is desirable that you should attend the Assembly session to represent the cause of the detenus. We were expecting a lively debate there, but there is a slight apprehension now that with your release, the popular wrath might be somewhat appeased. Your presence there should stiffen the public demand and strengthen the opposition. You will have to make your maiden speech if you attend and it is exceedingly necessary that the speech should be well-prepared. There is no harm if you read out a written speech, in case you do not like to speak extempore.

The detenu question is sure to come up before the Assembly. You will have a very busy time for at least a couple of months. There will be a continuous stream of visitors, I am afraid, including our friends of the C.I.D. incognito. Please manage to make time to think and write out your speech. The more thought you bestow on it, the greater effect it will have.

I do not know if we could meet before the Assembly sitting as I shall be here. However, if by any chance you can manage to come up to Shillong, you will be thrice welcome.

Please let me know about your future programme and movements when convenient.

Apart from attending the Assembly, it is not necessary that you should rush to the political arena. I am aware that you mentioned that point in your message to the Free Press. We shall have to act as peacemakers and try to settle differences as far as possible.

Hope this will find you quite well. I am improving steadily.

Yours affly
SUBHAS

P.S.

In writing to me, please do not forget that my letters are usually tampered with at the Post Office. Did you receive the Deshbandhu number of *Forward* at Mandalay which I sent you ?

S. C. B.

Satyendra Chandra Mitra Esq.

125. To Sarat Chandra Bose

Shillong
11.8.27

My dear brother,

I hope you have received by now the telegram I sent you yesterday re. Mr. Sengupta's proposal. I also wrote to you yesterday by ordinary post elaborating what I had mentioned in my wire.

I find in today's *Bengalee* (10th Dak edition) that the European Councillors will remain neutral on the occasion. If this be true then the votes of the Hindu Councillors will decide the fate of the resolution.

I have received a letter from Dr. Roy today. He is willing to allow me to go down for the no-confidence motion —but does not desire that I should take part in the proceedings—apart from voting for the no-confidence motion. I am replying saying that I desire to speak on the detenu question and the Jail Com. report—but if the party consider that to be unnecessary, I won't be obstinate. I am also saying that so far I have not committed myself about attending the Council (in spite of the questions and resolutions, which do not necessarily mean that I shall attend) and that I shall leave Calcutta as soon as the session is over—in case I do attend. I shall await the party mandate regarding my attendance.

I find in the Bengal Council rules that it is *not right* to give publicity to resolutions until they appear in the list of business (vide Rule 70 note). I believe this rule is observed more in the breach.

I am sending a letter to Rajen Babu (Dev) thanking my constituents for electing me etc. I shall ask him to have it printed and distributed to the voters. This will mean some expenditure in connection with printing and I shall ask Rajen Babu to send the bill to you. Rajen Babu thinks that besides publishing it in the press it is advisable to send it to the voters individually.

I know that Upen Babu would not lend his name as Editor of *Atmashakti*. However that does not matter—Taranath Babu will do. I believe Gopal will be back by the end of September.

Hemanta has not—I understand—written to Polly or Biswa since they arrived here. This means that he did not approve of her coming here. Mother says that she will have to stay as long as Polly will be here—otherwise Hemanta will object to Polly's staying here. I thought at first that Polly would not be allowed to stay here after August—but mother says that if Hemanta continues his silence and does not expressly demand that Polly should be sent down—she would like Polly to stay till the end of September or as long as I shall be here...Mother is not unwilling to go down in spite of what she says and Polly is prepared to stay here in her absence but unless some other lady (or ladies) comes up—mother will not go. The last word that mother has said on this point is that she will decide after Rangamamababu comes up. To sum up her attitude, if she thinks that she can go down without causing us any inconvenience, she will do so—otherwise not.

Kaloo Singh does not want to go down now but is prepared to stay here till the end of September. He only wants to reach Kurseong by the time the Pujah commences, that is, the 3rd October. I communicated what you wrote to me and told him that he was free to leave Shillong by the end of this month or to accompany me, if I went for the Council session. But he has of his own accord volunteered to stay here. He desires that you should send Rs. 100/- to his people to enable them to make Pujah purchases.

If I go down, I do not think it will be necessary to take any attendant with me.

I am thinking of asking Ramanath Babu to look out for a good cook to be engaged from September in case you come up.

I was suggesting that you should come to Shillong, from the point of view of economy and convenience. If you think that Kurseong would be preferable, I am quite willing to go up to Kurseong at the end of the Council session. In that case we can all go down about the 20th and leave Calcutta for Kurseong about the 1st of September. I can fall in with any proposal which may suit you.

I don't know why A. G. is delaying so much over the matter. It is a simple affair.

I think at each session of the Legislative Council you should do something to "nurse" your constituency. I don't know if you have done anything so far. It is hardly possible to do anything substantial but one has to make a show—by means of questions and resolutions. Bijoykaka neglected to nurse his constituency, with the result that at the end of 3 years he made himself unpopular with his constituents.

I am suggesting to Nalini Babu that meetings should be held all over Bengal on the 22nd August next to demand the release of the detenus and condemn the report of the Jail Committee.

We are pretty well here. Hope all well there.

Yours v. affly
SUBHAS

P.S.

It is likely that after removing the ban the Burma Government are contemplating prosecuting the Editor of *Forward* for sedition or some similar charges.

S.C.B.

Important

P.S.

Please consider if it would be desirable to publish a statement in the *Forward* on the following lines "A correspondent of *Forward* called on me at Shillong to enquire if I would attend the Council. I replied saying that I was entirely in the hands of my medical advisers but that personally I wanted to attend the Council for the sake of the Jail Com. report and the detenu question. I had consulted many of my friends and well-wishers and constituents and they all advised me to abide by the advice of the doctors. I was in communication with my medical advisers and their advice would decide the question. I had of course told them that in case they permitted me to attend the Council, I would leave Calcutta as soon as the Council was over. My doctors did not think that I was yet fit to resume my work and I entirely agreed with them. But if they allowed me to go down just for a few days I would gladly do so."

The above statement will be a message alleged to have come from the Shillong correspondent of *Forward*. I have indicated the general lines, Dr. Roy or any one else can make out a draft for the press.

*126. To Bivabati Bose**

Mother Durga be with us.

Shillong
11.8.27

My dear Mejobowdidi,

Your letter of the 5th instant was to hand on the 8th. The postal mark on the envelope shows "1 p.m." but the letter failed to catch the Mail the same day. Please get somebody to enquire by what time letters must be posted at the Elgin Road Post Office to catch the Assam Mail. Letters posted at the G.P.O. by 2 p.m. get the Mail the same day.

It has been raining heavily this month—so we missed our walks from time to time. Nevertheless, nowadays I do not mind being confined to the house so much as I used to do before.

You do not appear to have been able to finalise your plans as yet. It looks as if you are not so keen to leave Calcutta. But I have something to say : the house will after all not grow wings and fly away. Once it has come into existence, it will stay where it is. You will get plenty of time to organise the household—so why worry so much about it ?

The bad finger is still giving mother a lot of trouble. Mother says that she will probably have to be here so long as Polly is here.

My digestion has improved somewhat on Bengers food. The weighing machine has been repaired—but it does not record as correctly as before. I have gained some weight since coming here. Polly appears now to have improved in health and looks cheerful. Biswa is all right.

Please let me know how you all are. We are well. Please accept my *pronams*.

Yours affly
SUBHAS

* Translated from the original Bengali.

*127. To Bivabati Bose**

Mother Durga be with us.

Shillong
(1927)

* * *

If children could stay on here, they would have improved further in health. However, it was good that they went back —their studies will not suffer. I only thought that when so much is being spent on the establishment here, the more it was profitably utilised the better—at least that would make me happier. That so much money should be spent on my account hurts me very much ; this may just be one of my weaknesses. But, you cannot so easily change one's nature.

The Sarabhais (Ambalal Sarabhai) left on the 17th inst. by steamer. They will arrive there probably about the 25th. It will be nice if you will ask them to tea one afternoon. They will probably not be there for more than a couple of days. I have asked Bidhan Babu to show them round the Seva Sadan.

Please get all the children to read Kashiramdas's *Mahabharata* and Krittibas's *Ramayana ;* Jogin Babu's editions are perhaps the best. He has rendered the old Bengali of Kashiramdas and Krittibas into the current language and has written in verse. They are thus easy for children to read. The more I grow up the more I realise that the Mahabharata and the Ramayana provide the fundamental basis of our civilisation. It is a pity that I never read the Mahabharata and the Ramayana well and from end to end.

I have asked Asoke to keep apart the books I need and to send them on through somebody if possible. Among them he should include the Bengali dictionary (the one I brought from Rangoon) and Shakespeare's Works. I want the edition in small type of the Complete Works of Shakespeare. The book is probably in the old house.

* Translated from the original Bengali.

Have you finished reading "The Mother". How did you like it?

I felt rather uncomfortable after you all left suddenly. The empty house gave a forlorn feeling—the mind became restive—I seemed to have lost for a while the moorings of my daily life—it will be no exaggeration to say that I felt a pang in my heart. I have not had such a feeling for a long time. I used to think that I had risen above worldly attachments. Now therefore, Nature ordainded this blow to bring it home to me that I was not yet entirely non-attached. I shall not discuss for the present if this is a matter of joy or sorrow.

After the initial blow I started to deliberate within myself the cause of such a state of mind. The self-analysis is continuing. People like me must become completely non-attached; otherwise there will be only more and more sorrow in store for them. When the call from prison came three years ago and I rose from my bed one morning to proceed to Alipore Jail, my mind did not waver even for one moment; I went along quite unconcerned and then spent two and a half years in prison with equanimity. All this time I had all but shaken off my attachments to worldly life. But that never caused me any pain. Then, why am I in this state today? Is this weak-mindedness, or the effect of aging or is it the result of being away from home for a long time?

However, I have since been settling down again. Of course, I miss company. But that does not affect me much. The azure sky, green fields, the mountain ranges all around, the play of light and shade in the forests, the continuous roar of the waterfall,——all this keep me contented. They keep me satisfied both in body and mind. When it clears up a little, I move out and engage in a silent communion with Nature and the poet's words come back to me.

And this our life, exempt from public haunt
Finds tongues in trees, books in running brooks
Sermons in stones, and good in every thing.

I would probably not have this experience if I were in a crowd. To lose one's being in the beauty of Nature has a steadying effect on the mind. To try to understand the language of Nature is of course a difficult task. To be able to do so even to a limited degree fills one's heart with joy.

Well, I have said enough nonsense—I hope you will not mind. As a result of living with and arguing with the English, even a shy and diffident person like me has become garrulous.

I have not decided yet what I should do during the Council session. Please let me know your programme for the Puja vacation when it is finalised.

How are you keeping nowadays? Are you sleeping better—or is insomnia still persisting? Have you got rid of the pain?

What more can I write? Please accept my respectful *pronam* and convey my love to children.

Yours affectionately
SUBHAS

I am sewing up the letter (not the envelope) and sealing it. I should like to know in what state the seal reaches you.

SUBHAS

128. To Sarat Chandra Bose

Kelsall Lodge
Shillong
19.8.27

My dear brother,

I shall leave for Calcutta on the 21st by the mail. I shall not probably send you any wire.

One of my questions has been disallowed by the President. I am sending the question and the Secretary's letter for publication in *Forward*.

Forward published 4 or 5 of my questions. I had 11 (eleven) in all—why did not they publish all? Some of the questions are of general public interest and need publicity. Please remind Satya Babu about this.

In order to appease Dr. Roy I have sent you a wire today asking if the doctors have permitted me to go down.

I have not been able to complete my criticism of the Jail Com. report. In these circumstances I had better not publish it at all. An ineffective criticism is worse than no criticism. I and Harish have however written a criticism of the Borstal School Bill which should be published without delay.

I hope vigorous canvassing of each individual M.L.C. is going on with a view to turning out the Ministers.

I have received Rs. 300/- through Harish and Rs. 100/- by T.M.O.

More when we meet. We are pretty well here. Hope all well there.

Yours v. affly
SUBHAS

P.S.

I shall probably take the Borstal School Bill criticism along with me. Just received your wire re—doctor's permission.

S.C.B.

6 p.m.
19.8.27

*129. To Basanti Devi**

Kelsall Lodge
Shillong
12.9.27

Revered mother,

I duly received your letter of the 2nd inst. I wrote to you on my arrival here—I hope the letter reached you all right. It rained here continuously for a week after my arrival, —as if it was Bhadro[1] at its worst. However we are having sunshine since yesterday. The sky is still overcast—so I presume it will be raining, more or less, all through this month. My digestive troubles are still there—otherwise I am well.

I shall be here the whole of September. If the house is

* Translated from the original Bengali.
[1] The most rainy month in the Bengali Calendar. Ed.

available for another month, I may also spend the month of October here. If not, I shall return to Calcutta in the beginning of October. Thereafter I am thinking of going to Purulia or Sijua. Please let me know when you propose to leave for Purulia and how long you will be there. Who else will be with you at Purulia ? Where has Sudhir Babu decided to go with his family ?

How are you keeping ? Do you still have heart-trouble ? Will you please write about your health in some detail ?

Devotedly yours

SUBHAS

130. To Satyendra Chandra Mitra

Kelsall Lodge
Shillong
26.9.27

My dear Satyen Babu,

I have received all your letters—the first through Lalmohan Babu and the next two by post from Simla. Your letter of the 22nd inst. from Simla is just to hand.

I have not written to you by post purposely—because all our letters are being tampered with. I have been waiting eagerly for a personal interview and chat.

You should by all means go to Mymensingh since it has been represented that through your mediation Dr. Bipin Sen may be elected Chairman. But if Dr. Sen does not desire your assistance, please do not trouble about going there. You should decide after hearing from Dr. Sen.

I am here till the middle of October, since the house has been taken till Oct. 15. After that I go down to Calcutta. I may go down by steamer from Gauhati as the river trip will be pleasant or I may go by train. The details will be settled when Mejdada arrives here (he is due here this evening). I shall write to you more definitely as soon as we come to a decision and you can then decide whether you should come up to Shillong or await me in Calcutta. I understand that Dr. Roy will also be arriving here this evening. If I find that your presence here will be required here (sic) for any urgent consultation, I shall take the initiative and ask you to come up—instead of waiting for me in Calcutta. If I do not take the initiative, I shall leave it to you to decide whether you should come up. It is needless to say that in any case you are always welcome here. Only give us timely information so that we may make the necessary arrangements.

I have met Messrs. Sasmal, Satkaripati Roy, Abanish Roy, Sailesh Bishi, Pratap Guha Roy, Sushil Bannerji and Sja Urmila Debi since my release. I have called on Sja Urmila Debi twice. I shall leave no stone unturned in the attempt to compose all differences and unify the different groups.

Henceforward we should all make it a habit to write in sealed registered covers—at least in sealed covers—if at all we communicate through the post. The reason is obvious.

I shall certainly be going to the Madras Congress unless unforeseen circumstances prevent me.

Do you know exactly when Pandit Motilal will leave England for home ?

Do you know if Mahatma Gandhi is going to support Dr. Ansari in his proposal that Congressmen should accept ministry ?

Have you got the letter which I wrote to you at Mandalay just before your release ? I think that was the second letter I wrote to you after your release. If you have not yet received it, I intend to write to Mr. Lowman about it.

I am eagerly and anxiously looking forward to our meeting. Hope this will find you well. I am improving.

With love,

Yours affly
SUBHAS

131. To Satyendra Chandra Mitra

Kelsall Lodge
Shillong
1.10.27

My dear Satyen Babu,

I have written to you by *ordinary* post a few days ago under sealed double cover to your Calcutta address, 122 Bowbazar Street. I have received all your letters duly.

The weather is not satisfactory here as it has been raining here continuously. The place has become monotonous to me and we are going down about the middle of this month (October). I shall not venture on a river trip as I apprehend that weather will still continue to be unfavourable. I shall meet you in Calcutta on my arrival.

In the meantime I would suggest that you should do two things. Firstly, you may go and look up Anil Babu at Pondicherry. I had a talk with Abanish Babu in Calcutta and he told me that both of you would probably go to Pondicherry. Abanish Babu is very much interested in Anil Babu—and rightly so. Whatever the result may be, we should make an attempt to bring Anil Babu back and who could do this better than you and Abanish Babu ? I believe Abanish Babu will gladly meet all the expenses. So, as soon as you are free, you can take a trip to Pondicherry. You will be able to return by the middle of the month and we can then put our heads together and settle our plans. It will make a great difference if we are fortunate enough to get Anil Babu back amongst us.

During the last 6 or 7 months I have received 3 or 4 letters from Anil Babu but have not replied to them, as I apprehended that the letters would be tampered with in transit. If you do go to Pondicherry, I shall write to Anil Babu direct by registered post under sealed double cover—explaining my position and according him a most hearty welcome. You know I have the greatest regard and affection for Anil Babu and his departure from Bengal was a terrible blow to me, from which I do not think I have recovered yet.

My disappointment today is so keen because I expected so much from Anil Babu. You will certainly explain all this to Anil Babu verbally when you meet him.

There is one other matter regarding which you could do something immediately. Some young Zeminder M.L.C.s, mostly Hindus, have joined together and formed a party called the Union Party. The shining lights in this party are Nattore Maharaja, Messrs Satyen Ghosh Maulik, Sachin Sanyal (of Puthia), Srish Nandi, Altaf Ali etc. If we could influence them in our favour, we shall be able to turn out the next ministry. On the last occasion we moved earth and heaven and we failed—and with one or two exceptions, they all voted for the ministers. Soon after the Council session, this party was formed and they issued a manifesto saying that if the ministers were not chosen out of their party, they would oppose the formation of a ministry. No doubt Sir Pravash is one of their Party patrons—but he accepted office without consulting them and the Governor also did not care to consult them. Owing to this, the Union Party is at present smarting under a feeling of indignation and if they could be approached before Sir Pravash gets hold of them—they might promise to vote with us against the ministers. In this affair we shall have to forestall Sir Pravash. I am almost sure that if Sir Pravash gets hold of them before we could—it will be impossible to persuade the Union Party to side with us. You will have to begin this work by tackling Sj. Satyen Ghosh Maulik. On the last occasion I personally went to Sayten Babu's house but I failed to get him round. This time you will probably be able to do so. I also called on Nattore Maharaja twice and spent several hours with him but he was adamantine. These young Zeminders—or at least many of them—told us that they had already given their word to Messrs Chakravarti and Ghaznavi. If we approach them first on this occasion—they will not be able to put forward this plea, though they may be able to invent new ones.

If you are able to leave for Pondicherry, please drop me a line giving the date of departure. Please be very careful about what you write by post. We should take it for granted that they are tampered with and no letters should be preserved. We are so so. Hope this will find you quite well.

Yours affly
SUBHAS

*132. To Basanti Devi**

Kelsall Lodge
Shillong
1.10.27

Revered mother,

I duly received your letter of the 24th September. I wrote you three letters since coming here—the last two addressed to 2, Beltola Road. I hope you have duly received all of them.

I have been keeping well on the whole, in spite of continuing heavy rains. Two of the children have been taken ill—but there is nothing serious. Mejdada has come back. Dr. Roy has come also—Goswami was to have come but has not. Dr. Roy told me that you had written to Goswami for the house at Benares. Mr. Haldar arrived here with his family two or three days ago.

We shall go down by the middle of October—I have not decided where I shall go thereafter. Probably I shall spend the rest of the month in Calcutta. I need hardly say that I should like to come and stay with you. But I am worried about the crowd. I am not sure that I would like to be in a crowd. I did not request you to come here, also on account of the crowd—although I had initially expressed a wish to that effect. Anyway, I shall make up my mind after reaching Calcutta.

What you have written about Bihar *Khaddar* is true. But, will mere criticism lead us anywhere ? One must participate in the work.

Please give some thought to the duties and tasks awaiting me. When I see you, my first question will be about this. I hope you know how highly I value your opinion.

* Translated from the original Bengali.

I do not wish to take up any work now without consulting you.

I hope all is well with you. Please accept my respectful *pronams.*

Devotedly yours
SUBHAS

*133. To Basanti Devi**

Kelsall Lodge
Shillong
15.10.27

Revered mother,

I received your letter of the 6th on the 9th inst. I hope you received the two or three letters I wrote to you in the meantime at 2 Beltola Road.

Please, accept my respectful *Bijoya pronam.*

You have written: "Do not expect any help from me in any matter whatsoever." I was deeply hurt to read this. I felt hurt not for myself but for the sake of my country. These are critical days for Bengal. There is a serious dearth of "wholetime" workers. It will be no exaggeration to say that Mr. Sengupta has nearly given up Congress work. Kiron Babu has served me a notice that in October he will pass all the burden on to me and retire. I do not now find much enthusiasm or eagerness on Tulsi Babu's part in national work. You know the Big Five—excepting Tulsi Babu all of them are professional people, so they cannot devote much time to Congress work. At the moment only Bidhan Babu is interested in the work of the B.P.C.C. but even he has very little time. The treasury of the Congress is absolutely empty. None of Deshbandhu's relatives is available for national work. You happen to be our only hope but even you want to wash your hands of all responsibility. Having observed all this, I have been thinking for some time why must it all be my headache, why must I alone carry this unwanted burden to my own spiritual detriment? Politics

* Translated from the original Bengali.

is not a suitable field of work for me. It is only by chance that I have drifted into the whirlpool of politics. Now I can avail of this opportunity and go back to my chosen field. I have no attachment to the material world, so I chose not to enter wordly life. I do not see any reason why in the present condition of the country, I should leave the path of peace, create a new worldly snare and get myself enmeshed in it.

The country needs you—the political prisoners want you. They have requested me again and again that I should convey their wishes to you. I was also vain enough to think if I went to you as their emissary you would never be able to say 'No'. God has spurned my pride. I came out of jail full of hope but now I find that it was only a false hope. Many of those on whom I had relied most do not want to worry about national problems, not to speak of devoting themselves to national work. Tears come flowing from my eyes when I think of the present condition of the Congress. What a skeleton of the Congress we see before us today—is it for this skeleton that Deshbandhu laid down his precious life? Relations, friends, colleagues and followers of Deshbandhu who had the opportunity to know and understand him closely show lack of faith in national work most of all. What is the reason for all this?

You are foremost among those who have neglected to do their duty after Deshbandhu's death, because even though his body has perished, his unfulfilled hopes and dreams reside in you. Even though you are the symbol of that spirit and you have so much influence, you do not wish to do anything. I say this out of a deep sense of sorrow—please forgive my impudence. It is for the last time that I am expressing my heartfelt sorrow and regrets. I will not trouble you any more.

I had thought I would visit you at the beginning of this month or may be in the beginning of November. Now I realise that it would be useless to go to you. I have to find the way out all by myself. It is futile to try to achieve something which is beyond one's means. Bengal is most unfortunate, otherwise the Congress would not have degenerated like this within such a short period of time.

One word more and I shall stop. I have never flattered anyone in my life, I do not know the ways of saying things in order to please somebody. When our leader was living and everyone said the things that would please him, I said unpleasant truths and quarrelled with him. I did never say nor shall I say anything merely to please you. Your countrymen want you—they have immense respect for you and faith in you. All factions will obey you, accept you and do as you say. This is my sincere conviction and I have conveyed that to you. I have never said, nor shall I say anything just to please you or flatter you. I know where your place is in the hearts of your countrymen and your "position" in this country and I have simply told you about that. I do not want any party in the country to exploit you; if I had any misgivings that any party wished to establish its power by exploiting you, I would have told you so. It is not that any particular party wants you—the nation as a whole wants you. You are a big asset in national work, so we want to keep you away always from factionalism. The nation wants you—not in order to exploit you but to follow you.

You have an individuality of your own; even when Deshbandhu was living you had your individuality. That is why the public have so much faith in your capacity. The "better minds" of this country are not totally unreasonable. The 'better minds" do not claim from you anything that is improper. They do not want you to go about making speeches here, there and everywhere. They want your faith and inspiration in national work. They want your advice and counsel, they want to proclaim to the world that you have taken up the work begun by Deshbandhu as your life's mission, they only wish to see that Deshbandhu's unfulfilled hopes and desires achieve success and fulfilment in your life.

Those who followed Deshbandhu in triumph as well as in misfortune are prepared to follow you today with the same devotion. If you do not believe in what I am saying, you may find it out for yourself. You may easily find out if Bengal would not rise and fall at your command.

Anyway, I have written a lot. Please forgive me if I

have said anything improper. I am not a mercenary soldier. I do not pledge myself so easily but when I do I do not turn back. You will always have full claim on my "loyalty and devotion" whether or not you choose to "use" them. For the present I shall have to chalk out my path by myself. Where it will lead to I do not know.

Most probably I will not be here for long ; so, if you write it will be better to do so at my Calcutta address. I have not decided on my programme for November—I may spend it away from Calcutta (may be at Kurseong or somewhere in Upper India). I shall be glad to hear that all of you are well.

Devotedly yours
SUBHAS

P.S. I saw in the newspapers that Madame Zaghlul had herself taken over the work of Zaghlul Pasha. Madame Sun-Yat-Sen has been carrying on her late husband's work for a long time. The whole Egyptian Nation has accepted Madame Zaghlul as the "Mother"—she has not rejected the devotion, respect and trust placed upon her by them. But India alone is unfortunate !

*134. To Basanti Devi**

38/1 Elgin Road
Calcutta
20.10.27
Thursday

Revered mother,

I received your letter day before yesterday just when I was leaving Shillong. I arrived here yesterday. Mejdada, Bowdidi and others have not returned as yet—they are expected on Sunday or Monday next. They were held up as Neru developed fever. Ami and Mira came down with me. Parents are here now—they will probably leave for Cuttack on or about the 1st November.

* Translated from the original Bengali.

Bidhan Babu will be coming back on Sunday or Monday. How long more will you be there? All is well on the whole both here and at Shillong. Neru had remission of his fever even before I left Shillong.

Please accept my respectful *pronams*.

Devotedly yours
SUBHAS

*135. To Basanti Devi**

38/1 Elgin Road
Calcutta
24.10.27

Revered mother,

I arrived here safely this morning. All are well here.

Mejdada, Mejobowdidi and the rest of the children reached here this morning. Neru did not have fever again. He is well but very weak. Dr. Roy also arrived today. I hear Mr. Srinivas Iyengar will be coming tomorrow.

I shall be meeting Satyen Babu, Kiron Babu and others this afternoon. I hope all of you are keeping well. Please accept my respectful *pronams*.

Devotedly yours
SUBHAS

136. To Sarat Chandra Bose

38/2 Elgin Road
28.2.28

My dear Mejdada,

I think it is becoming increasingly necessary to decide whether or not we should discontinue the Associated Press service in *Forward*. It is clear that with regard to the Commission they have instructions from Delhi and London to carry on a violently pro-Government propaganda. On the other hand, the Free Press are standing us in good stead. The Associated Press have been suppressing facts and even

* Translated from the original Bengali.

giving lying reports about Calcutta and Bengal since the hartal. Satya Babu has warned Iyer but to no avail. Evidently he is helpless—because he is acting under instructions.

From the national point of view, we cannot do without the Free Press Service. Therefore we must keep it alive for at least 2 years by all the means at our disposal. Two courses are open to us :—(1) Finance the Free Press from the Congress Fund. This may help Free Press financially—but it will neither cripple the Associated Press, nor will it enhance the prestige of Free Press.

(2) Institute the Free Press Service in *Forward* in place of the A.P.I. This will help F.P. financially, enhance its prestige and at the same time hit A.P.I. If we give up A.P.I., the *Amrita Bazar* will certainly give it up and others are likely to follow suit.

I have had a talk with Satya Babu re—this and he thinks that between the F. P. Service and our own correspondents' service—we shall be able to do without A.P.I. If we give up A. P. I. altogether as the *Bombay National Herald* has done —we shall get a comprehensive service from the F. P. As matters stand at present, F. P. do not feel encouraged to arrange for a more expensive and comprehensive service without being sure of support.

Please have a talk with Satya Babu and call a meeting of the Board if my suggestion seems acceptable to you.

There is another matter re—which a decisive step should be taken by the Board viz. advertisements in *Forward* and *Banglar Katha*. The Board should have a discussion on this point as well—with a view to arriving at a decision.

I am sending some outside papers for your perusal. You will be able to compare the service given by A.P.I. and the F.P.—re—the Commission and Boycott propaganda.

Yours affly
SUBHAS

P.S.

Nirmal Babu is here now—but he will leave for Delhi on the 3rd. March I think.

137. *To Motilal Nehru*

1, Woodburn Park,
Calcutta
July 18, 1928

My dear Punditji,

I sent a wire to you yesterday morning regarding Congress Presidentship and I received a reply last night.

I cannot tell you how disappointed the whole of Bengal will feel if for any reason you decline the Congress Presidentship. Your close association with the work and policy of the Swaraj Party is one of several reasons for which your name is universally acceptable in this province. I will not refer to the other provinces but I am almost sure that when the final nomination is made, the whole of India will stand unanimously in your favour.

The situation in the country today is such and the year 1929 will be such a momentous one in the history of our country, that we can think of nobody else who can rise to the occasion. We have heard of some of the alternative names suggested and in other circumstances they would have been worthy of consideration but when serious attempts are being made for a rapprochement between different parties and for the drafting of an agreed Constitution, none of the alternatives suggested can be accepted. I am not exaggerating matters when I say that if for any reason you decline the Presidentship, the effect would be so disastrous in this province that it will seriously affect the success of the Congress session. At a time when we are passing through a serious crisis, may we not hope that you will respond to the nation's call?

With profound regards,

I am,
Yours respectfully
SUBHAS C. BOSE

P.S. I have received your wire regarding the voting strength of the District Boards. I am trying to collect them but I doubt if I shall succeed. It will take a lot of time to compile these figures after getting the electoral rolls from the different districts.

138. To Amrita Lal Chatterjee

1 Woodburn Park
7.8.28

My dear Amrita,

I have not met you for a long time. Enclosed please find a letter from Sj. Girija Sankar Chowdhury who was formally in-charge of the Orphange and was arrested under the ordinance. Is it possible for us to take him back? If so, what salary can we offer him? I would like to have a talk with you regarding this matter. Kindly come over to 1, Woodburn Park on Thursday next at 8 a.m. in the morning and bring Girija Babu's letter with you.

Yours affectionately,
SUBHAS

Srijukta Amrita Lal Chatterjee
83 Lansdowne Road
Local

*139. To Basanti Devi**

C/o S. K. Basu Esq.
E. Road
Jamshedpur
3.10.28

Revered mother,

I arrived here yesterday. I am fairly well. I am leaving for Nagpur tonight—and shall be back in Calcutta probably on the 12th. How are you all? I hope there was no discomfort on the way.

With *pronams,*

Devotedly yours
SUBHAS

* Translated from the original Bengali.

140. *To Basanti Devi**

C/o S. K. Basu Esq.
E. Road
Jamshedpur
15.10.28
Monday

Revered mother,

I hear it has been published in the newspapers that I was coming to Purulia on the 16th. I do not know how the news leaked out, because my trip is still uncertain. I wish to return to Calcutta this week and also visit Purulia on the way. But I cannot stay there long because from what I can gather from letters from Calcutta, my presence there is urgently necessary. What I apprehend is that if I go to Purulia, I shall be stuck up there and there will be more delay. I am therefore considering if I should return to Calcutta direct. Anyway, if I decide to come to Purulia, I shall let you know by wire.

I hope all is well there. I am well on the whole.

With respectful *pronams*,

Devotedly yours
SUBHAS

141. *To Basanti Devi***

1 Wooburn Park
7.11.28

Revered mother,

I returned from Delhi today. I am leaving for Jamshedpur tonight. I shall be there for a week. How are things over there ? I met Sudhir Babu—he has appreciably improved in health. My address will be—27 E Road, Jamshedpur. How long will you be there ?

Please accept my respectful *pronams*.

Devotedly yours
SUBHAS

* Translated from the original Bengali.
** Translated from the original Bengali.

142. To Amrita Lal Chatterjee

1, Woodburn Park
Calcutta
19.3.29

My dear Amrita,

There is an application on behalf of an orphan for admission into the Sevasram. I am sending Sushil Babu to you to narrate the details. Please admit him if possible.

Yours affectionately
SUBHAS

Sjt. Amrita Lal Chatterjee
83, Lansdowne Road.

*143. To Basanti Devi**

C/o. Dr. Bidhan C. Roy
Shillong
16.6.29

Mother dear,

Tday** I am here. After coming here I have had some physical rest. But I have had little time to think. It is necessary to have some time to think. I am rushing along like a storm—it is necessary to understand whither I am going—towards good or evil. Besides, I need self-analysis—it is not possible to carry out self-analvsis unless there is time enough for it.

Mother, do bless me today with all your heart. I know your blessings are showered upon me day and night without my having to ask for it. Still I pray—do bless me on this particular day; there is some other significance in such blessings.

Mother, I am an absolutely unworthy and useless son. Your love is taking me towards full manhood. Mother,

* Translated from the original Bengali.
** The day happened to be the death anniversary of Deshbandhu C. R. Das.—Ed.

bless me so that in lives to come I may have the good fortune of having a mother like you.

He who was at once my friend, philosopher and guide in my life's mission—is no more. Today I am utterly destitute. You are the only refuge of this helpless person. Even if I lose everything else while going through vicissitudes of fortune, conflict and struggle, may I not lose your affection ever!

And, please think it over and tell me the path I should take in future.

Your utterly useless but
loving son
SUBHAS

*144. To Kalyani Devi**

1, Woodburn Park,
Calcutta
On way to Calcutta
26.10.29

Dear Sister,

I received your letter quite some time ago—I felt both happy and pained to read it. I should have replied to you already, but I have been continuously on the move for about ten days now. I am trying to write to you today on the way from Delhi to Calcutta. Because I do not know what is in store for me in Calcutta—most probably I shall not easily get a chance to write. When you wrote to me, mother was in Purulia—but you did not know about it.

I have been shy by nature since my boyhood—and I continue to be so till today—in spite of the fact that I go about making speeches at public meetings. Whatever I may be—I am not a vain person—because I know that I have nothing to be vain about. Where I surrender, I do so with all my heart. You know very well how I look upon you all.

People of the Punjab have, on this occasion and everywhere, given me love, kindness and honour in an abundant

* Translated from the original Bengali.

measure. This was all due to Jatin Das's self-immolation. In fact, the atmosphere of the Punjab appears to have changed completely.

My programme is now so indefinite that I cannot say if I can make a trip to Purulia ; chances of that are very remote.

Please accept my love and *Bijoya* greetings and convey the same to Bhaskar Babu. Please convey my respectful *pronams* to your father-in-law and mother-in-law. My love to the children also.

Yours affly
SUBHAS

P.S. I am back in Calcuta. I was not arrested—the Magistrate let me off on bail.

SUBHAS
27.10.29

*145. To Basanti Devi**

BENGAL PROVINCIAL CONGRESS COMMITTEE

....
Calcutta..........19
5.11.29

Telegraphic Address
"BIPISEESEE"
Phone No. 2952, Barabazar
No..............

Revered mother,

I returned from Delhi yesterday. I am sure you have read news of all that happened there in the papers. Jawaharlal has now given up Independence at the instance of the Mahatma.

How are you all ? Who are staying there with you now ?

Preparations are well under way here for the fight—the elections are due on the 16th and 17th. Mr. Sengupta

* Translated from the original Bengali.

and his group are making a desperate effort to drive us out of the B.P.C.C. Let us see what happens. Most probably we shall not lose. I am fairly well. Please accept my respectful *pronams* and convey my love to all.

Devotedly yours
SUBHAS

*146. To Basanti Devi**

1, Woodburn Park
Calcutta
9.12.29

Revered mother,

I have not been able to write to you for a long time. For some time I have been going through difficulties. I think I have not had such trouble since my release. The feeling that your good wishes are always with me gives me limitless solace and strength. I hardly know what would have happened to me at this difficult time if you were not there. But, then, although I can always feel your presence, I need hardly say that I wish very much to be near you. I do not know when I shall be able to come.

I carried out effective propaganda among the youth when I visited the Central Provinces last. Meanwhile during my absence, they have elected me as the President of Trade Union Congress.

Sengupta's party tried repeatedly to outmanoeuvre and destroy us but so far without success. Our dispute is now in Pandit Motilal's hands. Even though we did not do anything unfair in the elections, I somehow apprehend that Panditji will support Sengupta and invalidate the elections to B.P.C.C. and A.I.C.C. from Sylhet.

I am now considering when I should go to prison—before or after Christmas. I think my conviction is certain. I do not know what will happen if there is a change in policy from higher quarters—but personally I do not entertain much hope of a general amnesty.

Well, what is the good of writing about dry political

* Translated from the original Bengali.

matters ? A meeting with you would be most desirable ; there was so much to talk about but I see no way of coming over.

May your love and blessings help me grow up to be a real man—is my hartfelt prayer. It looks as if I shall never be a real man.

The help that was expected of Dr. Roy at this time of our difficulty has not been forthcoming. Nirmal Babu is doing a lot.

How is your health ? How are all the rest there ?

Devotedly yours
SUBHAS

147. *To Basanti Devi**

On way to Lahore
24.12.29

Revered mother,

For some time now since you left Calcutta, I have been passing through all sorts of anxiety and struggle. Every day I feel like coming to you and seek your love and blessings. But that is perhaps not to be. It is so difficult to liberate myself from the trammels of work. Even so, the feeling that your love and blessings are always with me gives me sustenance. When I feel mentally tired out, your love and blessings bring me new life. It is indeed true that in my life there is no other treasure or refuge. I do not know if the course I have taken is the right one—you will please show me the path of truth. May I shake off all my failings and unworthiness with the strength that comes from your blessings ! What more can I write—I am on the way to Lahore. I hardly know what will happen there.

Time and again my opponents have banded together and tried with all their might—to defeat me. By the grace of some Unseen Power I have also been able to foil their attempts. I cannot of course say what the final outcome

* Translated from the original Bengali.

is going to be. But, please remember that the son's victory means a triumph for the mother ; the son's defeat is a defeat for the mother.

Your unworthy son
SUBHAS

*148. To Basanti Devi**

1, Woodburn Park
Calcutta
6.1.30

Revered mother,

I returned here this morning. The trial has started already today.

I have not had any news of you and all others for a long time. How are you all ?

I am fairly well. Is there any possibility of your coming here ?

Devotedly yours
SUBHAS

*149. To Basanti Devi***

Alipore Court
23.1.30

Revered mother,

I received all your letters. I could not reply to them timely on account of all sorts of trouble. I was today sentenced to one year's imprisonment. We are all well—we shall joyfully begin our victory march to the Royal temple. I believe deeply that your love and blessings will always be with me. I felt very anxious to learn of your poor health. You should come down to Calcutta without delay and let Dr. Roy treat you. This is my earnest request—please keep it.

Devotedly yours
SUBHAS

* Translated from the original Bengali.
** Translated from the original Bengali.

*150. To Basanti Devi**

1, Woodburn Park
Calcutta
7.11.30

Revered mother,

I received your letters but was unable to reply. You may have been angry or felt hurt. But I shall not offer an apology because you know my habits very well. I am often not able to reply promptly.

How are you all? I am well on the whole—although I cannot have a moment's rest. In spite of my desire to do so, I was not able to go away from Calcutta. When are you coming?

Devotedly yours
SUBHAS

151. To a friend

Seoni Sub-Jail
Seoni, C. P.
27.2.32

You must have been aware by now that I have been here for about two months and that Mejdada (Sj. Sarat Bose) has joined me of late. The climate has been pleasant so far, but before long the hot weather will, I am afraid, set in.

We are having plenty of rest here. I would have been more happy—had it not been for a physical ailment which has appeared occasionally during the last five weeks. Occasionally, I have been getting an acute pain in the region of the liver which lasts for two or three hours. This pain appears only after meals, sometimes several times after meals. When it followed my evening meal—the pain used to keep me awake at night. When it followed my midday meal the pain appeared in the evening and disappeared

* Translated from the original Bengali.

by 10 p.m. At first the pain used to appear only at night. When I cut down my evening meal, it appeared in the evening as a result of midday meal. Since then I have been practising rigid diet control and that has had a favourable effect so far the pain is concerned. But, on the other hand, it has brought about a reduction of weight to the extent of 10 lbs.

I have not been able to understand what the trouble really is and which organ is really affected but the superintendent assures me that it has something to do with my digestion, and is not more serious than that. He is doing his best in the matter.

The pain occurs only in the right side and above the waist line when the pain is acute, it causes very great uneasiness and also breathing difficulty on lying down—so that one feels more at ease on sitting up or walking up and down. Apart from this ailment I am well—and so is Mejdada.

However, let me stop talking about myself. How are you all keeping ? Remember us to all. By the way, you will be interested to know that I am trying my hand at cooking. As in the case of scientific experiments, the results obtained are sometimes flattering and sometimes disastrous. I think I could pick up cooking without difficulty—if I had some one to teach me. We are practising economy here, as we get a diet allowance of Re. 1 per diem inclusive of fuel. Mejdada is well and we are in the best of spirits. Please accept kindest wishes from both of us.

SUBHAS

152. To a friend

C/o, The Superintendent,
Seoni Sub-Jail,
Seoni, C. P.
22.4.32

Since I wrote to you last it has become hotter all over the country and we too have been experiencing it. There was a slight shower a few days ago which had a temporary cooling effect. We have still the whole of summer to negotiate and it is not a cheerful prospect at all.

Recently the civil surgeon of Chindwara came up to Seoni to examine me. He examined me very carefully. I have not been informed yet about his prescription and I am eagerly awaiting it. Since yesterday we have been allowed to have a walk in the jail garden in the evening for exercise and I am hoping now that it will do us good. Continuous confinement in a small place may not have any visible effect all at once but it undoubtedly has a cramping effect on the body as well as on the mind—and this is revealed gradually as the days roll by.

My physical condition is on the whole unchanged. Sciatica is still adhering to me as obstinately as ever, in spite of two injections. During the last fortnight I had acute pain only once but every day between meals and at odd hours I experience a burning sensation on the right side. It is not possible to increase my diet as long this sensation is present because from experience I have come to look upon it as a danger signal. Further increase in diet at this stage will aggravate the discomfort and agony. I have uptill now lost 20 lbs. in weight—but before I can think of recouping this loss I have to try and bring the stomach back to a normal condition (of course if that is at all possible under present conditions of confinement). I wish I could have a thorough examination of the inside—viz. X-Ray examination after bismuth meal, test meal examination etc.—in order to find out what exactly the trouble is due to. At present we are more or less groping in the dark. But while I am here, no such examination is possible either in the jail or in the civil hospital. So we have to do the best we can.

Mejdada is doing well on the whole—as far as present circumstances will permit except for an increase in the sugar.

I am trying to make the best use of my stay and my leisure here. I do not know when I shall be able to return to Bengal—but I have felt during my stay here, as I have never felt before (except once only when I was in Burma) what Tagore wrote in his exquisite style.

"সোনার বাঙলা ! আমি তোমায় ভালবাসি
চিরদিন তোমার আকাশ তোমার বাতাস
আমার প্রাণে বাজায় বাঁশী"*

And I long at times for the scenery which one can see only in Bengal—the ocean like rivers and the smiling fields of wavy corn. And I cannot help repeating in the poet's words—

"ওরে অঘ্রাণে তোর ভরা ক্ষেতে
কি দেখেছি মধুর হাসি..."**

Before my arrest this time I had toured in the interior of Maharashtra and I enjoyed heartily the wild and rugged scenery of the hills of Maharashtra. But much as I liked it—I felt simultaneously that the picture was not complete without the poetic scenery of Bengal—the vast rivers and the never ending field of Agrahayan† paddy.

Where an experience is denied to the senses—the mind has to conjure it up for self-enjoyment. That is my excuse for the digression.

Yours affectionately,
SUBHAS C. BOSE

153. To a friend

Seoni Sub-Jail
Seoni, C.P.
29.4.32

I was glad to receive your letter of the 20th instant which reached me on the 26th. I have received Bergson's "Creative Evolution" and Prof. Radhakrishnan's book. I have also received the copies of "Uttara" which you despatched me. I have received the four issues of *Parichaya* sent by the Editor. When I received the first three issues, I wrote to

* O my golden Bengal, I love you so,
your sky and the air ever play
the music in my heart.

**Oh what a picture of sweet smile came to my gaze
Reflected from the fields replete with corns in the month of Agrahayan.

† Eighth month in the Bengali Calendar.

the Editor thanking him for the same. I do not know if that letter reached him.

I have not been able as yet to go through all the issues of *Parichaya*, handicapped as I have been by my ailments. Consequently I shall write to you after some time as to what I think of *Parichaya* as a journal. In the meantime let me tell you that I have formed a very favourable impression of *Parichaya*. I wish the editor every success in his noble endeavour. We badly need a magazine of this kind. I only hope that the journal will maintain its individuality throughout and not try to imitate other magazines which may have a larger sale.

If you send us any more books you may include Trotsky's life and Memoirs of Alexander Herzen (in 4 vols.) which are in our library. Can you get hold of any literature dealing with Thoreau (the American) ? I am feeling interested in the farming experiments of Tolstoy. Is there any literature dealing with this subject ? Newmans are advertising a book "The Man from the Volga"—the latest biography of Lenin. Have you seen the book ? It may be in the Imperial Library.

You have put me a series of questions about my health. I shall try to answer them as satisfactorily as possible. At the outset let me tell you that I have received Kaviraj Mahasaya's letter and his kind offer to treat me. Please give him my warmest thanks and tell him that I shall write to him next week.

The civil surgeon of Chindwara who had been sent to examine me has opined that there is something wrong with the gall bladder. He thinks that the past history of enteric fever, the stomach complaints as well as the sciatic pain points towards this diagnosis. He further thinks that corroboration will be afforded by an X-Ray examination. I am therefore expecting now to be taken somewhere for X-ray and other examinations as there is no such arrangement here.

I am taking all possible care about my diet and I am in general agreement with what Kaviraj Mahasaya has recommended. But there is another risk involved in diet restrictions viz., loss of weight. I have lost uptill now 26 lbs, (twentysix pounds) since my arrival and this is no doubt a good bit. Sciatica is obstinate as ever and I feel that has a deeper origin and will not yield either to injection or to massage. I am trying to avoid internal pain by restricting and controlling my diet.

By the way, you may be interested to know that I have been taking vegetable charcoal by way of medicine. Who ever dreamt that he would have to eat charcoal while in the land of the living.

SUBHAS

154. To a friend

Seoni Sub-Jail
Seoni, C.P.
14.5.32

Good and bad are relative terms and this remark may very well apply to Seoni. So far as I am concerned, I have no grounds to say that Seoni is a healthy place. Others who are more fortunate as to the matter of health than I have been here, may say the opposite. Of course, I do not know how I would have fared if I have lived in Seoni as a free man and not as a prisoner. That might have made a lot of difference,—one does not really know.

I was interested to read your suggestion as to how to kill time. To sit up and go on writing day after day in the present state of my health is a task to which I cannot take kindly. There is much that I would like to write about and about which I have formed clear and definite ideas, but I cannot stand the physical strain.

Though I have been handicapped in the matter of writing and even reading, I am otherwise making the most of my time here. I cannot write while I am here all that I would like to but I shall only say this that I am now passing through an interesting—and in some ways a critical period of my life. What the ultimate consummation will be, I shall leave it to you to conjecture.

REALISATION OF TRUTH

I have always taken life very seriously, being of the opinion that life has value and meaning only in so far as it is lived for an idea as an ideal. But to consecrate one's life (which includes his emotions, volitions and thought) to one object is not an easy task. As a matter of fact the *Sadhana* has to be a continuous one and sometimes a lifelong one. Even when one has the ardour, devotion and tenacity which is required for self-consecration one may not have a realisation of Truth, and without this realisation one's life may very well go astray. To most men, the realisation of Truth does not come in a day. It has to be a continuous one spreading over a long period of time. Thus you will see that throughout our life a twofold *Sadhana* has to go on—the endeavour to "see" the truth and secondly, the endeavour to live in accordance with it.

LIFE AND TRUTH

To be able to live in accordance with the truth, one must be bold and courageous beyond description and be reckless in one's capacity to suffer and sacrifice. Nevertheless, I believe that God has given me the strength to 'live' in accordance with the truth. But the endeavour to do so would be altogether futile unless we realise the truth and our mission in life. This realisation is an inner experience to which one can attain only through intense struggle and through one's own efforts. Others may help you and inspire you, but you will have to fight your own battles unaided. When you are lucky and the truth flashes upon you—your whole life is transformed and transfigured. You undergo a new birth as it were and you then tune your whole life to the truth you have realised.

SPIRITUAL REBIRTH

This spiritual rebirth is what I crave for now. It will not do to accept blindly what other master-minds have said. Their experiences and teachings are like milestones or finger-posts on the road but the path has to be travelled by us if we want to know the truth. As Emerson would say, "We must live wholly from within,"—and only by living wholly from within can we ultimately reach the truth. We have to pass through all the experiences which those who attained the truth in the past had gone through. Then alone will truth become a first-hand experience—*Pratyaksha* and not merely *Aaptabaky*.

You may ask: "Why waste your time and energy in going over the same ground already covered by others? Why not blindly accept what other master-minds have already realised—just as we accept the laws, postulates and axioms of science in college?" To this my reply is that if you want the power to recreate life from the very bottom, you must have a *Pratyaksha* experience of truth. If you merely want self-satisfaction or self-complacence, you need not bother about *Sadhana* or realisation.

(Here about 60 lines have been deleted by the Censor)

You have asked about my health. Far from improving, it has been deteriorating. During the last fortnight there has been a further drop in weight, making the total loss 28 lbs. I am also getting the internal pain occasionally and during the last week it came on twice very late at night. The sciatic pain is still there, and we have not made any further progress in the matter of diagnosis. The civil surgeon of Chindwara opined that there was something wrong with the gall-bladder. I am now waiting for a thorough X-Ray and other forms of examination. Then only can we come to a correct diagnosis and begin proper treatment. Things are moving slowly and I have to wait and wait. In the meantime the loss of weight as well as the heat have made me very weak.

....(deleted by censor) already made their contribution and it now remains for India to make her contribution. In the eighteenth century France's contribution constituted an important landmark in the history of human progress and similarly Russia's contribution during the early part of this century is an important world event. I feel instinctively that during the next era India's contribution to the solution of the socio-economic problem will be another landmark in human history. Who among us will help India to fulfil her mission in this respect I cannot say, but one-thing is certain—India has not yet given any indication of the exact nature of her contribution in this behalf but she will do so before long and then alone will India be able to come to her own and regain the position which once was hers and which she rightly claims now.

Remember me to all friends.

SUBHAS

*155. To Santosh Kumar Basu**

Censored and Passed
Illegible
9/7/32
for D.I.G., I.B., C.I.D.

C/o. D.I.G., I.B., C.I.D.
(Bengal)
13 Lord Sinha Road
Calcutta
Jubbulpore Central Jail
5.7.32

My dear Santosh Babu,

Your kind letter of 9.4.32 was to hand duly but I was not able to reply to it.

Your "totka"** (টোটকা) regarding sciatica (lemon juice etc.) is good for the stomach—but I don't think it has much effect on sciatic pain. I have been taking it regularly for some time past. My mother, too, is a great believer in this—not for sciatic trouble, but for the stomach. Sciatica, in my case, is an offshoot of gall-bladder or similar trouble. Until this trouble is eradicated, sciatica will not go. This view of mine is indirectly confirmed by the provisional diagnosis made by the Civil Surgeon of Chindwara in April last.

How are you all keeping? How are Susthir Babu and his family? I understand that he has been officiating as Welfare Officer in place of Naoroji.

Amrita has written to me to say that he desires to stand for the Improvement Trust Tribunal, if sufficient support is

* At this time Netaji was confined in Jubbulpore with his brother Sarat.—Ed.

** Indigenous remedy.—Ed.

forthcoming. If he stands, I can warmly commend his candidature. I have known him sufficiently long and I have great regard for his character and his straightforwardness in particular. For the Tribunal, we want a man of sterling character with transparent honesty. Erudition alone will not do. Old men may come in to contest Amrita—but old age does not necessarily connote wisdom or erudition or experience or character. And youth is not a crime ! At the last election there was a feeling that the post should not be the monopoly of one person. I suppose that argument will hold good even now. You will not get a front rank lawyer from the High Court to stand for this job. Consequently among those who will apply I don't expect there will be any one with outstanding legal knowledge and experience. Besides, I do not think that profound knowledge of law is really necessary for the Improvement Trust Tribunal. What we really want is a strong and honest man who will do justice to the parties whose cases come up before the Trust. Amrita will eminently fulfil these conditions and I hope you will support his candidature. I am writing to Amrita to see you in this connection.

Have you proceeded any further with the Drainage Extension Special Committee ?

Some time ago I wrote to you about two employees of the Corporation. Please consider their application for promotion whenever a suitable opportunity arises. One of them —Jiten Bennerji—has written to me again. Please see if you can do anything for him.

Hope this will find you all quite well. Please tell Mr. Yakub that we were very glad to read his letter which we received some time back.

We are not keeping well at all— as you probably know. There has been a continued deterioration unfortunately.

Kindest regards from both of us.

Yours affly

SUBHAS C. BOSE

P.S. How are your boys ? When did you meet Susthir Babu last ?

S.C.B.

156. To Santosh Kumar Basu
Censored and Passed
Illegible
19/8
for D.I.G., I.B., C.I.D.
Bengal

C/o. The D.I.G., I.B., C.I.D.
(Bengal)
13 Lord Sinha Road
Calcutta
Madras Penitentiary
15.8.32

My dear Santosh Babu,

I wrote to you from Jubbulpore before I left for Madras. I trust that letter has reached you safe.

In that letter I wrote to you about Amrita Babu. Since then I have heard from him again. I hope you are helping him in the matter of the Improvement Trust Tribunal. I am writing to him asking him to get your advice as to how he should proceed etc. He says that he will stand a better chance if the matter is not made a party question. This is a point on which the men on the spot can alone give an opinion.

Nearly a month ago I got a letter from Susthir Babu. I shall not be able to write to him in all probability, as I can write a limited number of letters per week. Please write to him to say that I was very glad to receive his letter of the 13th July. I am anxious to hear of his wife's illness. How is she doing now ? Please give her my regards. Is her boy with her ? I forget his name at the moment. He is a playmate of Chotodada's girl Radhu—at Jamshedpur. Please ask Susthir Babu to tell Mani Babu that he has not written to me for a long time and has not replied to my last letter. One of Mani Babu's letters to me was withheld some time ago. I am sorry to hear of the drastic retrenchment at Tata's, causing unemployment to thousands. Why did Mr. Temple resign ? I was very sorry to hear of the death of Dr. Gopal C. Guha's wife. She was a high-souled lady. Please ask Susthir Babu to convey my sincerest condolence to Gopal Babu.

I hope you will remember the two employees of the Corporation about whom I wrote to you in my last letter—when any opportunity comes for bettering their prospects.

Hope this will find you all quite well though you have had an unusually busy time. With love and kindest wishes,

Yours affly,
SUBHAS C. BOSE

Santosh K. Basu Esq.
Calcutta

*157. To Bivabati Bose and her Children**

C/o. D.I.G., I.B., C.I.D.
13 Lord Sinha Road,
Calcutta
The Penitentiary
Madras
Monday, 29th August (1932)

My dear Mejobowdidi,

I was delighted to receive your letter. I received it on the 11th instant, but have been late in replying. I also received all the letters enclosed with yours; but large portions of Ami's letter were deleted. No other letter was tampered with in any way.

Nilratan Babu and Bidhan Babu have gone back after examining me. You will get detailed reports from them. The examination was held at the hospital. There were two other government physicians with them—Drs. Skinner and Keshab Pai. They have given an unanimous report. Their views, in short, are as follows:—

(1) Signs of tuberculosis are present.

(2) There is an abdominal mischief—probably appendicitis.

(3) I should be sent to a healthy place without delay.

(4) Arrangements for treatment should be made in

* Translated from the original Bengali.

Switzerland or in the Bhowali Sanatorium in India.
Detention in prison will aggravate the disease.

You will get detailed information from the doctors—I have only given the substance of their report. Now we have again to wait for some time for orders of the Government.

It is still warm here. The position regarding my diet remains as before. Unless my digestion improves, there is no possibility of any addition to the diet. Drinking water here is not good at all.

I have heard from father from Puri—the letter is dated the 12th. I wrote to father on the 16th August—I hope the letter reached his hand in due time.

Ami's letter of the 22nd has been withheld by the C.I.D. Office. However, Gita's letter that came with it has been delivered to me. Ami's previous letter (of the 3rd) reached me in a largely mutilated state.

My dear Ami, Mira, Neru and Gita,

I have received all your letters. It seems Mira and Neru are exhausted after writing one letter.

The local jail is smaller than that in Jubbulpore but the buildings are better. I live on the first-floor. The rooms are very small--just enough for one person—what they call "cells" in English. I am out on the verandah day and night. I could not bring any pets here; neither have I tried to get any locally due to want of space. Here I have not got a completely separate yard as at Jubbulpore. The space therefore is limited. Nobody has to bother about cooking here—because what I eat needs no cooking. It is possible to get my food ready just with a stove. I spend most of the time reading—so I have had to purchase some books.

I received an answer after a long time to the letter I wrote to Mejdada on my arrival here. I wrote back to him again some time ago.

Living in one place for a long time makes one feel bored. If one shifts to another place at that moment, he feels better initially. But then the feeling of monotony returns. The best and only way to pass time in prison is to read without respite.

Answering Gita's many queries has made this letter quite long. I find the kiddies are terribly worried as to the name to be given to the baby brother. If they all cannot agree—why do not we do something? Let all the names suggested be given to him—he will choose one for himself when he grows up.

I hope all of you are keeping well. Akshoy has written me to say that he wishes to come here to interview me. Please ask him not to come. What is the necessity of coming all this way for nothing?

How are parents? I have no idea how long I shall have to be here. It is desirable that somebody goes to Jubbulpore from time to time. Mejdada will be feeling very lonely there. Akshoy had better go to Jubbulpore instead of coming here.

158. To Dilip Kumar Roy

Censored and Passed
Sd/- Illegible
13/9
for D.I.G., I.B., C.I.D.,
Bengal

C/o. The D.I.G., I.B., C.I.D.,
Bengal
13 Lord Sinha Road
Calcutta
The Penitentiary, Madras
10-9-32

My dear Dilip,

Your affectionate letter of the 15th August reached me on the 29th ultimo. All my letters are now sent to Calcutta for censoring and this was partly responsible for the delay. In future you may send direct to the above Calcutta address any letters you may write.

In what you have done for me, you have acted like a true friend and you could not have done more. I do not know if I am sufficiently "open" to receive yogic force—probably I am not. Nevertheless, I think that even those who rule out the existence of a supra-mental order have to admit the existence and efficacy of what is popularly styled as "will-power". And this force—call it by what name you will—is bound to act, even if the receiver is not "open" or adequately and consciously receptive. I am grateful to Sri Aurobindo.

Yes, Madras is so near to Pondicherry—but the walls intervene—and that makes all the difference in the world. It does not look as if I shall be here long. The papers say that I shall be transferred to Bhowali sanatorium.

It is not necessary to bother you with details about my "physical" health—after all, you are not a medical doctor. I don't think I have suffered from "mental" ill-health as I have been suffering from physical—and my usual "spirits" are therefore unaffected. I have been studying a bit and thinking more ; at times I feel as if I am groping in the dark. But I cannot go wrong as long as I am sincere and earnest—even if my progress towards the truth be more zig-zag than straight. After all life's march is not as straight as a straight-line.

Have not each of us a sphere of work allotted to us (taking "work" in the broadest sense) ? And is not this sphere conditioned by our past *Karma*, our present desires etc. and our environment ? Nevertheless, how difficult it is to understand or realise our proper sphere of work ! This sphere of work is the external aspect of our nature or "*Dharma*". It is so easy to say—"live in accordance with your স্বধর্ম (*Swadharma*)"—but so difficult to *know* what one's ধর্ম (*Dharma*) is. It is there that the help of a "guru" becomes so necessary—and even indispensable.

I know that you will continue to feel for me and I also know that in the long run this cannot prove unavailing. This is a great solace to me—no matter where I may happen to be confined. I have appreciated (I cannot find the proper word !)—Sri Aurobindo's action. I shall not say more lest my language become conventional.

With best love,

Ever affly yours

SUBHAS

Dilip Kumar Roy Esq.
Sri Aurobindo Ashram,
Pondicherry

159. To Santosh Kumar Basu

Censored and Passed
Illegible
24/9
for D.I.G., I.B., C.I.D.
Bengal

C/o. The D.I.G., I.B., C.I.D.
(Bengal)
13 Lord Sinha Road
Calcutta
The Penitentiary
Madras
19.9.32

My dear Santosh Babu,

I hope you have received my last letter, which I wrote on the 15th August last.

I am sorry I am going to write to you again on a municipal matter. Unfortunately, people think that I carry great influence in matters municipal. Personally I have no illusions on this point—but it is not easy to make others share your point of view especially when you are away. And I do not like anyone to feel that I could help him—but that I would not. That is my only excuse for writing to you.

Sj. Sabitri Prasanna Chatterji has applied for the post of lecturer in Bengali in the Teachers' Training School. He is a graduate of the Calcutta University and would have also taken his M.A. Degree—but for the non-cooperation movement. He was a lecturer in Bengali at the "Kalikata Vidyapith" as long as that College was in existence. He was successful as a lecturer and was also popular among the students. Deshbandhu knew him personally and liked him.

He has made a name for himself among the new generation of Bengali litterateurs. He is a good poet also (though you do not require a poet for the job). Naturally he is a good critic of poetry as well. He has been connected with literary journalism for a very long time and I think this has sharpened his faculty of criticism and appreciation of literature—a faculty which is indispensable for a good lecturer.

In his private life he is a perfect gentleman and a kind-hearted man. There is nothing that I know against him.

I do not know what type of men you want or you will get. But I think that Sabitri Babu will be a very good man for the job. If you can appoint him, I shall be very glad indeed. And if he can get a living wage—it will help him to continue his literary pursuits—untroubled by worldly difficulties or worries. If you can sponsor his candidature, please speak to other friends also.

I need not write at length about my health. You must have heard everything from Dr. Roy. Since he left, there has been an aggravation of some complaints and a further drop in weight. I suppose there is no help and I must put up with whatever comes in my way. Hope all well there. Greetings to all friends.

With loving regards,

Yours affly
SUBHAS

P.S. I hope you have communicated my greetings to Susthir Babu. Hope he is doing well with his family. Have they gone back or are they in Calcutta now?

*160. To Bivabati Bose**

Mother Durga be with us.

Madras
1st October (1932)
Saturday

My dear Mejobowdidi,

Your letter of the 2nd September reached my hands on the 10th and that of the 14th September on the 30th (that is, yesterday).

Whenever I hear of anybody coming to see me, I feel disturbed. In short, I do not like the idea of anybody doing so. So, when Akshoy wrote to me that he wanted to come, I sent him word not to. Meanwhile, the police authorities refused him permission and so the matter was disposed of. I heard the other day that Bardada wanted to come, I therefore asked him not to come. I do not know how long I shall be here; perhaps I shall soon be transferred. Consequently, I do not see any reason why anybody should unnecessarily come all this way. People could perhaps come only after some sort of a permanent arrangement about me has been made.

No treatment has been started here—it is not possible to do it here. If I try to add to my diet, the pain returns. My weight is steadily going down.

The Superintendent is, in a way, helpless; he is trying so that some arrangement is made about me quickly. But so far there has been no result. It came out in the newspapers some time ago that I would be sent to Bhowali. However, no such orders of the Government have yet been received.

I have not been able to write to Didi since coming here, nor have I heard from her. Mother said in her letter that Didi and her family might go to Cuttack; but it appears to me now that they will be staying on at Gorakhpur for the time being.

I wrote to mother on Monday last at Cuttack. I wrote to

* Translated from the original Bengali.

father on the 8th. I have received his letter of the 17th. Father has sent me Mejdada's letter of the 2nd with his own.

Please inform Natunmamababu that the medicine sent by him arrived here today. I also received Bardada's letter yesterday.

I am having fever daily as before. It is still quite hot here. Rains have not arrived yet.

I read about your trip of Jubbulpore in the local papers. Later, your statement was also published in the local press. Please arrange so that somebody goes to Jubbulpore for interveiw every month.

How long will Gopali's leave last ? I received the letters of dear Mira, Neru and Gita. I have received Neru's second letter also. But why nobody except Neru has written this time ? Gita wants to know how many floors this jail has. Why, does she want to come and stay here ? The buildings here have two floors and there is separate arrangement for women. The space inside the jail is very small but are well-ventilated ; and there is a long narrow verandah. I spend most of my time out in the verandah. I am very happy to know Neru's examination results, but he must occupy the first place.

How are Sejobowdidi and her family ? I hope Chotodada and his family are well. I have not had any news of Nadada for a long time.

I hope all is well at home. Please accept my respectful *pronams* and convey my love to children.

Yours

SUBHAS

ADDENDA

[The following letters were discovered much later. As such these could not be placed according to our plan.—Ed.]

*161. From Haricharan Bagchi**

Sevak Samity
44 Choulpatty Road
Bhowanipur
Calcutta
25.2.25

Most respectfully Sir,

I got your letter in time. I just failed to reply duly because of my dilatoriness, and please excuse me for that.

We have been able to collect one thousand four hundred rupees by selling tickets for the variety entertainment organised by us.

We could save Rs. 1000/- out of that Rs. 1400/- after meeting all the necessary expenses. Gradually we are getting more and more monthly subscription. Our primary school is now having its classes inside the premises of National School of Bhowanipur. We have been able to recruit a few good workers for our primary school.

We are trying to keep engaged those persons whom we are helping by providing them with rice free of cost. As a matter of fact, we have made arrangements in such a way that they can learn and make bags, bottles etc. But unfortunately most of them are not at all prepared to do any work. Anyway, our Samity is now proceeding more or less in a satisfactory way. At present there is no need for renting a room for the library and spending money on that account. We have repaired and renovated the house of our landlord.

We have applied for Corporation grant. We have requested Kshitishbabu to see to it that the grant is given in time and he has promised that he would try his utmost.

I went to see Dr. Naren Law carrying the letter written by Mejdada. He promised that he would try for us so that we

* Translated from the original Bengali.

can have a good grant from the Calcutta Corporation.

I am keeping well now. I have decided to take some rest during the month of May and I have been provided with a free bed at the sanatorium of the Rajahs of Tajhat.

Please write to us from time to time. Write more than one letter. How are you keeping now ?

Yours sincerely
SRI HARICHARAN

162. From Janakinath Bose

Cuttack
17 March, 1925

My dear Subhas,

I have got your letter of the 27th February and am glad to know that you are doing well.

I went to Calcutta on the 8th instant and came back in the morning of the 12th. Your mother is still there.

It is getting warm and I am thinking of going to Puri as soon as I can.

People here and at Calcutta are doing well.

Please let me know how you keep.

Yours v. affectionately
J. N. BOSE

163. From Janakinath Bose

Cuttack
9.6.25
(Tuesday)

My dear Subhas,

I was very happy to receive your letter of the 16th of May.

Your mother, Sarala and her children and Sati are still at Puri. They are pretty well. Even Puri is very warm—not to speak of Cuttack.

It must be oppressively hot at Mandalay.

Sarat went to Kurseong for 4 or 5 days, he returned to Calcutta on Thursday last.

Sunil has arrived in London—he will do research work there for a year having secured Ghosh research Scholarship.

Sudhir joined his post at Jamshedpur on the 1st June—he is well.

Polly has been here for about 3 weeks—she is better.

Suresh and Gopali are busily engaged in setting up the machinery for the match factory in our Sikharpur garden.

We are all pretty well.

Our blessing to you. Trust this will find you in good health.

Yours very affly.
J. N. BOSE

*164. From Prabhabati Bose**

Jagannath Dham
Puri
10.6.25

My dear Subhas,

I received in due time your letter of 4th April.

Dolly will come from Gorakhpur very soon and Sarada too will come with her. Promila is now in Calcutta and is well. Aruna's marriage is being arranged.

Your father is now quite well and every week he comes here and stays for three or four days and goes back to Cuttack. Suresh, Sejobowma and Gopali are in Cuttack and they are well. Sarala and her children, Sati and Jogin came here a month ago and they are all well. They will stay here till the Car (Rathajatra) festival. For chronic piles it is advisable to take every day black sesame mixed with butter and sugar-candy (Misri). It is also advisable to take Ishapgul soaked into water and mixed with sugar-candy. Before evacuating your bowels and at night if you apply vaseline on your piles then it will reduce your pain much. How is your state of health now ? What happened

* Translated from the original Bengali.

to that application of yours which you sent asking the authorities to transfer you to Bengal as you are not keeping well there in Burma. We have got news of Sunil's reaching England. We got letters from him on his way to England from Eden and Port Said. Nadu is now sitting for the exam.

I wrote a letter to you before. Did you receive it ?

Everybody is well at our Calcutta home. Sudhir got a job at Tatanagar, went there and is now keeping well. I shall be happy if you write to me from time to time letting me know that you are well. Accept our whole-hearted blessings and affection.

Your

LOVING MOTHER

165. *To Sarat Chandra Bose*

Mandalay Jail
26.6.25

My dear brother,

I have not heard from you for some time past. The unfortunate event and the attending circumstances have not probably left you any time.

I have already written to you to ask Sudhir Babu to preserve carefully all the papers, letters, notes etc. belonging to the late Deshbandhu. These would be required for compiling a biography. It is a practical and matter of fact consideration which may not strike those who, owing to their proximity, are directly under the shadow of the great bereavement.

You probably know that Deshbandhu had a personal attendant called Mathur. Mathur was a prisoner in the Alipore Central Jail when he was there and he served him with great devotion. In spite of the fact that Mathur had seven or eight previous convictions he was liked by him and since his release Mathur had been living with him. I know that Deshbandhu had a soft corner for Mathur whom he had been able to reform and I am sure that Mathur is one of those who feel the loss most, so great was his devotion towards the great man. In spite of temporary exhibitions of wild temper—the mental relic of his past life—from what I have seen of him, he is a reformed man. I do not know what Sudhir Babu will do regarding this man. He will have to face the problem of applying the axe ruthlessly. In case Mathur has to leave, I should like to keep him—so you will have to give him shelter till I am back. Mathur is clever and hard-working—can do household work of all kinds and I think he will be useful. I feel that in giving shelter to Mathur I shall be acting in accordance with the wishes of the departed soul. You may have a talk with Sudhir Babu or Mrs. Das regarding this matter at your convenience.

I have been informed in reply to my application, that I cannot be transferred to Bengal. It therefore appears that Govt. do not believe what I wrote about my health. Such treatment inspires moderation and "sweet reasonableness"—does it not?

Have you heard in reply from Govt. about the loan? Whatever may happen later, I hope this loan will be sanctioned. Have you been able to appoint a Stores Supdt.? Are you going to have a separate Coal Controller or are the two posts going to be combined? I find that Santosh Babu is taking vigorous steps to improve the condition of the New Market. I hope he will be able to inspire confidence by his good work. Who is in charge of the Motor Vehicles Dept.? Have you got a good man to replace Wacha? Whatever you do, you must act in accordance with the dictates of Sir Ta....Hall Bannerji, otherwise he will hurl his thunderbolts at you from Dharamtala Street.

Hope this will find you quite well. How is Mrs. Das standing her bereavement? May God grant her strength.

Yours v. affly.,
SUBHAS (C. BOSE)

To S. C. Bose
38/1 Elgin Road
Calcutta

P.S. Bipin—one of the students I used to help has written

to say that since April he does not get free board and lodging as before. He has asked me to introduce him to some friends who may help him with at least a part of the total expenditure which he has to incur. I shall write to some friends next week. In the meantime please continue your help as before. He is feeling considerable hesitation in asking you to help him with the whole amount and that is why he wants to try and get a monthly stipend elsewhere as well. He is now sitting for one of the College Examinations.

S.C.B.

166. From Janakinath Bose

Cuttack
3.7.25

My dear Subhas,

I duly received your letter of the 13th June but I could not reply it in time as I was not very well. I had a severe nervous or rheumatic pain about my waist but I am almost free from it now. Your mother and Mejdidi are still at Puri—the Rathajatra is over. I expect them here in two or three days.

Polly and her boy are here—they have improved. Suresh and Gopali are busy with building the match factory and setting up the machinery. The monsoon has burst and we are having cool days. Trust this will find you in good health.

Yours very affectionately,
J. N. Bose

167. To Sarat Chandra Bose

Mandalay Jail
1.8.25

My dear brother,

I have not had any communication from you this week. I hope this will find you all in the best of health.

Please ask Ramiah to send me a complete list of the books that have been sent to me from the Corp. office up till now. I want to check the list and see if I have received all the books despatched from Calcutta.

In the 'Ashar' issue of the monthly *Basumati* there is an article on Deshbandhu from the pen of the historian Mr. Rakhal Das Banerjee. The article is interesting—and contains a lot of information re. Deshbandhu's last seven days on earth. How far the facts related are correct—I do not know—but I take it that Mr. Banerji being a historian is an accurate recorder of facts. Please make time to read the article—it won't take more than 10 minutes.

When you have time later on—you may also read in the same journal the article from the pen of the novelist, Babu Sarat Chandra Chatterji. It is worth reading.

Have you decided finally about your trip to the hills? I do not think you should cut it down—if you can possibly help it.

Most of the articles written about Deshbandhu are superficial and devoid of substance. There is a plethora of grandiloquent phrases but that is all. I wish the writers would write more about their personal reminiscences. It is these which really interest the public and serve to unfold the character of the man. Sarat Babu's article referred to above is an attempt in the right direction. By narrating and analysing his conversations with Deshbandhu and by skilful reference to events which on the surface appear to be of no significance—he has attempted to portray the man as he saw him in life. Mr. Banerji too has made an attempt in the right direction.

There is one aspect of Deshbandhu's work which is not ordinarily spoken of now but which in the years to come is bound to have a profound influence on Bengali thought. I refer to the line of thought which he tried to foster and develop in the columns of his *Narayana*. As you know his object was to revive the ancient and national culture of Bengal as revealed in the poems of Chandidas, Bidyapati and in the writings of a host of other writers—and at the same time to expose the hollowness of the shallow internationalism in life and literature of Tagore and his school which did not realize the fundamental truth in nationalism. I have been trying to study some of the articles which appeared in *Narayana* written by writers of the anti-Tagore School and I feel sure that in the days to come this school will come greatly into prominence. There is one gentleman whom Deshbandhu regarded as the best exponent of his thought in this particular field. He is Babu Girija Sankar Rai Chowdhury vakil of the High Court.

I am afraid I must curb my random thoughts as I have to be in time for the outgoing mail.

It looks as if it is going to be hot again in August.

Yours v. affly,
SUBHAS

*168. From Sailendranath**

19B, Dalimtala Lane
13.8.25

Dear Subhasbabu,

I got your letter last Saturday but could not manage to answer it so long. My younger sister is seriously ill, probably lying on her death-bed and we are not sure whether she will recover. That kept us all busy and so I failed to answer to your letter.

You have not written about your own state of health. Don't you know that there are so many persons who are so anxious to know about the state of your health now ? I think you have not yet realised how much you mean to the whole of Bengal and the Bengalees and in what kind of relationship you stand with them. This is why you ignore to write anything about yourself, taking it to be too much personal. I think I need not drive the point home that all should be anxious to know about the state of health of somebody for whom the youth of Bengal as a whole are waiting with much hope. Now I think I have been able to make you realise the significance of the whole thing. Yesterday Hemanta

* Translated from the original Bengali.

Sarkar raised questions regarding the persons who are now incarcerated in Mandalay Jail with special reference to their condition of health including you too. In answer Stephenson said that you have gained ten pounds of weight. But by reading your letter I can guess that you are not at all in a happy state of health.

Probably you have heard that Surendranath Banerjea died on the 6th of this month. Today the compatriots of Surendranath Banerjea did not even feel like sighing for him whom they once crowded to see. After all there was a person in Bengal whom the whole of India knew. Now, with his death Bengal has lost both her past and her future.

It is impossible to describe how overwhelmed with sorrow the people of this country became when Deshbandhu died. That day all became so much overwhelmed with sorrow that it appeared as if their own father had died. About 7 lakhs of rupees could be collected for Deshbandhu Memorial Fund and we are hoping that within this month we will be able to collect if not ten lakhs of rupees but nearabout that figure. You will be happy to learn that 9 thousand rupees were donated from the Municipal Office and six thousand rupees were donated by people of Ward No. III.

I am going to send by next post those books of Deshbandhu which you asked me to post. I could not manage to send them by this post because as I have mentioned before, I was busy because my sister was lying ill. It will be very helpful if you write what books you read following what method during your stay in Berhampore Jail and later in Mandalay. As I have a desire to read books so if you kindly write to me making a list of books to be read that will be a matter of great pleasure to me.

You will be sorry to learn that Swarajya Party was defeated in Council on 12th August last. Dr. Abdullah Suhrawardy contested at the poll as a candidate for Presidentship. He was defeated by the independent candidate who contested for the Presidentship.

You will be happy to learn that National Surviving (?) Association is making progress. A tent which was to be made as needed by this association is nearing completion at Cornwallis Square. Suhrawardy, the Deputy Mayor has been elected as the Vice-president of the Association and he is taking a great deal of interest in it at present. Sukumar is still now the Secretary and I have been also enrolled as a member.

Here all are well, I hope you are well at present. Accept the *namaskar* of all of us. Forget the difference of age and other differences and accept my humble offerings of respect to you. I pray to God to teach me to love the country as you are capable of loving it. After reading your letter today I have been able to realise somehow the kind of love which a devout vaishnava offers to his God without any reservation and how with that love in his heart he can see God everywhere, in the whole of nature, in the whole Universe. I want this blessing from you that I may inherit even a little portion of that love for the country offered without any reservation to the Motherland by you.

Yours
ever sincerely
SAILENDRANATH

169. From Janakinath Bose

Cuttack
16.8.25

My dear Subhas,

I have duly received your letter of the 25th July and am glad to know that you are doing well.

You need not at all be anxious for me as I have recovered from the attack of lumbago. At first I took some allopathic medicine but latterly I was under Homœo treatment.

The summer is nearly gone in the part of the country and September will not be warm at Bhubaneswar—moreover I wish to try the waters of that place.

I shall leave Cuttack for Bhubaneswar on the 26th August.

Your mother is somewhat unwell but there is nothing serious.

The factory has not yet started work. Suresh is working hard at it. Rest are pretty well. Trust this will find you in good health.

Yours v. affectionately
J. N. Bose

170. *From Janakinath Bose*

Cuttack
13.10.25

My dear Subhas,

I have duly received your letters of the 5th and 25th last and am glad to know that you are in good health.

Please accept my and your mother's hearty *Bijoya* blessings.

The Durga puja was duly celebrated at Kodalia and everything passed off well and smoothly.

A charitable dispensary has been established there and Kashinath Chatterjee M.B. of Bully has been placed in charge of it ; people are taking great interest.

At our Cuttack house Durga Puja was nicely celebrated and Suresh took great interest in it. This has become an annual affair so far as we are concerned.

Dolly and the children with Sarala have come down to Calcutta from Gorakhpur.

Satish and *Bowma* have gone to Waltair on a short visit.

I am free from lumbago and your mother is at Calcutta and doing better. I shall be leaving Calcutta on the 15th next.

I am glad you could celebrate Durga Puja in the Mandalay Jail. I have read a report of it with interest in the papers.

Our stay at Bhubaneswar was rather short. We arrived at Calcutta on the 21st Sept. and I came here on the 3rd Oct.

People here at Calcutta and at Kurseong are doing well.

I trust this will find you in still better health.

My blessing to you.

Yours v. affly
J. N. Bose

171. From Sarat Chandra Bose

Giddapahar
Kurseong
24.10.25

My dear Subhas,

Your letter of the 9th came in on the 21st.

We are happy that the parcel of Khaddar dhotis and chaddars reached you after all and that your fellow exiles appreciated the paltry puja present.

I read in the papers also that your image of the Goddess turned out to be the best. Have you received money from Government for your puja expenses ? I have not decided yet the nature or method of the campaign I should start for the abolition of the liquor traffic. The Government reply to the Corporation resolution has come (as I believe you have seen from the minutes) and it will be debated upon after I return to Calcutta next month. After the debate is over I shall indicate the steps we should take towards prohibition.

I shall place your views regarding Compulsory Primary Education before the members of the Corporation (specially the members of the primary education committee) and shall let you know what they say. That also must stand over till I return to Calcutta.

You have put it very mildly, when you say that "Hemendra Babu's biography of Deshbandhu will not be a success." I am almost certain that it will be a hopeless failure. I believe you have noticed in the papers that Mr. Prithwis Chandra Roy also announced that he would write a biography. It is difficult to guess what his will be like.

The latest report about village work in Kodalia is encouraging. On an average 15 to 16 persons are being attended to daily at our dispensary by the doctor. The poor and indigent are supplied with medicines free of charge. Those who, in the opinion of the village committee, are able to pay are charged the prices of medicines. Up to the 17th Rs. 64/- or Rs. 65/- was realised by sale of medicines. Up to that date the doctor attended 59 persons in their houses. It is not a bad record for 17 days.

I am going down to Calcutta this afternoon to attend the *Forward* Anniversary Celebration on the 26th. I shall inspect the grounds of 38/1 and the vacant land to the south of it and see if anything needs treatment with kerosene oil. 38/1 is quite clean. It might be that water stagnates in the vacant land.

Personal

Chiraranjan is doing practically nothing. He has rented a fairly decent house on Hazra Lane for his mother and family and first we thought that he was taking life seriously. But he soon relapsed into his old ways and was not heard of for 3 or 4 days. He has come back and is now staying at Hazra Lane. Mrs. Das is now staying at Mr.....Halder's House (20 Mullen Street) where Kalyani has been confined with a boy. Sudhir and his wife and children have gone to Ootacamund and that is why Mrs. Das removed to Mr. Halder's House.

Chiraranjan has made some arrangements with the *Basumati* for printing and sale of his father's books. The details of the arrangements are not known to me. But Nalini Sarkar told me that he would look into the agreement and if any variation in the terms of the agreement is necessary for conferring a little more pecuniary benefit on Mr. Das's family he would have the necessary variation.

Prithwis has not been able to get a job yet. I am reminding Mr. J. C. Mukherjee off and on.

When I am in Calcutta I shall make a search for your extra pair of spectacles to send it on to you if I find it. Gopali went down to Cuttack a few days ago. I don't know if he has returned.

Kiran Sankar Roy has written to say that he has filed your application for having your name on the voters list for the Council of state elections. I discovered only this morning that I was entitled to be a voter having paid income tax on an income of Rs. 12,000/-. I don't know if my name is there. If it is not nothing can be done now as the 20th was the last date of filing any objections.

I wonder what objectionable matter they found in my letter of the 25th September which needed treatment with ink.

I asked for permission from Government to send the Daily *Forward* to you regularly, but permission has been refused. As regards the Deshbandhu number I instructed the Manager *Forward* to send a copy to Mr. Armstrong for being forwarded to you and I learnt subsequently that it was passed on. The Deshbandhu number was a financial success also.

So long today. I shall go down with family on the 6th November. Hope you are all right. This leaves us well.

P.S. Ramiah's reply to my letter is enclosed herewith. Please let me have clear instruction on the point. I forgot to tell you—Baby is well. I got the news here. I am sorry. I cannot say Dada is well. He is at Waltair.

Yours affly
SARAT CHANDRA BOSE

*172. From Bivabati Bose**

Mother Durga be with us.

38/1 Elgin Road
5th December 1925
Saturday

Dear Chotodada,[1]

You have not written any letter to us for a long time and this makes us feel depressed. A letter from you is a

* Translated from the original Bengali.
[1] Bivabati Bose used to address Netaji as chotodada.

source of great joy to us which we all read collectively. You must inform us about your state of health. Are you taking the Kaviraji medicine regularly? Do you feel any good effect of it on your health? Is the climate cooler now in your place? Please inform us how others are there.

You must have heard that Sejodidimoni is here now. Sarada too has come with her. She often asks about you. Mejodidimoni and Barodidimoni are also here now. Shanti and Shova are here now. Now our house is pretty crowded. I am sending for you a *panjabi* which has been made out of yarns spun at home. I shall be very happy to learn that you are using it after it reaches you. Father has also been given a *panjabi* which he wears and is very happy to do so. This has inspired us all the more to spin more yarns. This is rather redundant yet if you cheer us up then we will be more enthusiastic about spinning. Moreover, we will get a letter from you.

Accept my affection. Give my *pronam* to all there. Father, mother and all of us are well.

Yours
MEJOBOWDIDI

*174. From Amulya Bhusan Bose**

9/1/1 Arpuli Lane
Calcutta
10.12.25

Revered Sir,

I got your letter a few days ago. While reading the letter my mind felt like crying and my eyes overflowed with tears, why I do not know. It was, as if after a long long time, I got the soft compassionate touch of somebody and somebody addressed my mind afflicted with suffering and pain—"I have not forgotten you." Probably I could not check my tears because many of my lost memories came back and I was reminded of the happy days of the past. How long shall I grope in the dark for finding the way and when

* Translated from the original Bengali.

shall we get you back amongst us ? Your letter has revived me whose mind was almost dead. Today I am thinking myself as one of the most fortunate fellows because now I am the owner of such a letter, a letter which has come from you. Your letter reminded me of Dr. Johnson, writing these words to Lord Chesterfield—"Is not a Patron, my lord, one who looks with unconcern on a man struggling for life in the water, and, when he has reached ground, encumbers him with help ?" Such treatment I did not expect for I never had a patron before—who knows, may be I shall have to express my disappointment like that. But every word of your letter, every sentence of your letter with scintillating brilliance, the ideas and the language of your letter have such a spirit which belies the sentiment expressed by Dr. Jhonson. A man like you have accepted me with great affection, this remains the greatest asset of my life. My prayer to God is this—may He allow me to lead my life in the way you ask me to lead it.

Today I have to move here, there and everywhere just to get a job and that too of a clerk. Now I have got to stand before persons very humbly to whom I never bowed down my head before. If I am to lead the typical life of a clerk then why did I boycott academic career, and who is going to solve this problem ? Is there any other way out ? Today we are in the state of Trisanku. Had I been able to get the stamp of the slave-making machine I would have been able to make a career for me, because it is essential for getting a job either to have a stamp of the slave-making machine or one must have some patrons. Alas! I haven't got any of these qualities. What have I got today ? With great hope I hitched my boat to a big tree and so today I am facing the bitterest of disappointments.

You asked me in your letter whether any post for which I am fit is lying vacant at the Calcutta Corporation. It is up to you to consider for what kind of a post I am fit. I harboured many high hopes and I think I can make claims on you. So far as my knowledge goes just at the present moment two posts are lying vacant at the Calcutta Corporation—that of a Clerk and also of a licence Sub-Inspector.

Later there might be a few more vacancies in the outdoor department. I would like to have a job in the outdoor Department, a kind of job which will fetch me enough money to contribute something to my family and to save some money every month. If I can do so then I think after being in the service for five or six years I will be able to open a shop and earn my living independently in that way. If you write a letter to Mr. Mukherjee or to Mr. Sengupta regarding me then I shall surely get a job either as a licence Sub-Inspector or something of that kind. This is my great hope that, taking into consideration my future and the condition of my family, you will not hesitate to do so knowing that it will be a great benefit to me. Sukumar Babu too talked to Mr. Mukherjee regarding me—yet your letter carries much weight and surely that will bring a job for me.

On the first page of your letter four or five lines have been struck out—probably the work of the I.B. Department. Please reply my letter with information of your state of health. When are we going to have days of joy again? Nothing more to add.

With respectful *pronam*,

Yours sincerely

AMULYA BHUSAN BOSE

*174. From Tarubala Roy (elder sister)**

Goddess Durga be with us.

38/2 Elgin Road
9.1.26

Dear brother Subhas,

I was so glad to get your letter. The news that you are well has made me very happy.

Mother is comparatively well. Father is well too. Father came here during Christmas holidays and went back to Cuttack last Monday. Everybody is well at Cuttack.

Polly is comparatively well. About a month ago, Polly's mother-in-law died. When the measured span of life of a

*Translated from the original Bengali.

person reaches its end that person has got to leave this world. Yet we feel the loss very much in the beginning but gradually grow accustomed to it.

Aruna's marriage has been fixed. She will be married to the brother-in-law of Nilu and the marriage will take place in the month of Falgun. If you can be present in the marriage ceremony with us, we all will be immensely happy. We do not know when by the grace of God we will have such a happy time. Oh! for so many days I have not seen you. Sarada is so anxious for you and she says "let me have the good fortune of seeing Subu before my death". Sarada loves very much my second son Rabi. I do not want to take Sarada to Gorakhpur again yet if she so wishes then I must take her. All of you were looked after by Sarada when you were children. I want to keep Sarada in Calcutta because where we live (Gorakhapur), there the river Ganges does not flow by the side of the town. She is very old now and falls ill very often and while she lives with me I take particular care in nursing her and treating her properly medically. So I want to do whatever Sarada likes. Sarada very often pines for you. I did not tell her that you were in prison, while she was with me at Gorakhpur. Now after coming to Calcutta she has come to learn everything. When you were in prison for the first time Sarada, after hearing the news, fell seriously ill. For that reason we did not tell her about your second imprisonment in the beginning.

Nothing has been arranged as yet in regard to Gora's marriage. I do not fancy much a Calcutta boy as her groom, but in Northern India many Bengalee families living there for ages have ceased to be Bengalees and so I do not like much the idea of getting her married in such a family. Moreover there are families who demand a high dowry along with the demand that the girl must be very beautiful. There is no harm in keeping a girl unmarried and if the girl shines in other fields of life that is quite praiseworthy. But the example should be set by great men first and then we ordinary persons can follow it. You know perfectly well the state of our society.

My children are all right. Gora is all right in other respects except the problem of marriage.

Accept my affectionate blessings. Answer the letter whenever it is convenient for you.

Yours affectionately,
DIDI

175. To Sarat Chandra Bose

Mandalay Jail
1.3.26

My dear brother,

I do not know whether you have received my last few letters. I purposely refrained from mentioning anything about the strike because I am afraid that the letters would be withheld and you would be put to anxiety from what has happened. I was not wrong in anticipating that my letters would be withheld if they contained any news about the strike.

I received your long telegram on 27.2.26 about 5 p.m. and sent the reply by express at once. I do not know when it reached you.

I am weak—but am otherwise well and there is no cause for anxiety as far as I am concerned. I had headache and slight brain-trouble for the first few days but I seem to be gradually accustomed to the fast. I am keeping to my bed as much as I can, in order to conserve my energy. The strike still continues and will do so for some time to come. Until you hear from me that I have broken my fast you can take it for granted that the strike is continuing.

Hot water with a pinch of salt is a great sustainer. I do get headache and dizziness now and again—but there is nothing alarming about it. Some of my friends here are very weak.

I expect Rangamamababu will be here on Wednesday next. I do not know how long he intends to stop here.

The weight on 27.2.26 was 144 lbs.

Please see by all means that father and mother do not

get alarmed. It is not possible, I am afraid, to prevent them from feeling anxious.

You are aware by now that our telegrams to relatives, friends and to India were held up for several days. We wired to the Govt.s of Burma and of Bengal and to the Governor General on the 18th the day we struck.

Hope this will find you all quite well.

Yours v. affly.
SUBHAS

P.S. I have seen the reports of the Corporation and Assembly debates in the Rangoon Papers. Though the religious question is the most important one, our grievances are many and are long standing. We did not write about these detailed grievances to the Govt. of India because after Sir Hugh Stephenson's speech of the 11th December 1925 we concluded that the whole matter was in the hands of the Burma Govt. and it was not necessary to write to the Govt. of Bengal or India. An Associated press statement—which amounts to an Official Communique—appeared in the Rangoon Papers of the 24th February (dak edition) to the following effect :— "....in connection with the report published by Forward regarding the Bengal detenus in Mandalay Jail, shows that the Govt. of Burma's position in respect of these detenus is that of the agent of the Govt. of Bengal. The Govt. of Burma is not responsible for the rules framed relating to allowances granted to these prisoners or to the conditions under which they are detained. The Govt. of Bengal, it is understood, make no contributions towards the celebration of their religious festivals by prisoners detained in Bengal itself". I wired to you and to Mr. Amarnath Dutta (at Delhi) on 21.2.26—and to Mr. Goswami (at Delhi), Mr. J. M. Sengupta, Mayor, Mr. Amarnath Dutta and yourself on the 25th February and to you on the 26th Feb. Our telegrams, I am afraid, were held up at Rangoon for several days—by the Inspector General of Prisons or the Rangoon Secretariat.

I received a telegraphic message from Messrs Lajpat

Rai and Goswami from Delhi via Home Govt. and Rangoon Secretariat asking us to give up the strike. Their message ran as follows—'Earnestly request you and other friends to discontinue hunger-strike—your health much more valuable to country than redress of any grievances'. We replied by wire stating briefly the circumstances under which we were forced to commence hunger-strike and that no other alternative was open to us.

Your wire to the Superintendent asking for daily reports about my health has been received. I believe daily reports are being sent through Intelligence.

Please let me know which of my telegrams you have received uptill now. If you quote the message I shall be able to compare with my copies and find out if any has been withheld. Please give me the dates of receipt as well.

S.C.B.

1/3

Besides these other joint telegraphic representations were also sent by us.

*176. From Tarubala Roy (elder sister)**

Mother Durga be with us.

38/2, Elgin Road
15.4.26
Thursday

Dear Subhas,

I am happy to learn that you have received my letter. Why was so much time taken by the letter to reach you? I thought that the letter might not reach you at all.

How are you nowadays? When it is summer and very hot we become more worried about you. What about you and your friends being transferred to another jail? It is quite hot here too but from time to time it rains and the weather becomes tolerable. Here riot broke out and there was much chaos but now things are comparatively quiet.

* Translated from the original Bengali.

It is more or less settled that Aruna's marriage will take place on the sixteenth of Baishakh. The way you have suggested to be adopted by us is the best way no doubt but to follow that way requires a great deal of strength of mind. Do we really possess that kind of mental strength ?

I hope all of you are well. Here, everybody is all right. Accept my affectionate blessings. Try to send a reply at your convenience.

Yours affectionately
DIDI

177. From Janakinath Bose

38/2, Elgin Road
Calcutta
16th April 1926

My dear Subhas,

I have received your letter of the 3rd instant. I arrived in Calcutta on the morning of Saturday last and I am going back to Cuttack tonight. I am better—you need not be anxious. Your mother will remain here for the present.

Aruna's marriage will be celebrated during Baishakh. I have a mind to go to Kurseong during the latter part of May but I do not know if I shall be able to carry out my wishes ; otherwise I shall be at Puri as much as possible.

Your mother will write to you soon. She and the rest are well. I shall remain anxious for you because you cannot bear the heat of Mandalay ; please let me know how you do as often as you can.

Trust this will find you better.

Yours very affectionately,
J. N. BOSE

178. *From Bivabati Bose**

Mother Durga be with us.

38/1, Elgin Road
28th April, 1926
Wednesday

Chotodada,

I got the letter written by you on the 9th of April, on 22nd April. By now I think you are suffering even at night from the heat because the summer is on and Calcutta too is having a terrible summer. Even if you do not take Kaviraji medicine will it not be good for you to use the Kaviraji oil at least ? Are you using the oil at present ?

Have you used the two dhotis sent by Asoke and Aruna ? Have you received the letters they sent along with the dhotis ? Please write to them a few lines at your convenience because they will be greatly happy if they get letters written with your own hands. After the dhoti which was woven for you, a stock of yarn could be made and I have arranged to have a broad piece of cloth woven by it. When it will be finished I shall get dresses made from that piece of cloth.

Have your parrot learnt to talk ? Unless and until it learns to talk, you will not get real pleasure out of it. Could you manage to have a *Mayna* ? Your younger brother who sat for the examination did fairly well. He told us that this time he would probably be able to get through and what he said is more or less convincing.

Asoke is now a student of first class. Mother is here now. She will probably go to Puri in the middle of May. Father is well. All of us here are well.

Please write how all of you are there. Give my *pronams* to the elders, who are there. My affection to you.

Yours affectionately
MEJOBOWDIDI

* Translated from the original Bengali.

*179. From Kulada Ranjan Sengupta**
Replied
S.C.B. 26/6
Despatched 28/6

101, Harish Mukherjee Road
Kalighat
8.5.26

Dear Subhasda,

This is the first time that I am sending a letter to you while you are in prison. Maybe I am disturbing you, yet I beg to be excused as one who is like your younger brother. Probably we have come to know quite a great deal from the letter of Trailokya Babu. You gave us the hope that you would arrange a ground which would be used as a playground for the boys of the school and where a gymnasium would be set up also for the physical exercise of the boys. We were so very sure all these days that we would certainly have such a ground, but unfortunately nothing of the kind has been arranged so far. From the letter of Trailokya Babu we have come to learn that you are going to write a letter to Santosh Bose regarding this arrangement of a ground for the boys. My earnest request is that you will kindly secure a ground for the boys of our school by writing to any person or any quarter which will be helpful to us. These boys will respond to your call everytime and will obey all your orders and this is the way we are trying to build them up. So, when these boys are asking for a playground, I am bound to write to you a letter while you are in far away Mandalay and disturbing you thus. You told us one day that we should not be too attached to sports for sports' sake and our real duty should be, "to serve the poor and to do work for the National Congress." So inspired by your words the boys collect rice every Sunday and they can collect about a maund of rice every week. At present, we are helping nine poor families by giving rice to them. The boys, every afternoon, play games which are indigenous—Ha-do-do, Bowbondi, Gadi, High jump, Long jump, flat race, drill and

* Translated from the original Bengali.

other games. After the games, the boys recite in chorus a devotional verse and thus worship God for five minutes. Then they go back home in the evening. This is the daily routine. But we lack a ground where the boys can come and play. This is the reason why we have been disturbing you for a long time. Please try again and arrange a playground for the boys. Write to the right person so that a playground for the boys can really be arranged. It is preferable that the playground should be near to the School and I think Hazra Park is the best place for it. This is a special request to you from myself and Chandi Babu.

The boys of the school had set up an organisation called Tarun Sangha. They have brought out a monthly journal and the journal is a quite nice one. Such prominent persons as Basanta Babu, S. N. Haldar and others were present on the occasion of the anniversary of Tarun Sangha. They were very satisfied with the activities of the Sangha and the monthly journal of the Sangha could win their praise. These gentlemen encouraged the boys of the Sangha. I hope that from Mandalay you, Satyen Mitra, Trailokya Chakraborty and others will send blessings to the boys, hoping that they will turn out to be real men as you and the others expect them to be. I expect that these boys will never hesitate to be guided by you and others and abide by your orders. I expect that these boys will come to the service of the poor of India and would also serve India—their motherland. If I have committed anything wrong in the matter of writing this letter, I beg to be excused by you as one who is like your younger brother.

The school has been able to clear all its debts and not a single paisa remains to be paid to the creditors.

Yours very humbly,

KULADA

180. From Sarat Chandra Bose

38/1, Elgin Road
11th June, 1926

My dear Subhas,

I hope you have by this time received my letter of the 27th May last. I have since received your letter of the 17th May and 26th May—former on the 28th May and the latter on the 5th June. In my last letter, I have told you why *The Statesman* applied for adjournment of the hearing of the case filed against them. The other day they mentioned to Mr. Justice Buckland that they wanted the further adjournment as Mr. H. R. Wilkinson, whom they wanted to call for the purpose of proving Lord Lytton's Malda speech could not come to Calcutta before the 20th of this month. We consented to the adjournment. If Wilkinson comes to the Witness-box the case is bound to take an interesting turn.

I did not know that you are getting the *Capital* there. The paragraph in the *Capital* you have quoted referred to a letter which Jones of *The Statesman* wrote to his successor in the editorial chair, Ray Knight from England with reference to *The Englishman* case. Jones tried his level best to pump out information from the India Office about you and in the effort he only succeeded in getting information from Mr. Hose (who is a retired civilian of the U.P.) now in the India Office that 'there was no documentary evidence against you.' Poor consolation for Mr. Jones.

I am sending in a separate cover a newspaper cutting containing the letters of Jones referred to by the *Capital*.

The question of hospital grant was on the Corporation agenda, the day before yesterday but was not reached. I am trying my best this time to see that no injustice is done to Kaviraj Shyamadas. I have also advised his son to apply immediately for a plot of land for the Vaidyasastrapith and shall try to pass it in the Exgt. Committee. The difficulty is—we have few committees in the Corporation who have any 'go' in them and I cannot be there always. Those who have go in them are championing Jamini's cause and there is no match for them.

I shall write to Srinagar to send me samples of suitings and shirtings made in Kashmir and shall send them on to you as soon as I receive them. The Police returned to me after several months the threatening letter which you have received and it is with me. I shall show it to Sarkar and take his advice as to whether that letter should be used in evidence on your side in *The Statesman* Case.

Yes, I also think that you might first as well take the Master's Degree of the Cambridge University. I shall forward the letter when I find I can spare the money.

I am sorry that I have not been able yet to speak to the Book Company about the books they have sent you. I shall do so at an early date, and let you know the result. Didn't you know that Arthur Avalon was Sir John Woodroffe ?

Yes, I know Rakhaldas Banerjee very well. In fact, we were in college together. I am sure he would feel interested in what is contained in Burma records. How did you get them ?

Mr. S. N. Mallick and Mrs. Mallick left for England last night. They would be fellow passengers in the same boat with Lord Lytton. No, I do not think I can take a holiday during summer this year. I don't need it either. In the last few letters you have not said anything about your health. Please don't be too reticent on that matter.

Yours affectionately

SARAT

APPENDIX 1

Home Deptt. Political Proceedings.
(Part B Deposit) Nos. 3, 7, 9.
Part II—1924 (Secret)

Telegram P.

From Viceroy (Home Department).
To
The Secretary of State.
No. 789
Dated the 27th August 1924.

2397-D. Mirzapur street bomb outrage. Reference our telegram dated the 25th August. Bengal Government report that as result of outrage their main source of information regarding the inner working of the Jugantar group is no longer available. They obtained recently from this source report of inception of plot directed against life of His Excellency the Governor. Their intelligence is none seriously crippled and at any moment without previous indication grave developments may take place. Source of information above mentioned was in close touch with Swaraj revolutionary leaders and it was for this reason that action against these leaders under Regulation III though otherwise regarded as extremely necessary was not recommended by the Government of Bengal. 2. The Bengal Government now urge the necessity of the immediate arrest of 18 persons under Regulation. These include Subhas Chandra Bose, Chief Executive officer of the Calcutta Municipality and one of chief lieutenants of C. R. Das, two members of the Legislative Council and other prominent revolutionary leaders. The matter is under our consideration and we have called for further information. We should be glad to receive any observations you may have to offer with as little delay as possible by telegram.

APPENDIX 2

Prison Dept. No. 406/6C
From Lt. Col. P. K. Tarapore, I.M.S.
I.G. of Prisons Burma.
To
The Superintendent of Jail
Insein
Dated Rangoon, the 6th April, 1927.

Sir,

I have the honour to forward a copy of a letter No. IF-24 Part-XXI dated the 2nd April, 1927 from the Deputy Secretary The Govt. of Burma for communication to detenu Mr. S. C. Bose.

I have the honour to be Sir
Your most obedient servant
Sd/- P. K. Tarapore
Lt. Col. Duns.
I. G. of Prisons, Burma

Miscellaneous dept. letter No. IF 24 Part XXI dated the 22nd April, 1927 from the Deputy Secretary, Govt. of Burma (Home and Political Dept.) to I. G. of Prisons, Burma.

I am directed to refer to your Prison Dept. letter No. 348/6C dated the 24th March, 1927 forwarding the petitions addressed to H. E. from S. C. Bose and five other letters.

With reference to the petitions dated the 19th March, 1927 H. E. while fully recognising the unusually complete command of the English language possessed by Mr. Bose is constrained to regard the terms of the message sent by Mr. Bose to the Chief Jailor, as of a peremptory character, viewed in the light of modern usage and consider that Major Flowerdew's intervention on behalf of the Chief jailor a senior official, was neither unnatural nor unreasonable.

With regard to the petition dated 21st March, 1927, you report as follows :— "Major Flowerdew's warning Mr. Bose about not communicating with anyone was quite a legitimate warning. Unauthorised communications from detenus to the outside world undoubtedly take place and a Superintendent is well within his right in warning all new arrivals on the subject. It is merely a question of discharging one's duty.

During the visit of Mr. Bose to Rangoon in Dec. 1926, Major Flowerdew was merely the custodian of the prisoner who had been brought down to be examined by Col. Kelsall. It could have been improper on the part of Major Flowerdew to have taken any steps either towards diagnosis or treatment unless, of course he had to deal with any emergency. Mr. Bose admits that he received attention from Col. Kelsall and that was the main object of bringing him down here.

With regard to Mr. Bose's complaint that he was not offered a chair by Major Flowerdew the latter states that as soon as Mr. Bose came into his office, Major Flowerdew asked the Chief Jailor to take him straight to the Ward as he thought Mr. Bose would like to take rest after the journey. Mr. Bose himself admits that he exchanged a few words which meant that the interview did not last any length of time and there was no particular occasion to ask Mr. Bose to sit down.

Major Flowerdew has no record as to how often he has seen Mr. Bose during the last few months. He states that he has seen him as often as he considered necessary and Mr. Bose has been visited by the Assistant Medical Officer every day. I think Mr. Bose is making an error when he imputes sarcasm to Major Flowerdew at the Monday inspection parade. Major Flowerdew does not remember the exact word—but—he thinks his usual question was "Are you all right?" and on certain occasions he has asked, "Is there anything you want?" These questions do not imply that Bose's ailments were trivial. No particular treatment was prescribed for Mr. Bose by either of the two medical officers who examined him beyond taking Mr. Bose out for fresh air which is being done. Any special thing he wanted by way of an experiment or a tonic has been given to him. It is unfortunate that Mr. Bose has had to be kept in Rangoon Jail where no proper arrangements exist for keeping him separate from the rest. The superintendent had therefore to make the best arrangements he could and see that communications did not exist between Mr. Bose and rest of the prison population. To my personal knowledge the superintendent of the Rangoon Jail and his staff had done what they could for the comfort of Mr. Bose during the short time he has been in Rangoon. I have interviewed Mr. Bose on several occasions but this is the first one on which I was made aware that he had any complaints to make about his treatment by the staff." His Excellency accepts your view.

In view of Mr. Bose's subsequent transfer to the Insein Jail and the changed circumstances, the other communications received with your letter have not been forwarded.

I am to request that Major Flowerdew and Mr. Bose may be informed accordingly.

True copy
Sd/- W. R. Brooks
Bench Clerk

APPENDIX 3

From : A. N. Moberly
To Sarat Chandra Bose

Bengal Secretariat
Calcutta, the 15th of April 1927

Secret
D.O. No. 2890 X

Dear Mr. Bose,

As I said this morning when acknowledging your letter, I am sorry for the delay which has taken place. I had hoped to be able to write to you definitely in time to enable you to catch today's mail to Rangoon, but was disappointed.

Perhaps it will be well if I recapitulate the position. We now hold your brother under the Criminal law Amendment Act. We do not think that it would be safe to release him at present and can, if we consider it necessary, continue to hold him until the Act expires. Owing however to the state of his health we sought possible means of enabling him to obtain the care and treatment necessary to his recovery. The result was my statement in Council which involved his release on his giving his word of honour to proceed direct from Rangoon to Europe and not to return to India, Burma or Ceylon, until the Bengal Criminal law Amendment Act had expired. When you saw me last Sunday, you pointed out the hardship which would be caused to him and his family especially to his parents, who are old, if he were to go right away from India for a prolonged period without seeing them and that if he had given his word of honour not to return to India, Burma or Ceylon, until the Act had expired he might feel that this would preclude him from asking for permission to return even if conditions were to change entirely. You therefore suggested that a house should be taken for him in Almora before his departure to Europe where he would stay for about three months in order to see his relatives. He would give his word of honour not to receive or communicate* with anyone whilst at Almora except his parents, brothers, brothers' wives and their children save with the previous permission of the Government of Bengal. After the three months had expired, he would be given a passport and go to Switzerland and would undertake not to return to India, Burma or Ceylon except with the permission of the Government of Bengal and to abide by any conditions attached to such permission if accorded. I may say at once that the Government of Bengal are prepared to agree to these modifications subject to it being understood that Mr. Subhas Bose would proceed direct from Almora to Bombay and that the condition regarding visitors and communications would hold good until he had embarked for Europe. Unfortunately I am not able to give you a final answer because the places to which it is proposed that your brother should go are outside Bengal and consultation is necessary. I had hoped to be able to inform you before this that the matter had been settled. If you leave for Rangoon on the 17th I will wire to you through the Government of Burma if you will let them know where to find you.

In agreeing to the change in the formula regarding his return I should, I think make it clear that it was not intended in advance to reduce the term of his absence, but only to meet the specific difficulty which you raised.

I have seen Mr. Subhas Bose's letters to you dated the 4th and 8th April. I think that the present proposals meet his strongest point —the hardship of proceeding abroad without seeing his relations.

Turning now to your letter of today Government would not be prepared as matters stand at present to release your brother unless he had first given his word of honour so as to cover his future movements while at large until the expiration of the Bengal Criminal law Amendment Act unless the Government of Bengal permitted him to return to India at an earlier date.

The question of extending the period of his stay at Almora is one which might be considered after he has been there for a month or two.

S. C. Bose Esq. M. L. C.
38/1 Elgin Road
Calcutta.

Yours sincerely,
Sd/- A. N. Moberly

---

* The words "or communicate" at the two places were marked and commented on by Mr. Sarat Chandra Bose in his own handwriting in the margin of letter as follows: "not mentioned at the time of conversation".—Ed.

APPENDIX 4

From O. M. Martin

16th April, 1927
57, Ballygunge Circular Road
Calcutta.

Dear Sir,

I am desired to inform you that Government accept the proposal made by you to the Hon'ble Mr. Moberly last Sunday, viz., that Mr. Subhas Chandra Bose's relations would take a house for him at Almorah for three months; that Mr. Subhas Chandra Bose would give his word of honour whilst at Almorah not to receive visits from, or communicate with anyone without the permission of the Govt. of Bengal except his parents, brothers, brother's wives, and their children; at the end of three months he would request a passport to London with a view to subsequently proceeding to Switzerland; he would proceed direct from Almorah to Bombay, and the condition regarding visitors and communications would hold good until he had embarked for Europe; he would further give his word of honour thereafter not to return to India, Burma or Ceylon before the expiration of the Bengal Criminal law Amendment Act, without the permission of the Govt. of Bengal, and to abide by any condition attached to such permission, if accorded.

If Mr. Subhas Chandra Bose agrees to these conditions, he should give his word of honour to a responsible officer of the Govt. of Burma, who have been asked to depute an officer for the purpose. On hearing from you, Mr. Bose, if he accepts, would be escorted to Almorah and, on arrival, orders of release would be served on him, and he would be handed over to his relations.

I have just received these orders from Darjeeling tonight and have been asked to communicate them at once to you. Hence the informal nature of the letter.

Yours faithfully,
Sd/- O. M. Martin
Addl. Deputy Secretary
Govt. of Bengal,
Political Deptt.

To Sarat Chandra Bose
Esq. M. L. C.

APPENDIX 5

Tel. No. 399 South.

18th April, 1927
57, Ballygunge Circular Road
Calcutta.

Dear Sir,

I am desired to refer to the modified proposals the approval of Govt. to which was intimated to you in my letter of the 16th instant and to request you to communicate them to Mr. Subhas Chandra Bose and let Govt. know as soon as possible what are his views on these proposals. I am to make it clear at the same time that Govt. are not prepared to go further than they have already gone.

The Govt. of Burma have been requested by telegraph to permit you and the medical man accompanying you to visit Mr. Subhas Chandra Bose in Insein Jail. In the meantime, however, I understand from your recent telephone message that you do not now intend to proceed at once to Burma and that you have not been able to arrange for a suitable medical man, but that your brother, Mr. Satish Chandra Bose intends to start for Insein tomorrow. If this change in the arrangements is confirmed, the Govt. of Burma will be informed according to telegraph and requested to arrange for the interview.

The modified proposals referred to above may of course be communicated to Mr. Subhas Chandra Bose by your brother who it is now understood is going to Burma in your place.

Yours Sincerely,
O. M. Martin

To Sarat Chandra Bose

APPENDIX 6

Insein Jail
23. 4. 27

To
Lt. Colonel Tarapore
I. G. Prisons.

Dear Sir,

My brother Subhas is prepared to accept the first condition subject to the modifications mentioned hereunder.

1) The period at Almorah to be extended if advised by M. O.
2) The Govt. shall allow all near relations and Mrs. C. Das to visit him except those whom Govt. consider on political grounds undesirable.
3) Correspondence with persons, other than near relations should be permitted through censorship as at present. It is understood

that there will be no censorship over correspondence with near relations.

I have the honour to be
Sir
Your most obedient servant,
Satish C. Bose

P. S.

My brother is not in a fit state of health to come to a final decision on the second part of the Govt. offer and requests that it may be left over for discussion till after he has recovered his health to some extent.

APPENDIX 7

To
The Secretary
The South Calcutta Sevasram,
Calcutta.

Sir,

We the members of the Sub-Committee appointed by Executive Committee of the South Calcutta Sevasram on the 25th of September last to enquire into the wants of the Orphanage and to suggest means for the better working of the institution have the honour to submit the following Report :—

1. The first thing that strikes us is the want of a proper person to take charge of the boys. Our attention was drawn to the want of any sort of co-operation between the two men who are now employed by this institution. This has had a very demoralising effect on the boys and it has been impossible to have discipline maintained. We therefore suggest that immediate steps be taken to secure the services of a whole time Superintendent, preferably an elderly man and one who would take up the work more out of love for the boys than for other considerations.

2. Next we find that out of the 16 boys now kept in the orphanage only 4 might be termed as genuine orphans. So long as the institution is not registered and recognised by Government we are afraid, there will always be difficulties in doing any real work or helping actual orphans in need of help. Hence we suggest that, with a view to have the Institution registered, the draft constitution that has been framed be at once circulated amongst the members of the Committee for consideration as previously resolved upon but not given effect to and the constitution be finally adopted.

3. The house in which the orphanage is at present located (108/2 Monoharpukur Road) is not in an ideally healthy quarter. The Secretary Babu Hemendra nath Das Gupta for for instant removal of it to some healthier place but taking into consideration all the circumstances we do not think the matter as so very urgent. The

house should however be at once whitewashed and the small repairs attended to. We also recommend a periodically liberal use of disinfectants as a preventive for diseases. Attempts should also be seriously made to create a building fund for the purpose of giving the institution a permanent house of its own.

4. Up till now there has hardly been any arrangement for the proper medical relief of the boys. This is a matter which cannot any further be neglected. We might note here in passing that we found more than half the boys suffering from skin diseases, and some rather from an aggravated form of it, and hardly any steps were so long taken to get them cured. We consider this state of things highly deplorable.

5. No attempt has yet been seriously made to give the boys some technical education or other training to make them self-supporting and useful member of society in future. We propose that the elderly boys be at once apprenticed to different shops. Cycle repairing, signpainting, picture mounting, carpentry, gold and silver smithy, tailoring, watch repairing are some of the works that we can think of which the boys can be taught with profit.

6. There has been some controversy about the standard of food to be given to the boys. We hold that Rs. 8/- per head is a very fair amount for an institution of this kind and that the messing expenses should not go beyond that scale. A great reduction can however be made if arrangements could be made for the free supply of rice to the institution. We propose that with this purpose in view the Rice Mill owners and merchants' Associations at Chetla be approached.

7. The boys we find remain generally very dirty and unclean. They have very scanty clothings and hardly anything called bedding. We have made a list of the articles that we consider necessary for the Institution and have already given it to the Secretary. We hope that the things will be procured without unnecessary delay. There should be a fixed standard of clothing and other necessaries and the standard should be maintained.

8. The daily bazar should not be left in the hands of the boys alone as is being done now.

9. Arrangements should also be made for regular physical exercise and outings for the boys.

10. New appeals and pamphlets should be printed with statement of accounts etc. for distribution amongst the supporters of the institution and the general public and genuine efforts should be made to increase the list of donors and subscribers to the Institution.

11. During the enquiry we learnt of various grievances and complaints including complaints of harsh corporal punishment on the boys. We enquired into all these matters and have already taken steps to prevent repetition of the same in future. We do not think any useful purpose will be served by mentioning all these things in this report.

12. The task of bringing up the orphans properly and making them useful members of society is of so complex a nature and to our mind it requires so much looking after that we propose that individual members of the committee be made responsible for and subject to general supervision by the Secretary, given charge of looking after special requirements of the boys (e. g. Education, Sanitation, clothings, medical relief, food etc.) as it is not usually possible for the Secretary to devote sufficient time to do all that is necessary.

13. Another thing we propose is the creation of a Board of Visitors to inspect the orphanage every now and then and suggest methods of improvement. The local gentry may also be requested to visit the institution in like manner and leave their suggestions in the visitors book to which the attention of every visitor should be specially drawn.

14. Last of all we find that there has been no general meeting of the Institution for a long time and we propose that it be held now and the whole thing reorganised and greater interest created among the general public in this institution.

1st November 26
Calcutta.

Copy forwarded to
Sri Subhas Chandra Bose.

APPENDIX 8

Registrar of Joint Stock Companies Bengal
Received on 30. 11. 28.
No. 11843

THE DAKSHIN KALIKATA SEVASRAM
Memorandum of Association

1. The name of the Society shall be The Dakshin Kalikata Sevasram. Its registered office shall be situated at Calcutta.
2. The objects of the Society shall be:—
   (a) To give necessary relief from want to Hindu orphans and helpless children.
   (b) To provide food, raiment, shelter and education for such orphans and helpless children.
   (c) To bring up such orphans and helpless children in such a way as to make them useful members of society.
   (d) To give a start in life to such orphans and helpless children as the funds of the Society will permit.
   (e) To make provision for girls in premises or blocks completely

separated from the male orphanage directly under the supervision of ladies only.

3. For the purpose of carrying on the objects of the Society into effect it shall be entitled to:—
   (a) Subject to conditions imposed by the donors and accepted by the Society, receive, administer, lease out, mortgage and sell, all properties, moveable and immoveable, at any time, given, bequeathed or in any way made over to it and collect all moneys or other valuables, due, fixed, intended or promised as subscriptions or donations to it.
   (b) Borrow on such terms and conditions as may be decided on by the Society.
   (c) Purchase, take on lease or in exchange or hire or otherwise acquire any moveable or immoveable property or any rights or privileges in such property.
   (d) Construct, alter or keep in repair from time to time, buildings or other immoveable properties belonging to the Society or under its control.
   (e) Invest moneys of the Society, not immediately, required for its purposes, in securities approved under the Indian Trust Act.
   (f) Sell, improve, manage, develop, lease, mortgage, dispose of or otherwise deal with all or any part of the properties of the Society.
   (g) Do all such other things as are incidental or conducive to the attainment of the above objects.

4. The Society shall consist of Patrons, Vice-patrons, Life members, Ordinary members and Honorary members.
   (a) Any person of eminence whom the Society may think deserving of the honour may be elected a patron or Vice-patron of the Society according to the rules framed hereunder and such Patrons or Vice-patrons shall be considered members of the Society.
   (b) Every donor of five hundred rupees or upwards, paying the amount in one or more instalments within two years, shall be a life member.
   (c) Every subscriber of not less than three rupees per annum, or four annas per month, shall during the currency of his subscription, be an Ordinary member.
   (d) Any earnest worker for the Dakshin Kalikata Sevasram and any person taking special interest in the society, shall be eligible to be an Honorary member, subject to the rules to be framed by the Society.
   (e) Each Honorary member shall be elected for one year and shall not be required to pay any subscription.
   (f) No member of the Society, as such, shall have any pecuniary interest or right to any of the funds of the Society; all such funds being intended to be devoted to the attainment of the objects of the Society.

5. The working year shall commence from 1st January and end in

31st December. A general meeting of the members of the Society to be called the Annual General Meeting shall be held once every year not later than the 31st of March provided that at least clear seven days notice of the time and place of such meetings shall be given by advertisement in at least one English and one Vernacular daily local newspapers. Ten members shall form the quorum at a general meeting.

Special General Meetings may be convened by the Executive Committee, the President or the Secretary himself and the Secretary shall duly issue notices as above calling such meetings.

6. The members of the Society shall at the Annual General meeting elect the office bearers viz. one President, not more than three Vice-Presidents, one Treasurer, one Honorary Secretary and not more than two Assistant Secretaries. The Executive Commitee shall also be elected at this meeting. The annual General meeting shall also appoint not more than two auditors.
7. The general management of the affairs of the Society shall subject to the supervision and control by the general body of members, vest with the Executive Committee of the Dakshin Kalikata Sevasram consisting of not less than twentyfive and not more than fifty members over and above the office bearers who shall be Ex-officio members thereof.
8. (a) Subject to the supervision and control by the general body of members, the Executive Committee shall be competent to do all acts mentioned in clauses (2) and (3).
   (b) Subject to the approval of the general body of members of the Executive Committee shall have the power to make bye-laws for the better management of the Society.
9. Five members of the Executive Committee shall form a quorum and all questions before it shall be decided by a majority of votes, the President or the Chairman of the meeting for the time being, having a casting vote if there be an equality of votes.
10. In case of vacancies arising in the Executive Committee within its year of office, it shall have power to fill up the vacancy or vacancies from amongst the members of the Society.
11. The Executive Committee shall meet at least once in three months and special meetings may be held whenever necessary.
12. Subject to rules to be framed hereafter and subject also to the control of the Executive Committee there may be a Working Committee consisting of not less than five members and not more than twelve members. The Working Committee, if any, shall be elected annually by the Executive Committee from amongst themselves the Secretary being an ex-officio member and also Secretary of it. The Working Committee shall ordinarily have no other functions except to advise and help the Secretary in carrying out his duties but it shall be competent to exercise any functions of the Executive Committee that may be specially delegated to it by a resolution of the Executive Committee.
13. The Treasurer shall deposit Government or other securities belonging

to the Society, if any, and all moneys received by him from the Secretary or from other sources in a Bank to be approved of by the Executive Committee in the name of the Dakshin Kalikata Sevasram and no money shall be drawn from such Bank except for the purpose of the Society and only by cheques to be signed by the Treasurer. During the temporary absence of the Treasurer or when his services are not available, it shall be competent for the Executive Committee to act as Treasurer during that period who shall perform all the duties of the office.

14. The Secretary shall at any time upon a written requisition by not less than ten members, stating the reason and object of calling the meeting, call a Special General Meeting of the members of the Society. Notice of such meeting shall be given as provided in rule 5 and such notice shall state the purposes for which such special meeting is called.

15. The President or in his absence any Vice-president and in their absence such person as the meeting may elect, shall preside at all meetings of the Society or its Committees. All questions before every meeting shall be decided by a majority of votes and the Chairman shall have a casting vote in case there is an equality of votes.

16. At the annual general meeting of the Society the Secretary shall present a report previously approved by the Executive Committee, dealing, with the working of the Society for the past year, submit an abstract of account, of the receipts and disbursements for the same period duly audited and present a budget for the coming year stating also the properties and investments of the Society.

The names and address and occupation of the persons who form the Executive Committee or Governing body of the Association are as follows:—

PRESIDENT—	Sj. Subhas Chandra Bose, M.L.C. President B.P.C.C. 1, Woodburn Park
VICE-PRESIDENT—	Sj. Basanta Coomar Bose, Advocate. 15, Harish Mukherji Road.
	Sj. Nagendra Nath Banerji, Public Prosecutor. 24 Parganas, Alipore.
	Sj. Kumar Krishna Mitter, Merchant. 1/1, Ahiritola Street.
SECRETARY—	Sj. Amritalal Chatterjee, Pleader. 83, Lansdowne Road.
ASST. SECRETARIES—	Sj. Nitindra Nath Roy, Service. 2/3, Rani Sankari Lane.
	Sj. Profulla Chandra Mukherji, Merchant. 7, Monoharpukur Road.
TREASURER—	Sj. Ramaprasad Mukherji, Vakil 77, Asutosh Mukherji Road.

NON-OFFICIAL MEMBERS—

Dr. Ramendu Roy, M.B.
10, Prana Nath Pandit Street.
Sj Ramesh Chandra Ganguli, Service.
22, Hazra Road.
Sj. Ekcowri Chandra Mukherji, Pleader.
21/1, Hazra Lane.
Dr. Avimat Bose, M.B.
Monoharpuker 1st Lane.
Sj. W. M. Roy, Zeminder.
12, Prana Nath Pandit Street.
Sj. Debendra Chandra Deb, Service.
108/2, Monoharpukur Road.
Sj. Janardan Chakraberty, Service.
108/2, Monoharpukur Road.
Sj. P. Banerjee, Banker.
80, Chowringhee Road.
Sj. Santosh Kumar Bose, Advocate.
10, Gopal Banerji Lane.
Sj. Monmohan Mukherji, Pleader.
2, Ashu Babu's Lane.
Sj. Phani Bhushan Bose, Service.
23, Nazir Lane.
Sj. Atul Chandra Gupta, Advocate.
86, Lansdowne Road.
Sj. Nirmal Chandra Chunder, Attorney-at-Law
Wellington Street
Sj. S. N. Halder, Bar-at-Law.
21, Mullen Street.
Sj. S. C. Bose, Bar-at-Law.
1, Woodburn Park.
Sj. Bipin Bihari Sadhukhan, Zeminder.
19/1, Corporation Street.
Sj. Madan Mohan Burman, Zeminder.
Harrison Road.
Sj. P. D. Himatsinkga, Attorney-at-Law.
P-81, Sayed Sally Lane.
Sj. G. B. Malik, Zeminder.
22, Brindaban Bose Lane.
Sj. Bhupendra Nath Banerji, Pleader.
3, Lansdowne Lane.
Dr. Narendra Nath Law, Zeminder.
Amherst Street.
Sj. Basanta Lal Saha, Merchant.
Hazra Road.
Sj. Satya Ranjan Bakshi, Editor, Forward.
19, British India Street.
Sj. L. M. Sen, Engineer,
98, Beltola Road.

Dr. S. N. Roy Choudhuri.
24, Kalighat Road.
Sj. Dhirendra Nath Roy, Vakil.
Rani Sankari Lane.
Sj. Dhiren Neogy, Merchant.
Lansdowne Market.
Sj. Nagendra Nath Choudhury, Vakil.
6, Lansdowne Lane.
Sj. Angshu Prakas Chatterji, Teacher.
7, Monoharpukur Road.
Sj. Amalendu Das Gupta, Head Master.
Monoharpukur Corporation School.
Dr. J. M. Das Gupta, M.L.C.
College Street Market.
Sj. Asutosh Das Gupta, Teacher.
Monoharpukur Corporation School.
Sj. Nalini Kanta Bardhan, Service.
31/2, Asutosh Mukherji Road.

We the following persons whose names addresses are Subscribed hereto are desirous of being formed into a Society in pursuance of the Memorandum of Association.

Subhas Chandra Bose,
1, Woodburn park, Calcutta.
Nagendranath Banerji
Public Prosecutor, 24-Parganas.
W. M. Roy, Zemindar
12 Prannath Pandit Street.
Ramaprasad Mookerjee
77 Asutosh Mookerjee Road, Calcutta.
Ekkorichandra Mukherji
27/1, Hazra Lane.
Amritalal Chatterji
83, Lansdowne Road.
Janardan Chakrabarty
41, Beltala Road.
Romesh Ch. Ganguli
22, Hazra Road.
30-11-28.

Witnesses to Signature— Sarat Ch. Chakraborty,
41, Beltola Rd.
Janardan Chakraborty
41, Beltola Rd.
Debendra Chandra Deb
41, Beltola Raod.
Amritalal Chatterji
83, Lansdowne Road.
Ekkori Chandra Mukherji
27/1, Hazra Lane.
Sambhunath Mukherji
172, Panchanantola Rd. Howrah.

Registrar of Joint Stock Companies Bengal
Received on 30. 11. 28.
No. 11844

THE DAKSHIN KALIKATA SEVASRAM
Rules and Regulations

1. Subject to the control of the Executive Committee the Secretary shall :—

(a) Admit children deserving of the benefits contemplated by the Society as inmates of the Dakshin Kalikata Sevasram.
(b) Manage the internal affairs of the Sevasram that is, supervise the board and residence, nursing and medical treatment, education and such other things as may tend to the welfare of the inmates of the Sevasram.
(c) Receive all subscriptions, donations, bequests and other moneys of the society including interest, dividend or other income of all Government and other securities for money belonging to it and give due receipts for them.
(d) Draw from time to time all such moneys as may be required for the purposes of the Society, from the Treasurer who shall remit the same on receipt of written requisitions duly signed by the Secretary.
(e) Keep or cause to be kept a full, true and correct account of all moneys received and disbursed by him in proper books of account and submit abstract of such accounts from time to time to the Executive Committee.

2. The Executive Committee of the Dakshin Kalikata Sevasram shall appoint at least one resident Superintendent, who shall be in direct charge of the inmates, on such terms as to pay, allowance, leave or otherwise as they shall think fit, they having the power to remove him from office at their own absolute discretion without being required to give any reason for their action on this behalf.

3. The Superintendent shall be a whole time officer and shall live in the premises of the Sevasram. He shall be in charge of the office, maintain all registers, keep proper and full account of the receipts and expenditure of the Sevasram and under the orders of the Secretary manage the internal affairs of the Sevasram and perform all such duties that may be delegated to him in writing by the Secretary.

4. Hindu children of both sexes who have no father and mother alive or who are unclaimed or whose father or mother or both being alive do not take care of them shall be eligible to be admitted to the orphanage of the Dakshin Kalikata Sevasram.

5. No boy or girl over twelve years of age shall be admitted as inmates of the Dakshin Kalikata Sevasram but the Executive Committee may for any special reasons admit children about that age.

6. Free board and residence, clothes and medical treatment shall

be provided to the inmates of the Sevasram so far as the funds of the society will permit.

7. Education of the inmates shall be provided in such manner as may enable the inmates to maintain themselves in life.

8. Male inmates may be maintained up to their eighteenth year, females, so long as they do not marry. They shall however be discharged as soon as the Committee is satisfied that they are able to earn an honest and independent living.

9. The Society shall not undertake the responsibility of arranging for the marriage of the male inmates but in the case of females it may make arrangements for their marriage subject to the control of the Executive Committee.

10. The Secretary shall have power subject to the sanction of the Executive Committee, to expel any inmate for misconduct or other good and sufficient reason.

11. The Executive Committee may create a Board of Visitors, not necessarily from within the members of the Sevasram, to inspect the working of the Society and suggest methods of improvement.

12. At any Annual General Meeting of the Society any member shall be entitled to propose names for election as Patrons and Vice-Patrons of the Institution provided the member has seventy two hours previous to the time of meeting, given notice to the Secretary of his intention to do so. Each name shall be put to the vote by the President of the meeting and votes for and against such election shall be taken and decided by a majority of votes.

13. If for want of quorum any meeting of the Society be adjourned then no quorum will be necessary for the adjourned meeting.

14. Subscriptions are payable not later than 15th of the month for which they are due. Members will forfeit their membership if they are in arrears for six months in spite of due notice from the Secretary.

15. No member whose subscriptions is in arrear for three months shall have the power to vote in any meeting of the Society its Committees or Sub-Committees.

We the undersigned members of the Executive Committee of the Dakshin Kalikata Sevasram do hereby certify that the above is a correct copy of the rules and regulations of the Dakshin Kalikata Sevasram.

Subhas Chandra Bose
1, Woodburn Park, Calcutta.
Nagendranath Banerji
Public Prosecutor, 24-Parganas.
W. M. Roy, Zemindar
12, Prannath Pandit Street.
Rama Prasad Mookerjee
77 Asutosh Mukherjee Road, Calcutta.
Amritalal Chatterji
83, Lansdowne Road, Calcutta.

30-11-28.

Witnesses to signature— Sarat Ch. Chakraborty,
41, Beltala Rd.
Janardan Chakraborty
41, Beltala Road.
Debendra Chandra Deb
41, Beltola Road.

TRUE COPY,
Sd./- Illegible
Registrar of Firms Societies &
Non-Trading Corpns. W. Bengal
9/12/80

NOTES

Abanish Babu—Abanish Roy
Akshoy—Akshoy Kumar Sarkar, a nephew
Ami—Amiya Nath Bose, second son of Sarat Chandra Bose
Amrita—Amrita Lal Chatterjee
Anil Babu—Anil Baran Roy
Aptabakya—Gospel like words accepted without reasoning
Armstrong—British Officer in Intelligence Branch, Criminal Investigation Department, Calcutta
Aruna—Niece, eldest sister's daughter
Ashathwa—Banyan tree (Ficus Indica)
Ashar—Third month in Bengali calendar marked by heavy rains
Asis: Blessing
Astanga—Astanga Ayurveda Vidyalaya, one of the Ayurvedic Colleges of Calcutta
Asoke—Asoke Nath Bose, eldest son of Sarat Chandra Bose
Atmasakti—*Swarajist Bengali daily*
Ayurveda—Hindu system of Medicine (Ayus = Life ; Veda = Science)
Baby—Sarat Chandra Bose's second daughter Gita
Balak Samity—Boys' Association
Banglar Katha—Bengali daily started by Deshbandhu Das in 1923 with Netaji as the editor
Bankim Babu—Bankim Chandra Chatterjee, eminent Bengali litterateur
Bardada—Eldest brother, Satish Chandra Bose
Baradidimoni—Eldest sister of Netaji, Promila
Basu, Kumudini—Bengali authoress
Basumati—a Bengali daily and monthly publication
Bengalee, The—English daily founded by Surendra Nath Banerjea
Bhadra—Fifth month of Bengali calendar
Bhagavad-Gita, Gita—Divine song, the essence of Hindu philosophy regarded as the Bible of the Hindus
Bhaskar
Bhaskar Babu—Bhaskar Mukherjea, younger son-in-law of Deshbandhu C. R. Das
Bhatri-Dwitia
Bhai Phota—a quasi-religious ceremony—more social than religious. On this occasion, sisters put sandal paste marks on their brothers' foreheads, praying for their long life, serving sweets to them and exchanging gifts
Bhombal—Chiraranjan Das, only son of Deshbandhu C. R. Das
Bidhan Babu—Dr. Bidhan Chandra Roy
Big Five—Sarat Chandra Bose, Nirmal Chandra Chunder, Tulsi Chandra Goswami, Bidhan Chandra Roy and Nalini Ranjan Sarkar
Bijoya Dashami—Tenth lunar day in autumn and last day of worship of goddess Durga

Bijoykaka—Bijoy Krishna Bose, Advocate, Councillor, Calcutta Corporation and Swarajist member of Bengal Legislative Council
Bimal—nephew, eldest sister's son
Bir (*Biru Buro*)—Domestic servant
Bir-Bani—Swami Vivekananda's "The Gospel of the Brave"
Biswa—Son of fifth sister of Netaji
Bose, Jitendriya—A leading advocate and Congress Councillor of Calcutta Corporation
Bose, Lady—Abala Bose, wife of Jagadish Chandra Bose
Bowdidi—Sister-in-law
Chhaya—Niece, elder daughter of Sudhir Chandra Bose
Chatterjee, Sarat—Sarat Chandra Chatterjee, eminent Bengali litterateur
Chotodada—Fifth brother Dr. Sunil Chandra Bose
Chotomamababu—Youngest maternal uncle R. N. Dutt
Chunder, Mr.—Nirmal Chandra Chunder
Dada—Eldest brother Satish Chandra Bose
Dakshin Kalikata Sevasram—South Calcutta Orphanage
Das, Mrs.—Mrs. C. R. Das, Basanti Devi
Das, Jatin—Legendary Bengali revolutionary who fasted unto death in Lahore prison in 1929
Desher Bani—Bengali periodical
Devi, Urmila—Sister of Deshbandhu C. R. Das
Dharma—Religion
Didi—Elder sister
Dolly—Third sister
Durga Puja—Worship of Goddess Durga
Dutt, Romesh—Bengali litterateur
Englishman, The—English daily of Calcutta
Findlay, Major—Superintendent, Rangoon Central Jail
Forward—English daily founded by Deshbandhu C. R. Das
Gita—Sarat Chandra Bose's second daughter
Ghaznavi—A. K. Ghaznavi, East Bengal Zemindar, who became an Executive Councillor, Government of Bengal
Goddess Manasha—Goddess of serpents in Hindu mythology
Gopal—Gopal Lal Sanyal
Gopali—Seventh brother, Sailesh Chandra Bose
Gora—Niece, third sister's daughter
Goswami—Tulsi Chandra Goswami
Guru—Religious teacher and guide
Haldar, Mr.—Surendra Nath Haldar
Hari Charan—Hari Charan Bagchi
Harish—Dr. Harish Chandra Sinha
Hemendra Babu—Hemendra Nath Dasgupta
Jamini Kaviraj—Kaviraj Jamini Bhusan Roy, leading Ayurvedic Physician and founder of Astanga Ayurveda Vidyalaya
Jitendriya Babu—A leading advocate and Congress Councillor of Calcutta Corporation
Jogesh Babu—Kaviraj Jogesh Chandra Sen, Councillor, Calcutta Corpo-

ration and Member, Bengal Legislative Council

Kaloo (Kalu) Singh—Caretaker of Sarat Chandra Bose's house at Kurseong

Kanak—Youngest sister Kanaklata Mitra

Karma—Work assigned by destiny

Karmi Sangha—Workers' Association

Kasiram Das—Translator of Mahabharata in Bengali rhyme

Kaviraj—Ayurvedic physician

Kaviraj Bimalananda—Son of Kaviraj Shyamadas Vachaspati

Kaviraj Mahasay

Kaviraj Shyamadas—Kaviraj Shiromani Shyamadas Vachaspati, leading Ayurvedic physician of Calcutta and physician and friend of the family

Kelsall, Col.—Senior physician, Rangoon Central Hospital

Khuku—Daughter of Netaji's second sister Sarala

Khuro—lit. uncle ; Sailendra Nath Bose, a relative and professional clerk of Sarat Chandra Bose

Kiron Babu—Kiran Sankar Ray

Kiran Sankar—Kiran Sankar Ray

Krittibas—Author of Bengali Ramayana

Kshitish—Khitish Prasad Chattopadhaya, Netaji's contemporary of student days, later Education Officer, Calcutta Corporation and Professor of Anthropology, Calcutta University

Kurseong—Hill station on way to Darjeeling

Lal Mohan Babu—Lal Mohan Ghosh

Manasha Mela—A fair, named after Goddess Manasha, organised in 1924 at Kidderpore, Calcutta

Mamima—Maternal aunt

Martin, Mr.—O. M. Martin, Additional Deputy Secretary, Government of Bengal, Political Department

Mejdada—Sarat Chandra Bose

Mejobowdidi—Second sister-in-law Bivabati, wife of Sarat Chandra Bose

Mejdidi

Mejodidimoni—Second elder sister of Netaji, Sarala

Minu—Eldest daughter of Chiraranjan Das

Mira—Eldest daughter of Sarat Chandra Bose

Mitra, S. C.—Satyendra Chandra Mitra

Mitter, Binod C., 1872-1930, leading Calcutta barrister, Standing Counsel and Offg. Advocate-General, Calcutta and finally Judge of Judicial Committee of Privy Council, London ; conducted Netaji's defamation case against The Statesman in 1928

Moberly, Mr.— A. N. Moberly, Home Member, Governor's Executive Council, Bengal

Muddiman, Sir Alexander—Home Member, Viceroy's Executive Council

Nabowdidi—Fourth sister-in-law, wife of Sudhir Chandra Bose

Nadada—Fourth brother Sudhir Chandra Bose

Nadu—Netaji's maternal uncle R. N. Dutt

Nalini Babu—Nalini Ranjan Sarkar

Nalu—Fourth brother Sudhir Chandra Bose

Namama
Namamababu—Fourth maternal uncle
Natundada—Fifth elder brother
Natunmamababu—Fifth maternal uncle
Neru—Sisir Kumar, third son of Sarat Chandra Bose
Nirmal Babu—Nirmal Chandra Chunder
Nripen Babu—Nripendra Chandra Mitra
Patel, Mr.—Vithalbhai Patel
Patterson, Mr.—A Prison Commissioner of England
Polly—Fifth sister
Prabhudayal—Prabhudayal Himatsingka
Pratyaksha—First-hand
Pravash, Sir—Pravash Chandra Mitter
Promila—Eldest sister of Netaji
Pronam—Obeisance
Purdah—The system of seclusion of women
Radhu—Eldest daughter of Dr. Sunil Chandra Bose
Ramaprosad—Ramaprosad Mookerjea, eldest son of Asutosh Mookerjea
Ramiah—Secretary, Calcutta Corporation
Ramtaran Babu—Ram Taran Banerjea, leader of Alipore Civil Court Bar and Councillor, Calcutta Corporation
Rangamamababu—Sixth maternal uncle, B. N. Dutt
Ray, Mrs.—Elder daughter of Deshbandhu, wife of Sudhir Chandra Ray
Roy, D. L.—Eminent Bengali litterateur Dwijendra Lal Roy
Roy Chowdhury, Girija Sankar—Distinguished Bengali writer closely associated with Deshbandhu C. R. Das
Sabitri Babu—Sabitri Prasanna Chatterjee, noted Bengali writer
Sadhana—Spiritual exercise
Sailesh—Seventh brother Sailesh Chandra Bose
Sandesh—Well-known Bengali sweet made of casein
Santosh Babu—Santosh Kumar Basu
Santosh—Youngest brother Santosh Chandra Bose
Sannyasa—Renunciation
Sanjeebani—Bengali newspaper edited by Krishna Kumar Mitra which played an important role during Swadeshi and Anti-Partition Movements
Sarada—Oldest family maid who looked after Netaji in childhood
Sarala—Second elder sister of Netaji
Sati—Youngest brother Santosh Chandra Bose
Satish—Netaji's eldest brother Satish Chandra Bose
Satya Babu—Satya Ranjan Bakshi
Satyen Babu—Satyendra Chandra Mitra
Saraswati Puja—Worship of the Goddess of Learning
Sasmal, Mr.—Birendra Nath Sasmal
Sejdada—Suresh Chandra Bose
Sejdidi
Sejodidimoni—Third elder sister of Netaji, Tarubala
Sejobowdidi—Third sister-in-law

Sejobowma—Third junior sister-in-law, wife of Suresh Chandra Bose
Sejojethamahashaya—Third senior uncle
Sengupta—J. M. Sengupta
Seva Sadan—Chittaranjan Seva Sadan, Women's Hospital in Calcutta, established in the house of Deshbandhu, bequeathed by him to the nation
Sevak Samity—Social Service Association
Sirajganj Conference—Annual conference of Bengal Congressmen held at Sirajganj in 1924
Sishya: Disciple
Shyamadas Kaviraj—see Kaviraj Shyamadas
Shraban—Fourth month of Bengali calendar
Smith, Captain (later Major)—Superintendent, Mandalay Central Jail
Statesman, The—English daily of Calcutta; for Netaji's defamation case against the paper, vide Calcutta Weekly Notes, 32, 490 (January 1928) and Indian Law Reports, 55,1121 (January 1928)
Sudhir—Fourth brother Sudhir Chandra Bose
Sudhir Babu—Dr. Sudhir Kumar Basu, elder brother of Santosh Kumar Basu
Sudhir Roy—Son-in-law of Deshbandhu C. R. Das
Sunil—Fifth brother Dr. Sunil Chandra Bose
Suren Babu—Surendra Mohan Ghose
Suresh—Netaji's third brother, Suresh Chandra Bose
Susthir Babu—Susthir Kumar Basu, younger brother of Santosh Kumar Basu
Swadeshi—National, Indigenous
Swadharma—One's own religion
Ta...Hall Banerjea—Surendra Nath Banerjea
Tarapore, Col.—Head of the Prison Department, Burma
Temple, Mr.—F. C. Temple, Chief Administrative Officer, Tata Iron and Steel Co., Jamshedpur
Tulsi
Tulsi Babu—Tulsi Chandra Goswami
Upanishads—Ancient Sanskrit Treatises on Hindu Philosophy
Upen Babu—Upendra Nath Banerjea
Vaidyasastrapith (Baidyashastrapith)—Ayurvedic College founded by Kaviraj Shyamadas Vachaspati
Viswa-kosh—Bengali encyclopaedia
Yoga—Union with Godhead; the word indicates the goal as well as the means

INDEX